TC
425
.Y4
B67

D1175115

Water Rights and Ene
in the Yellowstone Riv

Water Rights and Energy Development in the Yellowstone River Basin

An Integrated Analysis

Constance M. Boris and John V. Krutilla

WITHDRAWN

Published for Resources for the Future, Inc.
By The Johns Hopkins University Press
Baltimore and London

Tennessee Tech. Library
Cookeville, Tenn.

345630

Copyright © 1980 by Resources for the Future, Inc.
All rights reserved
Manufactured in the United States of America

Library of Congress Catalog Card Number 79-3741
ISBN 0-8018-2368-4

Library of Congress
Cataloging in Publication Data

Boris, Constance M.
   Water rights and energy development in the
Yellowstone River basin

   Includes index.
   1. Water resources development—Yellowstone
Valley.   2. Energy development—Yellowstone
Valley.   3. Water-rights—Yellowstone Valley
I. Krutilla, John V., joint author.   II. Resources
for the Future.   III. Title.
TC425.Y4B67   333.91'09786'3   79-3741
ISBN 0-8018-2368-4

RESOURCES FOR THE FUTURE, INC.
1755 Massachusetts Avenue, N.W., Washington, D.C. 20036

Board of Directors: M. Gordon Wolman, *Chairman,* Charles E. Bishop, Harrison Brown, Roberto de O. Campos, Anne P. Carter, Emery N. Castle, William T. Coleman, Jr., William T. Creson, F. Kenneth Hare, Franklin A. Lindsay, Charles F. Luce, George C. McGhee, Ian MacGregor, Vincent E. McKelvey, Richard W. Manderbach, Laurence I. Moss, Mrs. Oscar M. Ruebhausen, Janez Stanovnik, Charles B. Stauffacher, Russell E. Train, Franklin H. Williams

Honorary Directors: Horace M. Albright, Erwin D. Canham, Edward J. Cleary, Hugh L. Keenleyside, Edward S. Mason, William S. Paley, John W. Vanderwilt

President: Emery N. Castle

Secretary-Treasurer: Edward F. Hand

Resources for the Future is a nonprofit organization for research and education in the development, conservation, and use of natural resources and the improvement of the quality of the environment. It was established in 1952 with the cooperation of the Ford Foundation. Grants for research are accepted from government and private sources only if they meet the conditions of a policy established by the Board of Directors of Resources for the Future. The policy states that RFF shall be solely responsible for the conduct of the research and free to make the research results available to the public. Part of the work of Resources for the Future is carried out by its resident staff; part is supported by grants to universities and other nonprofit organizations. Unless otherwise stated, interpretations and conclusions in RFF publications are those of the authors; the organization takes responsibility for the selection of significant subjects for study, the competence of the researchers, and their freedom of inquiry.

This book is a product of RFF's Quality of the Environment Division, which is under the direction of Walter O. Spofford, Jr. Constance M. Boris is a fellow and John V. Krutilla a senior fellow in the Quality of the Environment Division.

The figures were drawn by Art Services, Inc. The index was prepared by Florence Robinson.

RFF Editors: Ruth B. Haas, Jo Hinkel, Sally A. Skillings, and Joan Tron-Ruggles

Contents

Tables

Figures

Preface

The energy crisis is doubtless a genuine crisis, but the phrase is a short-hand expression for a complex of difficult issues with energy supplies at its core. It is a truism that there is an abundance of energy if we are thinking only of carbonaceous, fissionable, or fusible materials for use as prime movers, or insolation which can be converted into other desirable forms of usable energy. What causes the problem are the complications by adverse side effects of various energy technologies or the community disruption that rapid development of some new source often entails. In addition, there may be shortages of cooperating inputs such as niobium, which might limit the production of energy from fusion, or other factors like the costs of fabricating components such as semiconductors, which prevent photovoltaic conversion of sunlight into electrical energy at economically tractable costs.

This study investigates one such problem associated with the development of the Fort Union Formation coal in the eastern portion of Montana. This portion of the Northern Great Plains Coal Province contains a vast quantity of suitable quality coal. Its exploitation and conversion to other usable energy forms such as synthetic fuels may be problematic owing to a variety of conflicting interests and competition for cooperating inputs by rival users and uses. It has seemed important to us to examine some of the possible constraints arising from considerations other than the amount and quality of the coal itself. In a companion RFF study by Krutilla, Fisher, and Rice (*Economic and Fiscal Impacts of Coal Development: Northern Great Plains*), economic and fiscal considerations were evaluated to determine whether providing for the growth in the demand for public services associated with rapid development of the Fort Union Formation in a quite sparsely populated region could be impeded owing to the requirements to fund infrastructure and community services necessary for a greatly expanded community structure.

In the present study we look to the relationship between coal extraction, transportation, and development of conversion operations on the one hand, and on the other the supply of, and rival demands for, water in the Yellowstone River Basin, where the most significant development of the Fort Union Formation in eastern Montana would be centered. There is always keen competition among contending parties for generally perceived scarce water throughout the arid and semiarid West. In the eastern Montana portion of the Fort Union Formation, the problem of competition among rival uses is intensified and greatly complicated by the overlay of Indian reserved water rights, other elements of the federal reserved rights doctrine, and the interstate compact for sharing water among the states, not to mention the overappropriation of existing flows and the determination of new water reservations only just completed within Montana.

Because of the panoply of laws and traditional water allocation institutions, market-mediated economic forces are substantially constrained in the allocation of water at least in the short-to-intermediate run. Because this is so it has been necessary to examine carefully the structure of rights and the interplay of institutions involved in the allocation of water as a basis for attempting to evaluate whether or not water may be available (and under what circumstances) for the expansion of the energy sector in this part of the country. Claims under the Yellowstone River Compact by the upstream state (Wyoming) determine the inflow into the Montana portion of the basin, and commitments to the downstream state may affect the extent to which the water can be used within the state of Montana. Accordingly, the hydrology as affected by interstate legal and institutional arrangements requires careful evaluation. Allocation of rights and reservations are similarly governed by Montana state law and the agencies established under these laws. Their operation must similarly be understood before a reasonably informed estimate of the amount of water, if any, is likely to be available for a range of coal extraction, transportation, and conversion developments in the Montana portion of the Fort Union Formation.

It is through an examination of the question of water rights and reservations that we approach the issue of allocating water supplies for use in energy development in this potentially important energy region of the United States. Next, attempting to infer the disposition of these rights from the economic motivation of the holders, we compare the sources available by tributary subbasin with the implicit demand for energy under a set of different plausible energy policy options. The purpose of this exercise is to illustrate under what conditions there would be water sufficient to carry out one or another energy development policy, even given the imponderables that presently shroud the ultimate outcome.

In this effort we have called on a large number of individuals over an extended period of time whose competence and cooperation have contributed greatly to what success this effort may ultimately enjoy. To Paul Gerhardt of the Department of Energy, and Robert K. Davis, Office of Policy Analysis, Department of the Interior, we are indebted for their sensitivity to our need for funding to complete the study begun under RFF auspices with support, provided in kind, from the state of Montana. Paul Gerhardt and Robert Davis were also helpful in reviewing an early draft of the manuscript and in enlisting the aid of specialists in their respective agencies to note the need for various corrections. To Montana, we owe a large debt of gratitude for making available a basic hydrologic simulator and for assistance in transferring to us much of what was contained in the heads of Donald Boyd of Montana State University, George Cawlfield of the Montana Department of Natural Resources, and especially, Satish Nayak, formerly with that department and now on the faculty of Southern Illinois University, for his indispensible help in getting their developmental model running on our computer configuration for further development.

Useful comments were received from several persons who reviewed the manuscript. Gary Weatherford of the John Muir Institute for Environmental Studies, David Marks of the Massachusetts Institute of Technology, Helen Ingram of the University of Arizona, Walter Langbein and Robert Hirsch of the U.S. Geological Survey, Leo Eisel of the U.S. Water Resources Council, Richard Wahl of Office of Policy Analysis, Mort Dreamer from the Bureau of Indian Affairs, Harvey Doerksen of the U.S. Fish and Wildlife Service, Gary Fritz from the Water Resources Division of the Montana Department of Natural Resources and Conservation, and Bob Anderson of the same department have been especially helpful at one period or another. To these individuals a large debt is gratefully acknowledged.

A large measure of thanks is also owed several individuals with professional competence in the law. Christopher J. Dunsky of the U.S. Environmental Protection Agency contributed his considerable legal talent tirelessly to this enterprise in continuing assistance to Constance Boris. We also are indebted to Richard Gordon, former legal counsel of the Montana Department of Natural Resources and Conservation, now with the U.S. Department of Energy in Washington state, for his special knowledge of the Montana legal environment. In addition, we thank Jonathan Reed, law clerk to the Wyoming State Supreme Court, and John Haigh, Resources for the Future and the Kennedy School. All of the above were very helpful in assisting the authors through the legal thicket surrounding the issues that could not be avoided in this study. While our debt to the attorneys and John Haigh is large indeed, we alone accept responsibility for any possible errors of interpretation or analysis.

Others who have willingly assisted at one time or another are Milton Schloss, formerly with the Department of Energy, and Louanne Sawyer, Winston Harrington, and Ruth Haas of Resources for the Future.

While our debts are many and we gratefully acknowledge them, there are doubtless some, perhaps many, whom we have failed to mention. Richard Rice, formerly at RFF, now at the University of Michigan School of Natural Resources, Philip Metzger at Interior, and Jo Zuboski narrowly missed omission. Such lapses of memory do not reflect well on the authors, but they should not suggest that we are any the less grateful for the assistance, even though we have inadvertently failed to acknowledge it.

There is a special debt owed Virginia Reid and Patricia Parker, whose competence, patience, and cooperation saw to completion a manuscript that, doubtless more than most, underwent a series of major revisions as litigation and sequential agency determinations moved the problem from one stage to another, requiring repetitious updating along the way. That we could rely on their assistance throughout is a credit to their mature perspective and sense of humor.

We have reserved to the end, and with special feeling, acknowledging the assistance of Doris Sofinowski, computer analyst at Resources for the Future, who worked with Constance Boris on the hydrologic simulator until her untimely death marred an otherwise gratifying venture.

April 1980

Constance M. Boris
John V. Krutilla

1 The Significance of Coal and Water in the Northern Great Plains

One of the major ways of increasing U.S. independence in energy supplies is to expand the production of coal. The coal deposits of the Fort Union Formation in Montana, North Dakota, and Wyoming are the largest in the nation, exceeding the combined reserves of the northern and southern Appalachian coalfields (see figure 1-1). Unlike the latter, they occur in very thick seams (ranging from 16 feet to as much as 200 feet, in contrast to the 5-foot thickness of the celebrated Pittsburgh seam). Moreover, these deposits have a general topography that lends itself more readily to rehabilitation of strip-mined areas than is the case in the Appalachian coalfields, and the precipitation is deemed adequate for revegetation.[1]

Because of its relatively low sulfur content and somewhat higher rank, coal from the Montana and Wyoming portions of the Powder River Basin of the Fort Union Formation has been sought by midwestern utilities as far east as Detroit. This is partly a response to Clean Air Act regulations governing sulfur emissions. Furthermore, because potential demand also exists for new electrical generating capacity in the Northwest and Southwest, the area's coal resources possess a significance quite apart from their low sulfur content.

In figure 1-2 we show the distribution of coal reserves by tonnage and heat content. Although the largest share of the reserves is in North Dakota, it is of the lowest rank (lignite); the higher rank (subbituminous) occurs in the so-called Powder River Basin of eastern Montana and northeastern Wyoming. Getting ahead of our story momentarily, we will concentrate on the Montana portion of the Fort Union Formation. The bulk of the higher rank coal occurs in the region stretching west

[1] Study Committee on the Potential for Rehabilitating Lands Surface Mined for Coal in the Western United States, Environmental Studies Board, National Academy of Sciences, National Academy of Engineering, *Rehabilitation Potential of Western Coal Lands,* a report to the Energy Policy Project of the Ford Foundation (Cambridge, Mass., Ballinger, 1974).

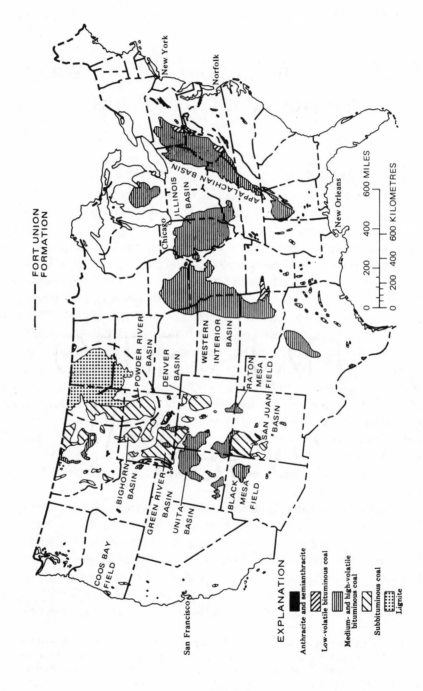

Figure 1-1. Coalfields of the coterminous United States   *Source:* U.S. Department of the Interior, Geological Survey, *Coal Resources of the United States, January 1, 1974*, Bulletin 1412 (supersedes Bulletin 1275) (1975) p. 5

2

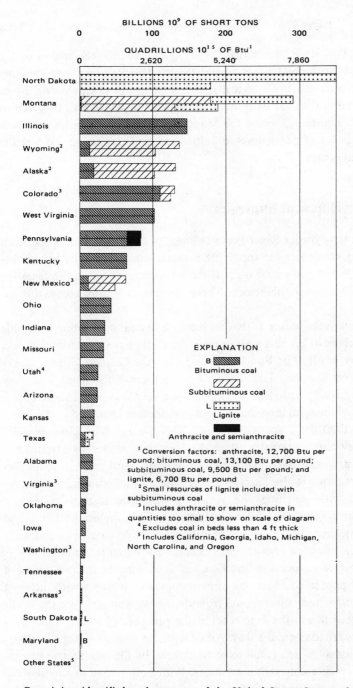

BILLIONS 10⁹ OF SHORT TONS

QUADRILLIONS 10¹⁵ OF Btu¹

EXPLANATION

B — Bituminous coal

Subbituminous coal

L — Lignite

Anthracite and semianthracite

¹ Conversion factors: anthracite, 12,700 Btu per pound; bituminous coal, 13,100 Btu per pound; subbituminous coal, 9,500 Btu per pound; and lignite, 6,700 Btu per pound
² Small resources of lignite included with subbituminous coal
³ Includes anthracite or semianthracite in quantities too small to show on scale of diagram
⁴ Excludes coal in beds less than 4 ft thick
⁵ Includes California, Georgia, Idaho, Michigan, North Carolina, and Oregon

Remaining identified coal resources of the United States, January 1, 1974, by States, according to tonnage (upper bar) and heat value (lower bar).

Figure 1-2. Coal resources of the United States, 1974   *Source:* U.S. Department of the Interior, Geological Survey, *Coal Resources of the United States, January 1, 1974,* Bulletin 1412 (supersedes Bulletin 1275) (1975) p. 21

from the Powder River, across the Tongue, and into the region of the Crow and Northern Cheyenne Indian reservations. This and the surrounding area are hydrologically identified as the Yellowstone River Basin, a more detailed hydrologic description of which will be given in chapter 4. Figure 1-3 shows the Montana portion of the basin on which our assessment of water flows, development, and competing water rights claims will center.

Coal Development Strategies

Although the Powder River Basin segment of the Fort Union Formation is a strong contender for supplying a substantial part of the needed increase in the nation's coal output, there is not universal enthusiasm for coal development in this region. There are several factors accounting for this.

One important reason is that an increase in coal production from this area anywhere in keeping with its potential could have a profound impact on the way of life. The Powder River Basin (the Colstrip-Gillette Oval) coal reserves are very large in relation to the nation's total, and they could conceivably be looked to to produce a very substantial share (up to one-half) of the total increment in coal production identified in the president's April 20, 1977 energy message.[2] This is a region of sparse population and few and very small settlements. It is characterized by a traditional native society associated with the Crow and Northern Cheyenne Indian reservations in the heart of the region, and a community structure associated with ranching and generally dispersed settlements in the non-Indian community. Thus, the increase in population that might accompany energy development in this region could change its character profoundly, affecting both the Indian and non-Indian communities.

There are two aspects to this. One has to do with the overwhelming of a sparsely populated region by large numbers of workers with different socioeconomic and cultural backgrounds. Those who embrace the traditional way of life in the area rebel at the prospect of having their lives altered in so fundamental a way. Allied with this is concern for the physical environment which is felt to be threatened by the prospective extraction and possible conversion activities. With both a way of life and the environment perceived as threatened, political alliances of what otherwise

[2] It might be noted in passing that the "allotment" to this region by the previous administration can be interpreted as being even greater.

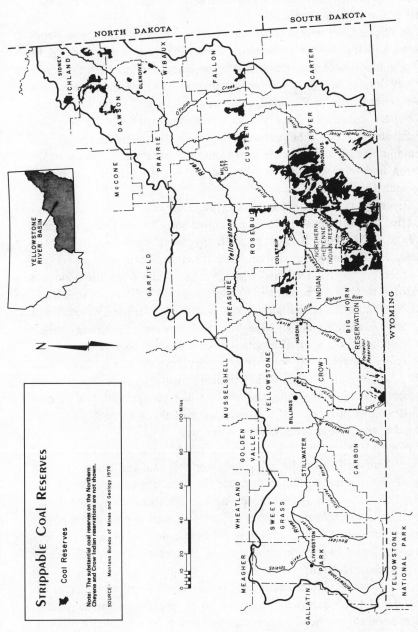

Figure 1-3. Strippable coal reserves in the Yellowstone River Basin. *Source:* Montana Department of Natural Resources and Conservation, *Draft Environmental Impact Statement for Water Reservation Applications in the Yellowstone River Basin, Volume I* (Helena, Mont., December 1976) p. 39

appear to be disparate interests have arisen, all eager to forestall actions they feel will be disastrous.

A different, but related concern is the recognition that the sparse population and the limited community service delivery systems would be wholly inadequate to cope with the population influx resulting from energy development. The resident population as well as the less hardship-tolerant members of the immigrant population could suffer a reduction in welfare that some believe will not be compensated for by development of the energy sector. The perceived limited fiscal capacity of the affected communities adds another element to the uncertainty of residents of the region and others about the ultimate justification for developing the Powder River Basin.

Given the mutual reinforcement of disparate concerns, significant opposition to development has been generated and expressed with particular strength in Montana. Because of relatively strong legislation, such as the Major Facility Siting Act, that prohibits the construction and operation of an energy conversion facility without a certificate from the Montana Board of Natural Resources and Conservation (BNRC), along with water use legislation which authorizes the board to determine or challenge existing water rights and allocate water reservations for future use within its boundaries, the state of Montana is in a position to greatly influence the scale, character, and rapidity of energy development in this pivotal area. Accordingly, because of the political controversy over energy development in eastern Montana, the power which resides with the state to influence the outcome, and the importance of this source of fossil fuel, we have centered our investigation on this area.

When there are significant changes, indeed cataclysmic changes for some, there are likely to be individuals who will gain and others who will lose. It is not our intention to evaluate the gains and losses or weigh the merits of the winners against those who fare less fortunately. Rather, our intention is to explore the implications of various energy development options that might be chosen—or may be the outcomes of political processes—in order to provide some sense of the quantitative significance of the difference in results.

An earlier study[3] reviewed several possible policy options to determine what might be the nature of the impact on the population, the increase in income and employment, the associated demands for community services,

---

[3] John V. Krutilla, Anthony C. Fisher, with Richard E. Rice, *Economic and Fiscal Impacts of Coal Development, Northern Great Plains* (Baltimore, Johns Hopkins University Press for Resources for the Future, 1978).

and the fiscal resources associated with each of the policies. These development alternatives involved coal mining and energy development consistent with the base level (20 million tons mined annually) existing in 1975, with the exception that the Colstrip power plant units 1 and 2, then rapidly nearing completion, were included in the calculations for the base line scenario.

A second scenario dealt with an increase in coal development from the 20 million tons in place in 1975 to 42 million tons to be achieved by 1980, an amount believed by informed state officials to represent plans and prospects of firms in the coal industry itself. Scenarios I and II (which are the numerical representations of strategies) largely reflected effects of decisions taken before Project Independence and suggested a shift to low-sulfur Powder River Basin coal in response to the sulfur emissions regulations of the clean air legislation.

A third strategy representing a "coal for export only policy," of which the state of Montana appeared to be in favor, postulated 60 million additional tons of coal extraction capacity in six 10-million-ton-per-year capacity mines located in the Montana portion of the Yellowstone River Basin by the year 1985. These three scenarios represented basically the mining of coal for electrical generation and conversion, and for use outside of Montana in order to minimize the impact of coal development within the state.

Finally, an alternative strategy that would abandon the "coal for export only" policy involved the addition of coal-fired electrical generating facilities consisting of two 2,600-megawatt units each, along with a coal gasification plant of a standard 250-million-cubic-foot-per-day capacity. (Note that this strategy encompasses the development activities of coal extraction, transportation, coal-fired electrical generation, and coal conversion. For convenience, we hereafter refer to the latter activities as simply coal "conversion.") This was done in order to evaluate the differences between a "coal for export only" and an "in-state coal conversion" policy regarding the demographic, economic, and fiscal impacts. One variant of the 100-million-ton annual extraction with conversion facilities involved extending the construction time for addition of the steam electric units to determine whether significant differences would occur in the peak and duration of employment and population during the construction cycles.

The study discussed above was performed to illustrate the quantitative implications of different levels and types of energy development and to determine whether economic or fiscal constraints would impinge on any of the postulated strategies and affect the rate, level, and character of development. One might note in passing that the revision of the Montana coal tax laws by the Forty-fourth Legislature (An Act Revising the Taxation of Coal Production)[4] adequately provides for state and county receipts to meet any reasonable fiscal obligations arising out of coal development that affects local communities.[5] This does not imply that there will not be prior residents who cannot avoid genuine uncompensable losses, namely, changes in personal lives and circumstances, destruction of a cultural milieu on which their welfare depends, and so forth. We mean to say only that the levies mandated by the revised coal tax legislation would provide adequately for the infrastructure and community services required, should coal extraction activities be expanded.

Although the coal resources are adequate for a significant expansion of coal production in this area of southeastern Montana, and the tax revenues provided for by the 1975 legislation appear to be ample, there are some other considerations that are also, and perhaps equally, relevant to the question of the capacity of the region to expand coal production significantly. One of these has to do with complementary resources; namely, the availability of water in a region which is not overly endowed— both with respect to the actual physical amounts available (for example, amount and pattern of stream flows) and the allocation of what water is physically available among competing claimants. The other question deals with the ability to expand energy production, assuming that both the coal and complementary resource inputs are available, without affecting the environment in a manner not permitted by legislation.

In this study we will address the first issue; that is, the availability of water as a cooperating factor input, and that part of the second that relates to water quality standards, in order to pursue the question of possible related resource constraints on coal development. We do not address the complex issue of air quality standards, nor the issue involving the desig-

---

[4] Chapter 525, *1975 Montana Laws,* Codified at Title 84, Chapter 13, *Montana Revised Code.*

[5] See Krutilla and Fisher, with Rice, *Economic and Fiscal Impacts of Coal Development.* It should be noted that while the aggregate receipts available to the state and counties from the severance and gross proceeds taxes respectively would appear quite ample, some attention needs to be given to the maldistribution of burdens and receipts involving those local jurisdictions such as towns and "in town" school districts which do not have the mining and related properties in their tax base but experience the demand for community services generated by the properties located outside their taxing jurisdictions.

nation of areas where air quality is not allowed to deteriorate significantly and which may be adjacent to areas where energy development might otherwise take place. This is a vital and difficult issue, but we defer it to another undertaking.

Preview of Problems in Evaluating the Adequacy of Water Supplies

With the prospect of coal conversion emerging as an expanding use for water in the Yellowstone River Basin and the possibility that water for this purpose could preempt or be preempted by traditional uses, primarily agriculture, several recent studies have examined the issue of water available for energy development. A review of typical studies indicates that there are differing conclusions about whether or not the physical supply of water is sufficient to support extensive coal development. For example, one study states: "The Yellowstone River Basin does not have enough water to satisfy all existing uses, reservation requests, and projected demands."[6] Consistent with this judgment, the final report of the Northern Great Plains Resources Program concluded: "The Yellowstone Basin should be considered an area where uncommitted and therefore available stored water is scarce."[7]

In contrast, the U.S. Bureau of Reclamation concluded that the 8.8 million acre-feet (MMaf) per year average yield of the Yellowstone River is adequate to serve all Montana's needs including one or more coal conversion facilities. Storage may be required to insure against occasional dry periods, but the "overall amount is far beyond all reasonable needs."[8]

---

[6] Montana Department of Natural Resources and Conservation, *Yellowstone River Basin Water Resources Situation Report 1975* (Helena, Mont., DNRC, 1975) p. 4.

[7] Northern Great Plains Resources Program, *Effects of Coal Development in the Northern Great Plains: A Review of Major Issues and Consequences at Different Rates of Development* (Denver, Colo., NGPRP, April 1975) p. 77.

[8] Phil O. Gibbs, "Availability of Water for Future Uses," in Montana Academy of Sciences, *Proceedings of the Fort Union Coal Field Symposium, Volume I* (Billings, Mont., Montana Academy of Sciences [at Eastern Montana College] 1975) p. 12; see also North Central Power Study, Coordinating Committee, *North Central Power Study, Report of Phase I, Volume I; Study of Mine-Mouth Thermal Power-plants with Extra-High Voltage Transmission for Delivery of Power to Load Centers* (October 1971) under the direction of Assistant Secretary of the Interior James R. Smith, p. IX-2.

Such a position is not consistent with the findings of a state study by the Montana Environmental Quality Council in which it was concluded that:

> A concise statement of future water demands and availability . . . in the Yellowstone River Basin will have to await additional research and legal and political developments. However, at this time it is fair to state that, at least for the Yellowstone River Basin, future water supplies, even with extensive damming, will be unable to meet both energy and irrigation needs.[9]

Because of the wide divergence of views concerning the water available for energy and other rival purposes in the Yellowstone River Basin, it is necessary to review the problem in greater detail, breaking down the geographic area into the relevant tributary subbasins in which the coal occurs and addressing the legal and institutional environment in which the decisions governing the allocation of water will take place.

Determining the amount of water that would be available as a complementary resource needed for energy production is complicated by several considerations, not the least of which are the legal and institutional arrangements that grow out of custom and tradition. Because for purposes of this book water is basically the surface runoff in the Yellowstone River Basin, we are dealing with a phenomenon that in its physical dimensions is the result of a random process. There is much variability in the amount of precipitation, by week, month, and year; indeed, at times it appears by cycles of years. This makes the amount of water available at any one time partly the result of unpredictable meteorological events and the recent history of precipitation that affects the condition of soil moisture runoff. The physical volume of water, therefore, may be couched in terms of an "annual average," but that means only that this statistic represents the total volume of runoff over a specified number of years, divided by the number of years. Whether any one of the next several years will yield a runoff equal to the "annual average" cannot be known, and is certain to be less during periods of drought. Moreover, even during a year in which runoff is normal with respect to the annual average, the rate of flow will vary greatly over the months of the year. To complicate the matter of evaluating whether water is available for energy development, the magnitude in which we are interested is the difference at any time between the flow and the demands made on the natural flow for beneficial uses. If irrigation agriculture is heavily dependent on a particular stream, then

[9] Montana Environmental Quality Council, *Montana Energy Policy Study* (Helena, Mont., 1975) p. 136.

it is likely that the heaviest draft on the stream will coincide with the period of lowest flow, since depleted soil moisture, which needs to be replenished for plant growth, is also likely to release a minimum of subsurface flow for runoff into the stream. "Water availability" then must be thought of in terms of the volume or rate of flow in periods of low flow in relation to the claims to rights of use at times of stringency.

If determination of the physical amount of water available is difficult because of the random nature of its occurrence and the often inverse relation between runoff and demand for surface waters, the situation is compounded an order of magnitude by the institutional setting in which rights to water use affect the availability for new uses. In the Yellowstone River Basin, determining the amount of available water is not as simple as ascertaining from the market transactions the supply price for a given quantity needed. Because of the interdependence between the amount withdrawn at an upstream diversion and the amount available through return flow to a downstream user, simple market transactions involving rights to water are not necessarily efficient in an allocation sense because they exclude effects on users downstream who are not parties to the transaction.[10] Accordingly, the criterion of noninjury to downstream users has been invoked to protect the interests of persons not parties to market transactions. This leaves the latitude in transfer of water rights very poorly defined, and correspondingly, the amount that could be purchased is left undetermined pending adjudication, which often involves litigation. Thus, the so-called transaction costs of a market exchange can become prohibitive unless one deals only with increments to existing supplies, for example, the unappropriated increment to low flow resulting from construction of storage reservoirs.

In the absence of conditions required for an efficient market for exchange of existing water rights, a very complex, and to many it would seem, cumbersome, administrative and litigative process has evolved. This process is both complicated and yet so essential to an understanding of the conditions governing the amount of water available for any given purpose in the Yellowstone that a substantial section in chapter 2 is devoted to its description.

[10] Perhaps the most esoteric treatment of the efficiency of water allocation by competitive markets is the article by H. Stuart Burness and James P. Quirk, "Appropriative Water Rights and the Efficient Allocation of Resources," *American Economic Review* vol. 69, no. 1 (March 1979) pp. 25–37. The article abstracts from the convexity conditions essential for the analysis to hold in reality. It is these conditions that give rise to the noninjury provision.

One feature of almost all western water rights involves the establishment of the rank or precedence of a right on the basis of whether one claimant's right was established prior in time to another's. Priority in this sense then refers both to the time at which a claim is made and to the superiority in rank, or precedence, relative to the claim of another when, because of hydrologic variability, the demands on the stream exceed the total flow. "First in time, first in right," then spells out the rationing rules when stringencies develop, but the question of *how much water* any party has a right to is not well established pending codification of water rights. This is currently being done pursuant to the Montana Water Use Act of 1973. This feature also is further developed in chapter 2.

Quite apart from the ambiguity associated with how much of the flow any individual possessing a water right is entitled to, and the priority of his right, there is the uncertainty about the rights granted under state law if the federal reserved water rights doctrine is asserted. The federal government maintains that it has reserved the rights to water for carrying out the purposes its various land reservations were intended to serve. Perhaps of greatest significance for our purposes is the application of this doctrine to the Indian reservations in the Yellowstone Basin. The crucial issue is related to what interpretation the courts may eventually place on the federal reservation in this respect. That is, whether because of the early establishment of their reservation, the Northern Cheyenne, and in particular, the Crow have the right to water sufficient to irrigate only their arable lands, or to water sufficient to carry on any economic activities on their reservations. The latter might include energy development because a very substantial part of the higher rank coal of the Fort Union Formation occurs on the Crow and Northern Cheyenne reservations.

The combination of the prior appropriation and federal reserved water rights doctrines may become crucial in the determination of what water is available for coal extraction and energy conversion. Under state law, the allocation of existing water rights tends to favor agricultural uses, if only because these rights were established prior to others in time. This could result in limiting the amount of water, if any, that would be available for energy development. On the other hand, if the liberal interpretation of Indian reserved water rights is sustained, and given the early date of the establishment of the Crow Indian Reservation (1851), Indian water rights would take precedence over others filed later. There is no reason to believe that water reserved by the Indians would be restricted in amount and application only to irrigation agriculture. The disposition of the Indian claims then, along with other aspects of federal reserved water rights, may be instrumental in the ultimate division of water between agricultural and energy pursuits. We address this matter in chapter 3.

A third matter involving the institutional setting within which water rights are allocated is the division of water in the interstate tributaries of the Yellowstone River between Wyoming and Montana under the Yellowstone River Compact. Quite apart from the internal allocation of water within the borders of Montana, the amount of inflow will depend significantly on the amount that will be used upstream in Wyoming under terms of the compact. It is likely that the water that will be awarded for use on the Wind River Indian Reservation in Wyoming (Bighorn tributary to the Yellowstone) under the Indian reserved rights doctrine will affect the amount that will be available for various purposes in Montana. This matter, along with the others identified above, will be reviewed in appropriate detail in chapter 4.

Regardless of the way in which the internal allocation within Montana is resolved by the institutional considerations, the physical volume with which we work, of course, is a combination of the institutional arrangements and the hydrology of the basin. The natural hydrology affects the volume and timing of flows. The problem is to adjust the rate of flow to make it more consistent with the timing of the demands that are made on the stream. This involves regulating stream flows by means of existing and proposed storage developments which modify the volume and timing of flows in selected subbasins of the Yellowstone Basin. As already mentioned, we also address the potential depletions from the flow into Montana that would result from the use of the compact's upstream allocation to Wyoming and from application of the reserved rights of the Wind River Indians.

Once we have detailed the physical volume and timing of flows under various conditions, we begin to estimate the water that would be required for various economic functions. In chapter 5, all of the possible coal extraction, transportation, and conversion options consistent with four development strategies that we postulate are examined to obtain a normalized complementary water input per unit of relevant output. We treat in turn coal mining itself, coal-fired electrical generation, coal gasification, and although not contemplated as a feasible Montana coal development policy (at least in present legislation), the export of coal by means of slurry pipeline. This exercise develops the normalized values that will be used in combination with the different levels and mixes of coal development operations reflected in the four scenarios previously described. Our integrated analysis in chapter 9 displays the results of the potential water demands for the range of coal development options and for the energy development projected for Montana by the U.S. departments of Commerce, Energy, and Interior.

As we have argued, the amount of water available for coal development in the basin will not necessarily depend on the amount which one would look to the market to supply at a price equal to its marginal value product in a given use, but rather on an intricate institutional mechanism which determines the allocation of water among competing uses. It is therefore necessary to evaluate the possible range of claims on stream flows by each of the different competing uses to which the water might be put. Accordingly, in chapter 6 we look at estimates of the potential use of water in agriculture based on three plausible working assumptions as to the extent to which requests for agricultural water could have been honored and the potential use for municipal and nonenergy-related industrial uses. Finally, we use the actual state water reservations for these purposes, determined by the BNRC, as published in their order of 1979. In chapter 7, we discuss the instream nonconsumptive flows on behalf of fish and wildlife, recreation, and water quality considerations. This completes the array of potential competing claimants and provides the quantitative information for our integrated analysis.

Chapter 8 addresses the methodology of the analysis, once the data have been assembled. Given that the decisions about allocation between Montana and Wyoming will not be known with certainty before the relevant administrative bodies and courts have made a final determination, and second, that the allocation of the resulting flow within Montana's portion of the Yellowstone Basin will also be dependent on actions yet to be taken by one or another adjudicative body, very little can be said with certainty about how much water will be available for any particular use. The object of our analysis, therefore, cannot be to "predict" what will happen all along the way where unpredictable political, judicial, and administrative decisions are pending. Rather, it is to acknowledge the intractable imponderables and to play out the consequences of some of the different ways in which the decisions may go.

Accordingly, this study represents a conceptual paradigm that draws on legal, institutional, and hydrological analyses and the formulation of an operational model to address the more important empirical questions the answers to which will be useful for public decision making. If the courts interpret the Indian reserved water rights issue according to a restrictive criterion, how will the allocation of water among economic functions be affected? Suppose the decision represents a liberal interpretation of the

Indian reserved rights doctrine, will this affect the allocation between agriculture and energy development? And how significant is the difference? What are the implications associated with each of several different economic functions being given priority in water reservations as a result of one or another outcome from litigation or negotiated settlement?

It is our belief that the results of different policy alternatives, judicial opinions, and so forth, might be altered if those making decisions or rendering opinions have a better understanding of the quantitative implications of different outcomes. "Rights" appear to be relative to a great number of considerations, among which may be foreknowledge concerning some aspects of the outcomes that enter into the final decisions on adjudication of competing claims. It is hoped that this analysis may play such a role.

The mechanism for carrying out the numerical analysis is the RFF/ Montana Yellowstone Basin simulation model, a large-scale hydrologic simulator that disaggregates the Yellowstone Basin into nine subbasins to pick up the implications of alternative policy and judicial outcomes for tributary basins. The model is designed—along with the analysis of the complex overlay of water rights, laws and doctrines, and the functional uses—to provide a more discriminating tool for analysis of a larger universe of questions that federal, state, and Indian planning personnel may wish to investigate than has been available until now. The characteristics of the simulator are described in chapter 8.

The numerical results of the analysis of our questions about the matter of water supplies for various beneficial uses are presented in chapter 9. These represent a very substantial number of questions to which answers seemed important, but certainly do not exhaust the universe of questions one or another jurisdiction might wish to ask. Because the model itself is fully documented and available to the public, we trust that it will be put to additional use beyond our application. The model also has a subroutine that addresses the effects of various water allocations among the several functional uses in terms of water quality maintenance or deterioration. It is thus useful as an indication of whether water quality standards, apart from the physical limitation of water, may pose constraints to the further expansion of economic activity. This aspect of the problem is analyzed along with the quantitative aspects in chapter 9.

Chapter 10 summarizes the analysis, highlights our conclusions, and presents our evaluation of the implications of the analysis for policy and action. We do not feel we have exhausted every question that could conceivably be of interest to some party. Indeed, the entire process of analysis, the structure of data assembly, and the documentation of the simulation model were undertaken to allow others to run through questions with different nuances. It stands to reason that almost everyone who may be interested can draw on the data and analysis, and the model, which is a tool for further analysis, to address questions having policy implications. Accordingly, we invite the interested reader to review this study with that purpose in mind.

2 The Legal and Institutional Setting of State and Interstate Water Rights

In Montana's portion of the Yellowstone River Basin, the physical supply of water available for development for any use depends not only on the hydrologic conditions in the basin, but also on the outcome of a host of complicated legal and institutional issues. Current water laws and institutions may be the most important factors in determining how, and if, water will be available for coal development in the basin and, more generally, the state.

This chapter addresses the legal and institutional setting on the state and interstate level that affects the supply of water for coal development, particularly for coal conversion facilities. This setting includes: (1) "old" state water law that protects existing water uses, primarily irrigation agriculture; (2) relatively "new" state water law that allows for reserving flows for future expansion of existing withdrawal uses and for the protection of instream uses *prior to* action on pending water right applications for energy development purposes; and (3) interstate water rights as governed by the Yellowstone River Compact, which allocates unappropriated flow (as of January 1950) between Montana and Wyoming and gives veto authority over out-of-basin diversions to those states and North Dakota.

A water right is a right to the use of water—a usufructuary right.[1] Almost all western water rights law is based on the doctrine of prior appropriation, the "first in time, first in right" principle, for allocating water. The basic thrust of this doctrine is protection of an existing water right against a later appropriation. Generally speaking, the appropriative water right is considered as real property.[2] Even though the appropriative right

[1] The right that attaches to the flow of a natural watercourse is not an ownership of the "corpus" of the flowing water. Water in a natural stream belongs to the public. See Wells H. Hutchins, *Water Rights Laws in the Nineteen Western States,* Volume 1, U.S. Department of Agriculture, Economic Research Service, Miscellaneous Publication no. 1206 (1971) p. 151.

[2] In Montana, the appropriative right "partakes of the nature of real estate insofar as a conveyance of the usufruct is concerned." Ibid., p. 153.

is associated with property aspects and is generally transferable, western water law subjects the proposed transfer of water rights to the criterion of noninjury to third parties, thereby restricting the role of the market in allocating water rights.

The market concept, however, can be applied to allocating rights to stored water via a competitive bidding process. In this vein, use of the market is being considered by Montana's Department of Natural Resources and Conservation (DNRC) to allocate the addition to the supply of usable water provided by the federally owned Fort Peck Reservoir of north central Montana. The prospect of the state auctioning stored water from a federal reservoir arises from legislation prohibiting the federal government from auctioning water from its reservoirs. Making stored water from the Bighorn River (Yellowtail Dam) in the Yellowstone River Basin available to the state sometime between 1977 and 1981 also seems to be under consideration,[3] and were this to occur, the institution of market transactions for stored water would introduce a measure of economic flexibility into the water allocation process.

Nevertheless, almost all of the existing water rights in Montana are held by agriculture, a use in which the marginal value productivity of water is lower than it would be in energy development. It is generally accepted that if it were not favored by allocation priorities, agriculture would not be able to compete economically with industry for water. In coal conversion operations, the demand for water is highly price inelastic within the relevant range. Thus energy developers could bid water away from agricultural users if efficiently functioning markets were in operation. Therefore, it is important to recognize that public action may be an important factor in determining flow or what, if any, additions to the usable supply of water can be made available for coal development. We will begin with a discussion of how water use for energy development is affected by Montana's water law and system of water rights; then we will discuss the interstate water right implications of the Yellowstone River Compact for the flow from the upstream state of Wyoming into Montana.

State Management of the Water Resource

EXISTING WATER RIGHTS

The Montana state legislature passed the 1973 Water Use Act and the 1974 Water Moratorium Act in order to permit more time to quantify ex-

---

[3] E. R. Wilde, U.S. Bureau of Reclamation, Billings, Montana, to Constance Boris, March 31, 1978.

isting water rights in light of the emerging demand for water for coal development and to assess the environmental impacts of coal development in the Yellowstone River Basin. The primary purpose of the 1973 Montana Water Use Act is to establish a system of centralized records of all existing water rights in the state in order to provide for the continued development of the state's water resources for future beneficial uses.[4] The establishment of a system of centralized records of existing water rights is a culmination of past legislative efforts to "recognize and confirm" existing water rights by their quantification and recordation.

Water law in Montana is based on the doctrine of prior appropriation, the essential concepts of which are that water rights are acquired by appropriation—diversion, impoundment, or withdrawal—from a watercourse for legally established beneficial uses. Property rights in water consist of not only the amount of water appropriated but also its "rank" or "priority" when rationing is required during low flow. The latter is governed by the date of the appropriation. The value of the water right is usually governed by the date of its original acquisition or establishment. Under the state constitution, a water right is granted by the state for a beneficial use subject only to the rights of any prior appropriator to the waters of the stream. The problem is that in the past the water right may not have been quantified or if it had been, there was no guarantee of judicial recognition of the right except through statutory adjudication, which requires joining of all parties along a particular watercourse. Hence, the water right was not necessarily secured because a prospective appropriator would naturally seek a redetermination of the rights of all parties involved in order to obtain water for his own use. A frequent problem with quantification of rights *after* adjudication was that the decrees would often specify a flow right, but make no mention of maximum quantity. Therefore, the private water right was well defined in terms of title, but not in terms of quantity.

The reason for not quantifying a water right dates back to the time when Montana was still a territory. At that time, the method of water appropriation was the "use right," whereby water was appropriated on an

---

[4] The existing water rights refer to those rights prior to July 1, 1973—the effective date of the Montana Water Use Act (Montana Sessions Laws 1973, chapter 462). A water right is the right to appropriate (divert, withdraw, impound) water for a beneficial use. In the 1973 Water Use Act, the meaning of "appropriate" was expanded to include a reservation of water by a public agency.

Beneficial uses include (but are not limited to) agricultural, irrigation, domestic, fish and wildlife, industrial, mining, municipal power, and recreational uses. It is interesting to note that the use of water for coal slurry export from the state is explicitly stated not to be a beneficial use of water.

unadjudicated stream by simply using it without posting or filing. The use right did not establish the use of a definite amount of water. The actual determination was established through litigation with other affected parties whenever a dispute occurred. In 1885, the Legislative Assembly, apparently recognizing the need to make future water rights certain and publicly recorded, enacted the statutory method of appropriating water. The law provided that the prospective appropriator "must post notice" at the point of the intended diversion and file a notice of the appropriation describing the right to be acquired with the county clerk.[5] By filing before rather than after the water diversion, the new appropriator usually filed a claim for water in excess of the need; in some cases, for even more water than was in the stream. In several cases, no diversion of water was ever made. Hence, this effort did little to establish and secure a water right. There was no assurance of the value of the water obtained under this system until the stream was adjudicated by the court, particularly since this method was held *not* to be exclusive; that is, one could still obtain a use right just as before even if one did not file, or if the filing were defective.

The basic method of protecting an existing water right, therefore, was through adversary proceedings between opposing claimants in order to determine the relative rights of all the parties involved.[6] The provision for the initiation of private litigation whenever a water rights dispute arises is expressly authorized in Montana law. As a consequence, this method has been used frequently in the past to adjudicate the same water rights over and over again. The lack of a provision binding all parties who might claim an interest in the stream has led to multiple litigation between the same parties over the same water.[7]

In response to the uncertainty about how rights will be quantitatively defined, Montana's new constitution, enacted in 1972, states that "the Legislature shall provide for the administrative control and regulation of water rights. . . ."[8] Responding to this constitutional mandate, the legislature passed the 1973 Montana Water Use Act. In order to establish the needed centralized record system of water rights, the law provided for the determination of all existing rights prior to July 1, 1973. Existing rights

[5] 89-810 R. C. M. 1947.

[6] There are two other provisions in Montana law for adjudicating water rights disputes: (a) the Department of Natural Resources and Conservation may bring actions to adjudicate streams; and (b) the DNRC may bring actions to adjudicate its sources of supply for state projects.

[7] Albert E. Stone, "Montana Water Rights—A New Opportunity" (Bozeman, Mont., Montana University Joint Water Resources Research Center, 1972) p. 18.

[8] Montana Constitution, Art. 9, section 3c(4).

are to be quantified through the use of all available data such as court decrees adjudicating water rights (commenced before July 1, 1973), recorded declarations of existing rights,[9] other filed statements, and the findings of water resource surveys and investigations conducted by the Department of Natural Resources and Conservation.[10] After gathering all the data necessary, the department will file a petition with the district court for determination of existing rights in the area under study. In the Powder River subbasin alone, the DNRC estimates there are about 11,000 water rights that will be recommended to the district court. The court will in turn issue a preliminary decree determining existing rights. If no individual objects, the preliminary decree will become final. The final decree in each existing right determination is "final and conclusive as to all existing rights" in the area under consideration.[11] Once the final decree is entered, the DNRC issues to each holder decreed an existing right a certificate of water right.

TRANSFER OF WATER RIGHTS

Particularly important for our discussion is whether appropriation rights can be transferred from one use, say agriculture, to another use

[9] Each individual claiming an existing right to use water was required to file a declaration which includes the date of the appropriation, the date the water was first put to beneficial use, the amount of water appropriated, the purpose of the appropriation, the place and means of diversion, the place of use, the time during which the water is diverted and used each year. Note that water as defined in the Water Use Act means all water of the state, surface and subsurface.

[10] The DNRC selected the Powder River subbasin first for a hydrographic survey because the need for a determination of existing water rights was considered urgent, given the proposals for interbasin transfers of both coal and water from Montana. The hydrographic survey of existing water rights was to have been done in two phases. Phase I consisted of the filing of declarations by the holders of existing rights (this has been completed). Phase II consisted of the hydrographic field survey for each filed declaration that had been undertaken. Of the 3,000 water rights investigated as of the end of 1976, about three-fourths were use rights, that is, rights which have not been filed. (Montana Department of Natural Resources and Conservation, Water Resources Division, *The Future of the Yellowstone River . . . ?* [Helena, Mont., DNRC, 1977] p. 63). The Tongue subbasin was the next subbasin selected for a similar water rights adjudication.

[11] 1973 Montana Water Use Act, section 13(5) (85-2-208 R.C.M. 1978). On May 11, 1979, new legislation (Senate Bill 76 [Chapter 697, Laws of 1979]) became effective which replaced the sequential subbasin adjudication process (as delineated in the 1973 Water Use Act) with a state-wide adjudication process. Under this new system all water users in the state must file a "statement of claim" during the two and a half year filing period. At the end of the filing period, a preliminary decree will be issued. Time will be set aside for formal objections and hearings. A final decree will then be issued.

such as energy development. Although the state water laws are designed to protect existing water rights, they also inhibit transfers of water rights in a way to reflect the changing relative value among uses as water becomes increasingly scarce in relation to the demands placed on it. The legislature, in changing the allocation of water among users from primarily a judicial process to primarily an administrative process, did not leave much scope for the market in allocating water. Under the Montana Water Use Act, the transfer of water rights is not governed by economic criteria.

Specifically, the act states that the "right to use water under a permit or certificate of water right shall pass with the conveyance of the land," but an "appropriator may not sever all or any part of an appropriation right from the land to which it is appurtenant, or sell the appropriation right for other purpose or to other lands . . . without obtaining prior approval from the department."[12] The condition for approval of a transfer of the appropriation right is whether the proposed change adversely affects the rights of other persons. If a valid objection to the proposed transfer is filed by a party whose rights may be affected, the DNRC is required to hold a hearing prior to making a decision on the proposed change.[13] If hearings are held, transaction costs for the transferee may be substantial and the amount of water to be received uncertain in advance. This is not to say that the administrative or judicial process used in water allocation is necessarily undesirable from a public standpoint.[14] However, the protection afforded in the act to holders of existing rights implies a policy of giving heavy weight to the state's major economic use, agriculture.

Since the majority of existing water rights are held by agriculture, the impact of an emerging consumptive use like energy development is generally perceived as a confrontation between the demand for water by irrigators and the demand by energy developers. Concern has been expressed that, being unable to compete for additional water with energy on economic terms, holders of agricultural rights will sell off their water to the higher paying use. If energy development does occur on a large scale during the next decade (the time frame of our study), it may involve the use of large quantities of water. At this time, however, holders of existing water rights are protected from the adverse effects of water right transfers

---

[12] Montana Water Use Act, section 29(1) and section 29(3) (85-2-403 R.C.M. 1978).

[13] In addition to an appropriation transfer—change of use, place of use, or severing water rights from the land are also subject to DNRC consent.

[14] In fact, the department's hydrologic surveys and investigations, combined with active negotiations with affected parties, conceivably could approximate economically efficient decisions.

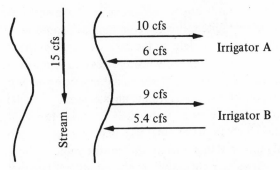

Figure 2-1. Example of integration of agricultural water rights

because freely transferable rights in water simply do not exist under present state law. Specifically, Montana water law states: "an appropriator of more than fifteen (15) cubic feet per second may not change the purpose of use of an appropriation right from an agricultural use to an industrial use."[15]

Transfers in water use are subject to the criterion of noninjury to existing water right holders. It is difficult to meet this criterion when transferring water use from irrigation agriculture to energy development, particularly since agricultural water rights are closely interrelated,[16] via irrigation return flow.

For example, suppose the flow of a given stream is 15 cubic feet per second (cfs). At an upstream reach, suppose irrigator A has a right to divert 10 cfs. Assume 4 cfs are consumptively used and 6 cfs are returned to the stream at some downstream location. Also, assume no other diversions or return flows take place between irrigator A's point of diversion and the point of return flow. Assume irrigator B, downstream, has a right inferior to A for 9 cfs. The remaining stream flow is utilized among other downstream users. Even though irrigator B's right is junior to A's, B is protected from any action which would infringe on his water right. Therefore, if irrigator A were to transfer his water right of 10 cfs to energy developer C where all of the 10 cfs would be used consumptively, this would eliminate the return flow upon which irrigator B depends (figure 2-1).

[15] 85-2-402(3) R.C.M. 1978.

[16] This, and the following discussion, deal with the transfer of appropriation rights and do not apply to additions to the usable supply of water from federal reclamation projects. Note also that the law dealing restrictively with the transfer of private water rights should not be viewed as permanently remaining inflexible.

Irrigator B would suffer injury, and transfer of the entire water right of 10 cfs would be prohibited. Present common law would restrict the transfer of irrigator A's water right to the historical consumptive use (4 cfs) to protect the right of irrigator B who depends on A's return flow.[17] Therefore, any transfer of a water right would entail a determination of the consumptive portion of the water right, an assessment on the part of the potential agricultural seller as to whether the price for the 4 cfs is worth more than the 10 cfs in his original use, and an assessment on the part of the potential industrial buyer as to whether the value of the 4 cfs obtained by a transfer of water rights is worth the additional transaction costs incurred by protest and judicial review when compared with other means of obtaining water.[18]

Any change in a water right that involves a change in use, place of use, point of diversion, or place of storage is subject to approval from the Department of Natural Resources and Conservation. Approval can be given only if there will be no adverse effects on the rights of other appropriators. Interestingly, there have been no applications for water right transfers for a change in use from agricultural to industrial in the state as of this writing.[19] Even though there are similar restrictions on water right transfers in some western states governed by the appropriation doctrine, there is evidence that rudimentary, sometimes *sub rosa,* markets are beginning to emerge in some parts of the West.

NEW WATER RIGHTS

As in the past, the right to appropriate water after July 1, 1973, must also satisfy the criterion of beneficial use. However, now the would-be

[17] It can be shown that there are cases in which it is impossible to protect the bypassed junior right without reducing the transferred right to zero. See Willis Ellis, "Water Transfer Problems: Law" in Allen Kneese and Stephen Smith, eds., *Water Research* (Baltimore, Johns Hopkins University Press for Resources for the Future, 1966).

[18] The potential buyer of a water right may be unable to determine exactly what quantity of water a given right may represent because the amount of water withdrawn, say for irrigation, depends on the type of crop grown, the type of soil, and so forth.

[19] In addition, given the Montana Environmental Policy Act, an environmental assessment would probably have to accompany an application for a water right transfer involving such a change of use (from Laurence Siroky, Chief Water Rights Bureau, Helena, Montana to Constance Boris, April 26, 1978).

appropriator must submit an application for a permit to appropriate water to the DNRC. The department issues a permit if the following criteria are satisfied:

1. there are unappropriated waters in the source of supply
2. the rights of a prior appropriator will not be adversely affected
3. the proposed means of diversion or construction are adequate
4. the proposed use of water is a beneficial use
5. the proposed use will not interfere unreasonably with other planned uses or developments for which a permit has been issued or for which water has been reserved
6. an applicant for an appropriation of 10,000 acre-feet a year or more or 15 cubic feet per second or more proves by clear and convincing evidence that the rights of a prior appropriation will not be adversely affected.[20]

If these conditions are met, the DNRC may issue a permit to the prospective appropriator subject to the conditions, restrictions, and appropriation or diversion construction modifications it may consider necessary to protect the rights of other appropriators.

Upon actual application of water to the proposed beneficial use according to the conditions stated in the permit, the DNRC will issue a certificate of water right to the holder of the permit. Existing water rights are protected from infringement of new appropriations because a new water right certificate for appropriation from a particular watercourse cannot be issued prior to a general determination of existing rights to that watercourse. Protection of existing rights is further secured under the law because priority of appropriation is based on the first in time, first in right principle.[21] While the Water Use Act ranks priority of appropriation with respect to time, it does not rank priority with respect to type of beneficial use. However, the explicit protection of existing rights granted under the act does implicitly rank agricultural over energy uses.

Deserving of special mention is one feature in the 1973 Montana Water Use Act that is unique in the water law of the Northern Great Plains states—the granting of *legal standing* for instream uses and their protec-

[20] Montana Water Use Act, section 21 (85-2-311 R.C.M. 1978).

[21] Priority of appropriation under the Water Use Act dates from the filing of an application for a permit with the DNRC. Note, however, that failure to make beneficial use of an appropriation for ten years will be interpreted as abandonment of the appropriation right.

tion through water reservations.[22] Instream uses are usually interpreted in connection with fish and wildlife for which a minimum flow is required seasonally or monthly to maintain the existing aquatic resources and associated wildlife and riparian habitat. Other instream uses also include a minimum flow to maintain stream-water quality standards, to maintain irrigation pumping, and to generate hydroelectric power. In a general sense, instream uses also include navigation and aesthetic purposes.

The inauguration of a legal water reservation process for instream use is particularly significant. Reserving flows for instream uses will affect the amount of water that can be made available for new or additional withdrawal uses. Specifically, section 26 of the act authorizes the Board of Natural Resources and Conservation (BNRC) to act upon any application to reserve waters "for existing or future beneficial uses, or to maintain a minimum flow, level, or quality of water." The board may adopt an order reserving water, provided the applicant (which can be the state, the federal government, or any agency of the state or federal government) establishes the following to the satisfaction of the board: (a) the purpose of the reservation, (b) the need for the reservation, (c) the amount of water necessary for the purpose of the reservation, and (d) that the reservation is in the public interest.

Complementing the 1973 Water Use Act that authorized the board to act upon flow reservation requests was the 1974 Water Moratorium Act which called for the reservation of water to preserve and protect both existing and future beneficial uses. Given the numerous water use applications filed by the coal developers during that period, and the volume of water applied for (over one million acre-feet annually), the moratorium act emphasized the urgent need to reserve water for irrigation, municipalities, and fisheries flows. The Yellowstone Moratorium suspended action on all large water use applications (diversions exceeding 20 cubic feet per second or storage of over 14,000 acre-feet per year) in the basin until March 1977, but later extended by legislative amendment and by subsequent state supreme court action to December 1978. The legislation passed in 1973 and 1974, which calls for instream flow reservations for irrigation, municipalities, and fisheries together with the suspension of large use applications (almost all from energy developers), is important for its effect on availability of water for energy development given simultaneously competing uses.

[22] There is no existing legal mechanism to protect instream flows against excessive future diversions in the neighboring coal-bearing states of Wyoming, North Dakota, and South Dakota.

The call for instream flow reservations was heeded by irrigators, state agencies concerned with the maintenance of fish and game and water quality, municipalities, and subsequent to the 1977 amendments to the moratorium act, federal agencies concerned with reserving flow for storage for future industrial use as well as maintenance of instream flows for preserving the riparian habitat.

Water reservations can be made for both instream and withdrawal uses, and therein lies the conflict. On the one hand, significantly large instream flow reservations have been requested by state agencies for the maintenance of fish and wildlife resources and water quality. Recognizing that substantial future stream depletions could damage fish and wildlife resources in the Yellowstone River Basin, the Montana Fish and Game Commission requested reservation of a given volume of water by month for each of the subbasins of the Yellowstone Basin, including some sixty tributaries to the mainstem. Likewise, the State Department of Health and Environmental Sciences requested instream flow reservations on the mainstem Yellowstone for the maintenance of water quality standards. On the other hand, substantial flow reservations have been requested for the withdrawal uses of irrigation and industrial (energy) purposes. The latter two uses compete with each other for the limited supply of water in the basin as well as with the instream uses.

During the Yellowstone Moratorium, initially set to expire in March 1977, thirty applications for the reservation of water on the mainstem Yellowstone and its tributaries were received. To a large extent, the reservation applications reflected a bias toward requesting very large amounts of water. This is quite apparent even in the applications of the municipalities. Procedural delays for the holding of hearings on the reservations required under the Water Use Act prevented the Board of Natural Resources and Conservation from acting on the pending reservation applications by the expiration date (March 16, 1977). The Forty-fifth state legislature extended the Yellowstone Moratorium until January 1978, and the state supreme court granted several extensions to December 1978. The legislature allowed the federal government to apply for reservations in the Yellowstone Basin, something which had not been allowed previously under Montana law. Consequently, two federal agencies, the U.S. Bureau of Reclamation and the U.S. Bureau of Land Management, submitted water reservation applications. Their reservations, however, reflected different uses of water. The Bureau of Reclamation requested offstream storage water from the mainstem for industrial purposes—primarily energy development—while the Bureau of Land Management requested water for instream flows to support riparian habitats in some forty streams in the basin.

Even the state Department of Natural Resources and Conservation applied for a water reservation for onstream storage on the Tongue River. While stating that the stored water would be for irrigation as well as energy, it is generally acknowledged that only industrial or energy developers could reimburse the reservoir cost.

With the extension of the moratorium deadline, four reservation applications were amended, one withdrawn, and eight new applications were received from the federal Bureau of Land Management, Bureau of Reclamation, and one conservation district. This raised the total number of reservation requests to be considered by the board to forty, consisting of eight municipal applications, four for instream use, twenty-three for irrigation, and five for multipurpose use. Considering first the nonconsumptive, or instream uses, two major state agencies' applications requested large volumes of water for fish and wildlife resources and the maintenance of water quality. The instream flow request of the state Fish and Game Commission totaled 8,207,000 acre-feet per year on the Yellowstone River at Sidney to preserve the fish and wildlife habitat in the basin. At the same outflow point, the state Department of Health and Environmental Sciences requested an instream flow of 6,643,000 acre-feet per year for the maintenance of water quality. For comparative purposes, from 1929 through 1975 the average flow of the river at this point was 8,345,000 acre-feet per year, adjusted for the 1975 level of depletion.

To a lesser extent, the federal Bureau of Land Management requested minimum instream flows in some forty streams in the Yellowstone Basin. In addition, instream flows have been requested in all the conservation district applications to maintain a minimum flow for irrigation pumping. However, only one conservation district (North Custer) quantified this minimum flow.

Considering next the withdrawal use applications, water for future irrigation was requested by fourteen conservation districts, two irrigation districts, the Department of State Lands, and the federal Bureau of Land Management. Irrigation diversion requests of these applicants amount to 1,186,561 acre-feet per year. In addition, there are multipurpose requests (municipal, industrial, and fish and wildlife) by both the state Department of Natural Resources and Conservation and the federal Bureau of Reclamation. Multipurpose requests represent a storage capacity of 1,179,500 acre-feet. Municipal water reservation requests indicate a surface water diversion of 390,911 acre-feet per year, which appears high considering the basin's sparse population.

The largest water withdrawal reflected in the reservation applications is 1.18 million acre-feet for future irrigation in the basin. A slightly smaller amount is requested for multipurpose storage. The largest instream use request is 8.2 million acre-feet for fish and game. Accordingly, the water reservation process, although originally intended to reserve water for all uses except energy development, has now become a process for allocation between instream and withdrawal uses.

Because of the large flows requested for reservation, the priority of one reservation over another and the priority of the reservations over new appropriations become important. If the application for a reservation for instream use is granted first, it takes precedence over all suspended industrial applications even if the latter have been filed before the instream flow reservation request. The monthly instream flow reservations would be protected from diversions of any water rights granted after the date of the board's approval, but the instream flow reservation cannot affect any rights in existence before board approval.[23] Accordingly, the first reservation granted by the board has priority not only over other reservations granted later in time but also over subsequent water rights or permits (including those applications of the energy companies that have been filed before the instream flow reservation request), but not over actual water rights existing prior to action by the board.

Therefore, the sequence in which the board approves water reservations is particularly crucial for withdrawal as against instream use allocations. Since a water reservation becomes a water right at the time it is adopted, the use which has the later priority will bear the brunt of water shortages. The order of adoption of the water reservations also establishes the preference for future water use. The results of the order of adoption of the reservations during periods of low flow cannot be overemphasized.

Hearings (at times spirited) were held on the reservation applications in the summer of 1977. Transcripts were then compiled and other documents containing a proposed opinion, "findings of fact," and "conclusions

---

[23] Specifically, section 85-2-316(6) R.C.M. 1978 states that "a reservation adopted under this section . . . shall not adversely affect any rights in existence at that time." If the right is existing, there can be no reservation priority. Pending suspended applications are not existing rights, they are at best "inchoate rights" which have not as yet ripened. Mr. Richard Gordon, Legal Counsel, Montana Department of Natural Resources and Conservation to Constance Boris.

of law" were prepared. Finally, on December 15, 1978, the Board of Natural Resources and Conservation rendered its decision on the reservation applications.[24] The board adopted the reservations in the following sequence: municipal reservations have first priority; instream flow reservations have second priority; and irrigation reservations have third priority in some subbasins, with the order of priority reversed for these two uses in the remaining subbasins; multipurpose storage reservations were given last priority. Not all reservations were granted all the water requested in the applications, nor were all reservation applications granted. In fact, eight applications were denied. With the board's decision on the reservations, the Yellowstone Moratorium officially ended.

Summarizing, these adopted water reservations have priority over the pending industrial permit applications suspended by the Yellowstone Moratorium. This holds true even though the pending industrial (energy-related) applications, if eventually granted, would otherwise have had an earlier priority date.[25] An evaluation of the effects of these newly adopted reservations on the availability of water for energy development in the coal-bearing subbasins is presented in chapter 9. Of the coal-bearing subbasins, the tributary subbasins, the Tongue and Powder rivers, have the greatest potential for conflict among competing water uses because of the relatively limited water supply, the magnitude of the water reservations, and the presence of coal.

In addition to the matter of state water rights and water reservations, interstate water right allocations as given in the Yellowstone River Compact are also important to the analysis of the issue, since the amount of water flowing from Wyoming into Montana will be determined in part by the allocation rules laid out in the compact.

[24] A brief summary of the board's order was issued. However, the detailed decision on the reservations contained in *Order of Board of Natural Resources Establishing Water Reservations* (Helena, Mont., 1978) was not publicly available until mid-March 1979. Also, see the earlier document entitled *Proposed Opinion, Findings of Fact, Conclusions of Law and Order Submitted by the Montana Department of Natural Resources and Conservation before the Board of Natural Resources and Conservation* (proposed opinion, findings of fact, conclusions of law, and order submitted by the Montana Department of Natural Resources and Conservation).

[25] Although approval of the water reservations could negate the use of water for energy development, energy development could still occur in the basin if the operators of proposed coal conversion or coal combustion plants were to install air-cooling systems, or develop alternative sources of water such as underground aquifers, or transport water via pipelines from the existing large Yellowtail Reservoir on the Bighorn River to the point of use in the coalfields. Each of these alternatives, however, would be more costly than diverting water directly from a neighboring surface water source.

Interstate Water Rights

As the territories of Montana and Wyoming approached statehood, it was clear that water would be a critical factor in both consumption and production activities in these states. As a consequence, both territories moved to obtain greater control of their water resources within their respective boundaries by enacting water codes and laws. By 1950, the two states and North Dakota entered into a compact to allocate water between the common borders of Montana and Wyoming. Although North Dakota is also a signatory state, there is no water allocation involving it because the interstate tributaries originating in Wyoming empty into the mainstem in Montana rather than North Dakota. The compact, however, confirms existing water rights (those prior to January 1, 1950) in North Dakota and grants opportunities such as water development in upstream states as long as such development is in accordance with the provisions of the compact. The Yellowstone River Compact, ratified by Congress on October 30, 1951, was specifically designed to allocate the surplus flow of the interstate tributaries on a percentage basis between the states of Montana and Wyoming.[26] According to Article V of the compact, Wyoming and Montana are entitled to the following percentages of surplus flow:

	Compact allocation (percentage)	
Interstate tributary	*Wyoming*	*Montana*
Clarks Fork Yellowstone	60	40
Bighorn	80	20
Tongue	40	60
Powder	42	58

Besides confirming water rights existing as of January 1, 1950, the compact provides the opportunity for holders of these rights to obtain supplemental water. This is an expression of the preference given agriculture since most of the existing rights in the signatory states apply to irrigation. This preference is explicitly stated in the preface of the compact: "The great importance of water for irrigation in the signatory states shall be recognized."

Division of water according to the provisions of the Yellowstone River Compact has never been implemented but the ever increasing interest in

[26] 65 Stat. 663. The surplus flow is defined as the average annual flow based on the water year (October 1 to the following September 30) minus existing water rights as of January 1, 1950, less supplemental water for the 1950 water rights.

using the basin's water for coal development is beginning to test at least one of the provisions. Article X prohibits the diversion of water from the Yellowstone River Basin without the unanimous consent of the three signatory states. One energy development company, Utah International Corporation, applied to the compact commission for permission to divert water from the Powder River in Wyoming to a coal development site in Montana. In another case, Intake Water Company (a subsidiary of Tenneco, Inc.) proposed to divert water from the Lower Yellowstone River in Montana to land outside the basin in North Dakota for a coal gasification plant. When Intake did seek the required approval of North Dakota, North Dakota filed a complaint against the company because any diversion could reduce the water available to North Dakota consumers. It was dismissed after Intake agreed to seek the consent of the Yellowstone River Compact Commission for its proposed interbasin water transfer.[27]

Another important article in the compact from the standpoint of evaluating water supplies for Montana is Article VI, which provides that the compact shall not adversely affect any Indian rights to the use of the waters. In it, the states of Montana, Wyoming, and North Dakota are prohibited from taking actions, either singly or jointly, that would adversely affect Indian water rights in the basin. Therefore, Indian reserved water rights have priority over any interstate water rights allocated in the basin by the Yellowstone River Compact.

On the assumption that the provisions of the compact will be implemented in the future, a portion of the surplus flow allocated to Wyoming will be depleted and unavailable to users in Montana. The reserved water rights of the Wind River Indian tribes are also relevant in this connection. This situation will be reflected in evaluating water supplies for competing uses and is discussed later in this study. Wyoming's estimates of its entitlement under the compact are on an annual rather than monthly basis without specification of the uses to which the water would be applied. In view of the lack of information for our computational purposes, we have estimated Wyoming's share of water of the interstate tributaries in the basin from water planning studies issued by the Wyoming state engineer's office. This is treated in detail in chapter 4. However, another facet of water rights that requires attention is the federal water reservation doctrine. We address this matter in the next chapter before attempting our quantitative analysis in the chapters to follow.

[27] In a 1973 action, Intake filed suit against the compact commission so that the commission would be enjoined from enforcing the unanimous consent provision.

3 The Legal and Institutional Setting of Federal and Indian Reserved Water Rights

Introduction

The federal government, Indian tribes, and downstream states also have some rights to the basin's water and this, in turn, may limit the amount of water not only for coal development, but for other state water uses as well. The reserved water rights of the federal government and those of the Indian tribes have their basis in the Winters Doctrine established in *Winters v. U.S.*, a 1908 U.S. Supreme Court decision.[1] The doctrine resolved a conflict between those who claimed water as appropriators under state law and the Indians of the Fort Belknap Reservation who claimed water as beneficiaries of an implied federal reservation. The court held that it was the "undeniable" constitutionally established power of the federal government to "reserve the waters and exempt them from appropriation under the state laws."[2] This conclusion was based on the opinion that anticipated future use of water for irrigation was an important element in the treaty that created the Indian reservation; therefore, the bench held that this implied a sufficient amount of water to develop the reservation when the treaty was made. The upshot of the Winters Doctrine was to give claimants of Indian reserved water rights a superior status to many state water rights claimants. In addition, the Indian claimants had a right to an unquantified amount of water which accrued as of the time the reservation was made even though no water had ever been applied to a beneficial use on the federal reservation. In subsequent court cases the reserved water rights doctrine was extended to all federally reserved or withdrawn lands.

[1] 207 U.S. 564 (1908). For an extended discussion of the doctrine see Harold Ranquist, "The Winters Doctrine and How It Grew," *Brigham Young University Law Review* vol. 639 (1976) pp. 640–652.

[2] Ibid., p. 576.

The court opinion in the Winters case shook the foundations of western state water law. It is not surprising that most western states take strong exception to the Winters Doctrine.[3] Since the 1908 case, the court has decided on the merits of only a few federal reserved water right cases—*Arizona v. California, Cappaert v. U.S., California v. U.S.,* and *U.S. v. New Mexico.*

In *Arizona v. California,*[4] the Winters Doctrine was expanded to include reserved water rights for all types of federal reservations: national parks, forests, wildlife refuges, and the like. In addition, state water rights were held subject to the reserved rights associated with federal withdrawals from the public domain.

In the highly publicized *Cappaert v. U.S.*[5] in which the existence of a unique species of fish (desert pupfish) in Devil's Hole National Monument (Nevada) was threatened by a declining water table caused by expansion of irrigation groundwater pumping, the Winters Doctrine of implied federal reservation was again expanded—this time to apply to subterranean as well as surface water. In addition to the fundamental significance of such an extension, the court's decision tacitly recognized an *in situ* (leaving water in place) use of water as part of a governmental purpose that can be served by the implied reservation doctrine.

There are several important consequences of the Cappaert decision. The court concluded that Congress, in giving the president the power to reserve portions of the federal domain for specific federal purposes, impliedly authorizes him to reserve "appurtenant water then unappropriated to the extent needed to accomplish the purpose of the reservation.[6] On the one hand, *Cappaert v. U.S.* reaffirmed the implied reservation doctrine to virtually all types of federal reservations in the arid West. The apparent immediate consequence of this is to increase the uncertainty caused by the existence of unquantified federal rights that enjoy a priority dating from the time of withdrawal from the public domain. Once federal lands are withdrawn from the public domain for a particular federal purpose or purposes, all future appropriators under state law obtain uncertain water

---

[3] In Monte Stewart's article, "The Winters Doctrine as Federal Common Law," *Natural Resources Lawyer* vol. 10, no. 3 (1977) Stewart states, "In every Supreme Court case since Winters having any relation to the doctrine of federal reserved water rights, every western state has separately or together with other western states filed an amicus brief in opposition to the position of the federal government." (p. 482)

[4] 373 U.S. 546, 600–01 (1963).

[5] 426 U.S. 128 (1976).

[6] Ibid. at 138.

rights, although state water rights acquired prior to the date of the federal reservation remain unaffected. On the other hand, while it stressed an implied reservation of water, *Cappaert v. U.S.* did so for an expressed federal purpose—to preserve Devil's Hole as an object of scientific interest. The court noted that the pool "need only be preserved, consistent with the intention expressed in the Proclamation to the extent necessary to preserve its scientific interest."[7] Therefore, the court limited the scope and quantity of the federal reserved water right in *Cappaert v. U.S.* to the amount of water needed to preserve an adequate water level for the desert pupfish to spawn.

Another important consequence is that the Cappaert decision represents a major departure from the modes of recognition traditionally given reserved rights by acknowledging *in situ* use of water as a beneficial use. The decision also dispenses with the requirement of actual diversion as a step toward securing legal protection of *in situ* uses of water. The legal recognition of *in situ* uses raises the likelihood that implied reservations may be recognized to protect minimum instream flows, since many federal acts authorizing water storage projects generally recite fish, waterfowl, and wildlife conservation as an explicit purpose. It is clear, however, that applying the implied reservation doctrine to secure instream flows for fish and wildlife conservation in national parks and forests, on Indian reservations, and in the operation of federal water storage projects could significantly affect existing junior water right holders in Montana, and future water rights designated for coal development.

Two thorny issues immediately surround any application of the implied reservation doctrine: (1) lack of clearly defined authority in administering and adjudicating federal reserved water rights for natural flow and (2) the uncertainty of the amount of the federal water right, particularly in light of expanding the purposes for which the reservation was established, for example, for minimum instream flows for the maintenance of fish and wildlife resources.

The first involves the authority, whether state or federal, to control, adjudicate, and administer federal reserved water rights, as such rights are applied to both natural flow and stored water. Two recent Supreme Court cases, *California v. U.S.* and *U.S. v. New Mexico,* are concerned respectively with the issues of the authority of federal and state governments over the waters of the western states and scope of federal reserved water rights.

[7] Ibid. at 141.

Both the federal government and the state assume a position of self-interest in defining the scope of the federal reserved water rights. Federal officials tend to favor the position that authority in quantifying these rights should reside in federal administrative and judicial bodies, and that there should be allowance for further expansion of reserved water rights for previously identified uses. For example, when legislation subsequent to the Organic Administration Act of 1897,[8] such as the Multiple-Use Sustained-Yield Act Act of 1960,[9] includes supplemental purposes like outdoor recreation and protection of fish and wildlife resources as management objectives in national forests, the federal government argues that it has a reserved right to use water for these additional purposes with the priority date being the date of the original act creating the federal reservation.

The states, on the other hand, contend that quantification of federal reserved water rights should be confined only to the purposes in the original, not subsequent, legislation and that the authority to quantify such rights should reside with a state administrative or judicial body. In its most recent decision, the Supreme Court in *U.S. v. New Mexico* (1978) significantly tipped the existing balance of federal versus state authority in favor of the states by confining the application of federal reserved water rights in a national forest to those purposes in the originating legislation (the Organic Administration Act of 1897) and excluding the purposes stated in the Multiple-Use Sustained-Yield Act of 1960 from a priority date of 1897. This is discussed further later in the chapter. State officials also hold that a federal reserved water right attaches only to the natural flow of a watercourse and not to stored water and cannot be used for the maintenance of minimum stream flow.

Examination of the statutory history preceding the Winters Doctrine indicates that while Congress allocated the ownership of water rights and the authority to administer them between the states and the federal government, it never clarified the proper balance between state and federal ownership and authority.[10] Legal arguments relating to the federal ownership claim to water have been made using various constitutional provisions. For instance, in relation to natural flow, the property clause in the

---

[8] 16 U.S.C. 473 *et seq.* (1974).

[9] 16 U.S.C. 528–531 (1974).

[10] The acts providing the statutory background of the Winters Doctrine are the 1866 act (which granted the right of way to ditch and canal owners over the public lands), the subsequent amending of the 1866 act in 1870, and the 1877 Desert Land Act (which severed all remaining unappropriated water rights from federal western lands).

Constitution is cited as granting the federal government the power to reserve water for present and future use in watercourses that cross or abut land areas reserved for federal purposes.

Another federal ownership claim arises from the commerce clause which is frequently cited as granting authority to the federal government to engage in water resource development. By its power to regulate inter-state commerce, the federal government is authorized to make regulations preempting state law, a power which is independent of the question of water ownership. This authority was made explicit in *First Iowa Hydro-Electric Coop. v. Federal Power Commission.*[11] In this case, it was held that the Federal Power Commission, which authorizes hydroelectric projects on waters subject to the commerce power, was not required to submit to state rules and regulations as to how the water should be used.

Subsequent court cases on the issue of state control over water rights versus the supremacy of federal preemption of state water rights have supported contradictory positions. With respect to stored water, the state has control over the licensing process for federal water resource projects (in which it is determined whether a project will be built and how the water is to be managed), with the federal government retaining rights to the waters to be stored behind a federal dam.[12] Generally speaking, where Congress has expressly addressed the question of whether federal entities must abide by state water law, it has almost invariably deferred to state law while generally upholding federal preemption of state water rights in the allocation of stored water behind federal projects. While Congress directed the federal government to comply with state law under section 8 of the Reclamation Act,[13] the courts have on occasion interpreted this section in a manner strongly favoring the federal government.

[11] 328 U.S. 152 (1946).

[12] See Joseph L. Sax, *Water Law, Planning and Policy* (New York, Bobbs Merrill, 1968).

[13] Section 8 of the 1902 Reclamation Act lays out the terms of federal–state relationships:

> That nothing in this Act shall be construed as affecting or intended to affect or to in any way interfere with the laws of any State or Territory relating to the control, appropriation, use, or distribution of water used in irrigation, or any vested right acquired thereunder, and the Secretary of the Interior, in carrying out the provisions of this Act, shall proceed in conformity with such laws, and nothing herein shall in any way affect any right of any State or of the Federal Government, of any landowner, appropriator, or user of water in, to or from any interstate stream or the waters thereof; provided, that the right to the use of water acquired under the provisions of this Act shall be appurtenant to the land irrigated and beneficial use shall be the basis, the measure, and the limit of the right.

In the *Arizona v. California* case (1963) about the title to the water stored behind a federal project, the court failed to accept the position that state laws should govern priority in intrastate allocation between water users. The U.S. Supreme Court held that water was implicitly reserved by the executive order that created the federal reservation and, therefore, such water is reserved from appropriation under state law. That is, the court held that Congress did not intend to relinquish its authority to reserve unappropriated water in the future for use on lands withdrawn from the public domain for specific federal purposes.

More recently, the Supreme Court in *California v. U.S.* decided the state can, however, attach conditions to the allocation of stored water in a federal reclamation project. In the predecessor *U.S. v. California* case (1974),[14] the federal government (Bureau of Reclamation) contested the attachment of minimum flow conditions by the state (when the state granted a federal government request for a water right) in federal district court. The federal district court in California entered a judgment declaring that the federal government can impound all unappropriated waters necessary for a federal reclamation project without complying with state law. As a matter of comity (harmony), the court held that the federal government must apply to the state for an appropriation permit, but that the state must issue the permit without conditions if there is sufficient unappropriated water. Upon appeal by the state, the federal appellate court in California ruled that while the federal government must go through state channels in appropriating the water, that is, apply for a state permit, states must grant appropriation permits without any conditions if public water is available, since permit procedures with conditions on water use did not exist at the time that section 8 of the Reclamation Act was passed. California appealed the decision to the U.S. Supreme Court, which agreed to hear the case on the limited issue of whether California can place conditions on the allocation of water in a federal reclamation project.

On July 3, 1978, the Supreme Court held that, under section 8 of the Reclamation Act, a state may impose conditions on the "control, appropriation, use or distribution of water" in a federal reclamation project that are not inconsistent with clear congressional directives authorizing the federal reclamation project.[15] The court referred the case back to the lower court to resolve the issue of whether any of the state-imposed con-

---

[14] 403 F. Supp. 874 (E.D. Cal. 1976).
[15] *California et al. v. United States,* 438 U.S. 645, 674 (1978).

ditions were inconsistent with congressional directives authorizing the New Melones Dam. The Supreme Court, in effect, re-stated the congressional principle of federal deference to state water law, that is, the federal demands for water can be modified by state-imposed conditions of beneficial use of appropriated water if those conditions are not inconsistent with congressional directives.

Water stored behind federal reservoirs in the Yellowstone Basin is important because it provides a dependable supply of water for energy or other industrial development projects. A water marketing program for industrial use had been initiated in 1975 for water stored in the Bureau of Reclamation's Yellowtail Reservoir on the Bighorn River, a tributary of the Yellowstone mainstem. The authority of the Bureau of Reclamation to market water for industrial purposes from a federal reservoir for which authorizing legislation specified the purposes of irrigation, hydropower, flood control, silt retention, and flow augmentation was challenged in *Environmental Defense Fund v. Andrus.*[16] The ownership of unappropriated water impounded by a federal reservoir on the basis of ownership (federal or state) has not been addressed by the Supreme Court. The argument can be made that the constitutional powers of the federal government coupled with the supremacy clause are broad enough to at least allow the federal government to market stored waters in federally constructed projects. By means of section 6 of the 1944 Flood Control Act,[17] Congress granted the secretary of the army implicit authority to market surplus water "provided, that no contracts for such water shall adversely affect then existing lawful uses of such water."[18] If existing uses such as irrigation or hydroelectric power generation are affected, then the qualification is not met.

There are other acts restricting the marketing of water for industrial use such as the Reclamation Project Act of 1939[19] and the Water Supply Act of 1958,[20] which requires congressional approval for any modification of existing projects to include storage for industrial use, when such use would seriously affect the original purposes of the project. The issue of industrial water marketing from federal reservoirs was decided in

---

[16] 596 F.2d 848 (1979). This is more fully addressed in chapter 4. See also George W. Pring and Laurence Edelman, "Reclamation Law Constraints on Energy/Industrial Uses of Western Water," *Natural Resources Lawyer* vol. 8, No. 2 (1975).

[17] 33 U.S.C. 708 (1970).

[18] See John M. Dunn, "Marketing of Surplus Water from Federal Reservoirs," *Land and Water Law Review* vol. 13 (1978) p. 845.

[19] 43 U.S.C. 485(c) (1964).

[20] 43 U.S.C. 390(b) (1964).

Environmental Defense Fund v. Andrus (discussed more fully in the next chapter).

State control over federal water rights versus federal preemption of state water rights may possibly become a moot issue in Montana if federal–state cooperation results in selling water in federal storage projects to the state. The federal government is prohibited by legislative mandate from auctioning impounded water because it can only charge an amount necessary to defray costs of building the dam that impounds the water. Because of the desirability of avoiding the legal problems associated with this restriction and also because of the pressure brought by western governors who want a greater say in allocating stored water to industrial users, the federal government made available to the state of Montana approximately 300,000 acre-feet of water from the Fort Peck Reservoir (on the mainstem Missouri River) for resale in October 1976. Under contract with the Interior Department, Montana will be receiving the water at $20.00 per acre-foot. The state in turn will likely make this water available under a competitive leasing process that is favorable to industrial uses. Montana would use the realized revenue from the competitive sale of its water to benefit agriculture, timber, and recreation in the state. By letting the state resell the federally stored water to the highest bidder, the market value of the stored water can be realized.

Adjudication of Federal Reserved Water Rights

Although consistency may have been elusive in judicial decisions regarding the supremacy of federal authority over federal reserved water rights, the uncertainty of jurisdiction in adjudicating such rights has generally been resolved in favor of the state courts. The McCarran Amendment[21] of 1952, in essence, waived sovereign immunity of the federal government only for its proprietary rights in water. The amendment subjected the federal government to suit in a state court for the determination of federal water rights, though it did not preclude the federal government from initiating a proceeding in federal court. On a related matter, in the 1976 case, *Colorado River Water Conservation District v. U.S.* (Water Conservation District No. 7),[22] the U.S. Supreme Court held that the McCarran Amendment "provided consent to determine federal reserved rights held on behalf of Indians in state court."[23] By thus permitting state

[21] 43 U.S.C. 666 (1970).
[22] 424 U.S. 800 (1976).
[23] Ibid. at 809.

courts to adjudicate Indian reserved water rights, the court opened the door for state court determination of all federal water rights. This case is significant since it could become the basis of a states' rights battle for water in the West. We will have more to say about Indian reserved water rights later in the chapter.

Administration of Federal Reserved Water Rights

Besides the power to adjudicate federal reserved rights in the state court, another important form of state control is administration of federal reserved water rights. The unresolved and potentially critical issue is the extent to which a state can integrate the administration of the federal reserved right into the state's appropriation system as illustrated in *California v. United States*. That is, it is not clear how far a state can go in restructuring the transfer of federally developed water. The law governing federal–state relations in the administration of water rights is certain to become increasingly important as the states seek to exert control over water use. It may become particularly acute in a state such as Montana if there is a political consensus to preserve an existing life-style and to protect agriculture as the economic base. As part of its administrative power, the state can restrict the transfer of water rights. Such a restriction could possibly impede coal conversion developments on federal mineral reservations or force the federal government to build new storage reservoirs. As mentioned in the preceding chapter, Montana does not allow a water right transfer greater than 15 cubic feet per second (cfs) to be changed from an agricultural use to an industrial use.

Although federal–state cooperation (in, for example, the sale of storage water to a state) may alleviate uncertainty over control and administration of federally stored water, the issue of unquantified federal reserved water rights with respect to natural flow—minimum instream flows for fish and wildlife resources and coal development on Indian reservations—still remains.

Uncertainty of Federal Reserved Water Rights

Widespread agreement exists on the need to quantify federal reserved water rights with respect to purpose, priority date, amount and right of diversion, and place and season of use. Generally speaking, however, the major stumbling blocks to such quantification are determining which federal land reservations and withdrawals are accompanied by reserved rights and identifying the purposes for which the federal reservations were made.[24] It is not clear at this time exactly what federal acreage is entitled to reserved water rights. While some reservations such as national parks and military reserves clearly carry reserved water rights, other federal lands, such as those withdrawn pending classification, do not.

The U.S. Bureau of Land Management (BLM) lands are a case in point. These constitute the "nonreserved" public domain, a part of which has been set aside for uses such as stock grazing, watershed protection, and so forth. One could argue that in addition to having limited reserved rights (public water holes and springs), the BLM lands also have federal nonreserved water rights (for which no specific reservation has been made). Federal nonreserved water rights are rights to use water for congressionally sanctioned purposes, for example, for stock grazing pursuant to the Taylor Grazing Act of 1934. The extent of such a right is limited by the time of its actual use and the purpose and quantity of the use.[25] Until binding adjudication takes place, however, the extent and priority of federal reserved and nonreserved water rights will remain unresolved.[26] This is not an irrelevant point. In Montana alone, for example, it is estimated that as much as 19 million acres of federal land may carry reserved water rights.[27]

Under the present implied reservation doctrine, no determination of the quantity of the federal reserved water rights is made until litigation of some form is completed. Therefore, no federal declaration of specific in-

[24] It is important to recognize that not all federally owned land is part of a federal reservation; in fact, most of the federal lands in the West are simply public lands. The distinction between federal public domain and federal withdrawn land is explained in *Federal Power Commission v. Oregon,* 349 U.S. 435, 443–444 (1955): Federal public domain—land owned by the United States by virtue of sovereignty, that has never been in state or private ownership, and that is available for disposition or use under the general laws applicable to federally owned land. Federal withdrawn land—land owned by the United States that has been formally designated for a particular purpose—therefore, is withdrawn from disposition or use under the general laws applicable to federally owned land.

[25] The U.S. Solicitor, Department of the Interior, rendered an opinion (Solicitor's Opinion M-36914) on this issue on June 25, 1979. See also a previous opinion by U.S. Solicitor Mastin G. White on November 7, 1950 (Solicitor's Opinion M-33969).

[26] In discussing the federal (non-Indian) reserved water rights, the National Water Commission in *Water Policies for the Future* (pp. 464–468) recommended that the future application of federal reserved rights should take its priority from the date the use is initiated rather than the date of the reservation in order to avoid divestment to state right holders without compensation.

[27] U.S. Department of the Interior, *Public Land Statistics* (1976) p. 31.

tent and proposed future use need be made at the time of the reservation. By deferring such declaration, the federal government does not foreclose options that may be related to the specific purpose of the withdrawal from the public domain. The lack of an explicit-purpose definition for a federal reservation is illustrated in the *Mimbres Valley Irrigation Co. v. Salopek* case[28] in which the Forest Service contended it had an implicit reservation of water on its forested lands for instream needs such as fish habitat maintenance and recreation, even though recreation was only explicitly included as a purpose for Forest Service management in the relatively recent Multiple-Use Sustained-Yield Act of 1960.[29]

Application of the reservation doctrine to the maintenance of minimum instream flows for fish and wildlife resources, aesthetic uses, and recreation is a relatively new concept derived from an emerging recognition of the social value and benefits of such uses. Current statutory bases for federal minimum instream flow rights include the Organic Administration Act (1897), the Multiple-Use Sustained-Yield Act (1960), and the Wild and Scenic Rivers Act (1968).[30] Few western states (Montana, Colorado, Washington) have recognized the maintained minimum instream flow as a beneficial use. Although authorizing statutes for federal water storage projects often cite the maintained minimum flow for fish and wildlife and recreation as an explicit purpose, most western states have not historically recognized the maintained minimum flow as a beneficial use. A successful challenge to the implied reservation doctrine as applied to minimum instream uses was made by New Mexico in *Mimbres Valley Irrigation Company v. Salopek* (1977).[31] The federal government claimed reserved water rights for "minimum instream flows and for recreational purposes" within the Gila National Forest. The New Mexico Supreme Court held that under the implied reservation doctrine, the United States may claim

[28] 90 N.M. 410, 564 P. 2d 615 (1977).

[29] It is unclear if the Winters Doctrine applies to federally "acquired" land (lands purchased or condemned by the federal government) or lands donated to the federal government. (See Ranquist, "The Winters Doctrine," p. 673). The draft report of the Task Group (see Federal Reserved Water Rights Task Group, "Draft Report," submitted to The Policy Committee of the Water Resource Policy Study, report prepared as part of the President's Water Resources Policy Review [November 7, 1977] p. 8) flatly states that the reserved rights doctrine does not apply to acquired lands. The answer is particularly important since substantial tracts of the National Forest and other federal-owned lands were acquired from private owners by land exchange programs or eminent domain.

[30] It should be noted that a portion of the Yellowstone River is being considered for inclusion in the national wild and scenic rivers system.

[31] 90 N.M. 410, 564 P. 2d 615 (1977).

that amount of water necessary to meet the specific purposes of a national forest. Since the statute establishing the Gila National Forest provided for the withdrawal of land only for the specific purposes of improving the forest, protecting the watershed, and providing timber supply, the state court held that although the Multiple-Use Sustained-Yield Act provided for supplemental purposes such as fish and wildlife, recreation, and aesthetics, it could not serve to broaden the above-mentioned specific purposes. Since minimum instream flows and recreational purposes were not contemplated at the time of the establishment of the Gila National Forest, the court held that the federal government is not entitled under its reserved water rights to use water for those purposes in that forest. The federal government appealed the state's supreme court decision to the U.S. Supreme Court in the renamed case, *U.S. v. New Mexico* (No. 77-510, 46 U.S.L.W. 3243). The central issue was the question of whether the federal government is entitled under the implied reservation doctrine to reserve water in the Gila National Forest for maintaining minimum instream flows for wildlife preservation and aesthetic, recreational, and stock-watering purposes.

On July 3, 1978, the Supreme Court in a 5 to 4 decision in *U.S. v. New Mexico* held that the federal government reserved the use of water out of the Rio Mimbres only where necessary to preserve the timber in the forest or to secure favorable water flows, and hence *not* to have a reserved right for aesthetic, recreational, wildlife-preservation, and stock-watering purposes.[32] The majority opinion said that federal reserved water rights, in this case, are based on the "relatively narrow" purposes for which the national forests were originally established in the Organic Administration Act of 1897. As stated in the Organic Act, Congress provided the following purposes for creation of the national forests:

> No national forest shall be established, except to improve and protect the forest within the boundaries, or for the purpose of securing favorable conditions of water flows, and to furnish a continuous supply of timber for the use and necessities of citizens of the United States.[33]

While agreeing that the Organic Act cannot fairly be read as congressional intent to reserve water for recreational or stock-watering purposes in the national forests, the dissenting opinion did express the view that the United States is entitled to as much water as is necessary to sustain the wild flora and fauna of the forests.

[32] 438 U.S. 696 (1978).
[33] 16 U.S.C. 475 (1974).

The question arises as to whether the act states two or three purposes for authorizing the national forests. There is no disagreement that federal reserved water rights can be applied toward securing favorable conditions of water flows (primarily watershed protection) and furnishing a continuous supply of timber. While the majority opinion cites evidence that "to improve and protect the forest" is not a third purpose, the dissenting opinion cites other evidence that Congress did intend improvement and protection of the forest as a third purpose. If it is a third purpose, then in the words of Justice Powell:

> I do not agree . . . that the forests which Congress intended to "improve and protect" are the still, silent, lifeless places envisioned by the Court. In my view, the forests consist of the birds, animals, and fish—the wildlife—that inhabit them, as well as the trees, flowers, shrubs, and grasses. I therefore, would hold that the United States is entitled to so much water as is necessary to sustain the wildlife of the forests as well as the plants.[34]

The question is, was there an implicit understanding that the forest included its wildlife? The 1960 Multiple-Use Sustained-Yield Act does appear to meet the requirements of the reservation doctrine—including the need for an express intent required by the court:

> That is the policy of Congress that the national forests are established and shall be administered for outdoor recreation, range, timber, watershed, and wildlife and fish purposes. The purposes of this Act are declared to be supplemental to, but not in derogation of, the purposes for which the national forests were established as set forth in the [Organic Administration] Act of 1807.[35]

This act broadened the purposes for which national forests are reserved and conceivably expanded the federal reserved water rights on national forest lands with a priority date for the additional reserved rights of 1960.[36]

---

[34] *U.S. v. New Mexico,* 438 U.S. 696, 719 (1978).

[35] 16 U.S.C. 528 (1974). Note, however, that it was in the 1963 *Arizona v. California* case that notice was given that the implied reservation doctrine would apply to all federal enclaves.

[36] In the *U.S. v. New Mexico* case, whether the 1960 Multiple-Use Sustained-Yield Act gave rise to additional federal reserved water rights with a priority date of 1960 or later in the Gila National Forest was never a question before the U.S. Supreme Court. The state supreme court concluded that the 1960 act did not give rise to any federal reserved rights not previously authorized in the 1897 act: "The Multiple-Use Sustained-Yield Act of 1960 does not have a retroactive effect nor can it broaden the purposes for which the Gila National Forest was established under the Organic Act of 1897." The U.S. Supreme Court, in its majority opinion, concluded that, while the 1960 act did broaden the purposes for which national forests

The Custer National Forest lies in the area of the coal resources between the Tongue and Powder rivers and the federal government could assert reserved rights for minimum instream flows for timber or watershed protection. The Montana Fish and Game Commission has already taken the lead in quantifying minimum instream flows for the maintenance of fish and wildlife habitat for each of the nine subbasins of the Yellowstone Basin. State water reservations for instream flows for fish and wildlife preservation are discussed in chapter 7.

The applicability of the reservation doctrine to wildlife refuges is, however, fairly well settled. The measure of the federal reserved water right for a wildlife refuge should be the amount of water needed to meet the needs of the fully developed refuge.[37]

Another important but still unresolved issue is whether or not the federal government has reserved water rights to develop its reserved mineral interest in coal (coal-fired electrical generation and coal conversion) and other fuels when they are withdrawn from the public domain. If it does, can the federal government grant the reserved water rights that carry an early priority date to private energy developers? The questions are as yet unanswered but the nation's demand for energy may encourage the federal government to quantify its reserved water rights. To date, little of the public domain has been reserved for the purpose of coal development and therefore, it appears that the issue of whether the reservation included water to develop the coal is not a major one for us, since there are so few federal reservations in our study area.[38] The major issues,

---

had been administered, Congress did not intend to expand federal reserved rights. It is unclear if the court means that Congress did not expand those federal water rights for the additional purposes (fish and wildlife, stockwatering, and the like) or that the 1960 act did not give the United States additional reserved water rights with a priority date prior to 1960. However, since this was not a question before the court, its opinion on the effect of the 1960 act on federal reserved water rights appears to be dicta, rather than a setting of legal precedent.

[37] In 1934, Congress authorized the establishment of refuges within national forests provided there was consent by the state legislatures. See also Ranquist, "The Winters Doctrine," pp. 678–79. It is interesting to note that the reserved water rights established for some of the wildlife refuges in the *Arizona v. California* case were insufficient to meet the requirements of the refuges because evaporation and seepage losses were incorrectly estimated.

[38] There is a naval coal reserve southwest of Colstrip in Rosebud County. This is a mineral reservation only because the surface was patented by private owners. The court has not decided whether federal reserved water rights would attach to a mineral reservation. However, there are at least two cases (oil) which would suggest a precedent for applying federal reserved water rights to mineral reservations in order to develop the minerals.

however, will likely revolve around whether Indian water reserved by the Winters Doctrine can be used for coal development, something which was not foreseen at the time the reservation was made. Closely related problems arise when the Indians, owing to a lack of capital, allow non-Indian developers to apply Winters' water to coal development.[39]

Indian Reserved Water Rights

To consider fully the legal constraints upon water available for competing uses in the basin, it is necessary to discuss Indian reserved water rights. Indian reserved water rights are significant for two reasons: (a) the volume of water to which Indian tribes have rights may be large, inducing uncertainty about how much water is legally available to state water right holders; and (b) the future utilization of early Indian reserved water rights on fully appropriated streams will deprive users with rights junior to the Indians. This has potentially serious implications for beneficiaries of both state and federal rights.

For the purposes of this study, who are the Indian tribes in the basin and do their reserved rights affect the legally available supply of water? The tribes are the Crow and Northern Cheyenne in the Montana portion and the Arapahoe and Shoshone (Wind River) tribes in the Wyoming portion. Their reserved water rights are relevant to this study. The flow of the Wind (Bighorn) River into Montana will be affected by the amount depleted as a result of the Wind River Indians' use, and this depleted inflow has to be reflected in our simulation model runs. In addition, the future utilization of the reserved water rights of the Northern Cheyenne and Crow tribes in Montana, if used consumptively, would lessen the amount of water available to non-Indian users in the Bighorn and Tongue rivers because of the priority arising from the early establishment of the reservations. Accordingly, estimates of Indian reserved water rights are included in our subsequent analyses to account for a possible constraint (depending on Indian choice of water use allocation) on the availability of water.

The existence of unquantified Indian claims on the tributaries in the basin thus makes determination of the legally available water supply difficult. With the exception of one government report, official estimates of

[39] Similar legal issues arise when the federal government allows transferees to use reserved water in the development of resources (for example, coal found on reserved or acquired lands).

Table 3-1. Estimated water requirements 2020 A.D., by Indian reservation (acre-feet)

	Indian reservation		
	Montana		Wyoming
Water uses	Crow	Northern Cheyenne	Wind River
Agriculture	1,080,000	109,200	1,920,000
	540,000	54,600	960,000
Domestic	1,800	1,400	1,400
	400	300	300
Industrial	7,000	300	300
	1,540	60	60
Minerals	0	0	3,000
	0	0	660
Energy	196,500	196,500	4,000
	196,500	196,500	4,000
Wildlife	828,300	178,800	300,000
	0	0	0
Recreation	500	300	300
	110	60	60
Total	2,114,100	486,500	2,229,000
	738,550	251,520	965,080

Note: Double entries indicate diversion requirements and corresponding depletions, if any.

Source: U.S. Department of the Interior, Water for Energy Management Team, *Report on Water for Energy in the Northern Great Plains with Emphasis on the Yellowstone River Basin* (January 1975) p. V-17.

Indian reserved water rights are not available, and the tribes are reluctant to provide any information while litigation over water rights for the tribes in Montana and Wyoming is pending. A 1975 Department of the Interior report projected water withdrawals for the year 2020 for the Crow, Northern Cheyenne, and Wind River Indian tribes to be roughly 2.1, 0.5, and 2.2 million acre-feet. From table 3-1, it appears that it was assumed that the same level of coal development would occur on both Montana reservations, and that water for energy purposes would exceed that used for agricultural purposes on the Northern Cheyenne Reservation. Recent information indicates a near universal feeling against immediate coal development on the Northern Cheyenne Reservation, while the Crow tribe is split on coal development. Moreover, it appears that the majority of both tribes oppose generation and conversion plants on the reservation. We will say more about this later in the chapter after describing the Indian reservations themselves.

THE NORTHERN CHEYENNE AND CROW INDIAN
RESERVATIONS—MONTANA

The relatively small Northern Cheyenne Reservation in the Tongue subbasin is adjacent to the expansive Crow Reservation (figure 1-3) in the Bighorn subbasin. The Crow Reservation was established by the Fort Laramie Treaty of 1851. The Northern Cheyenne Reservation was established in 1884 by executive order of President Arthur. The Northern Cheyenne Reservation was taken from lands previously granted to the Crow tribe after the Northern Cheyennes made their return to their Montana homeland after a forced removal to the Oklahoma Territory. The Northern Cheyenne Reservation was later enlarged by executive order in 1900. The reservation comprises 433,434 acres, compared with the 1.5 million acres of the Crow Reservation.[40] Grazing and timber production provide income on the Northern Cheyenne Reservation.

Present uses of reservation land on the 1,567,827 acres of the Crow Reservation are: (a) open grazing—1,217,311 acres; (b) commercial timberlands—34,281 acres; (c) noncommercial timberlands—73,331 acres; (d) other wild lands—9,732 acres; (e) dry farmlands—200,761 acres; and (f) irrigated farmland—39,892 acres.[41] A relatively recent source of income to the reservation is the mining of coal by Westmoreland Resources on the Crow Ceded Area, where the Crow own mineral, but not surface rights.

Substantial amounts of coal underlie the neighboring Crow and Northern Cheyenne reservations. It has been estimated that as much as 5 percent of all the nation's mineable coal lies beneath the two reservations. Roughly, 4 to 5 billion tons of coal underlie the Northern Cheyenne Reservation alone.[42] A U.S. Geological Survey estimate placed coal re-

[40] Approximately 277,636 acres are held in trust for the Northern Cheyenne tribe. Individual allotments of about 156,103 acres and 11,650 acres are held in patent fee. American Indian Policy Review Commission, *Report on Tribal Government, Task Force Two: Tribal Government Final Report to the American Indian Policy Review Commission* (Washington, D.C., GPO, 1976) p. 168.

[41] See U.S. Department of the Interior, Bureau of Indian Affairs, *Indians of Montana-Wyoming* (n.d.) p. 5. See also American Indian Policy Review Commission, *Report on Tribal Government,* p. 163. The exterior boundaries of the Crow Reservation encompass about 2,282,000 acres. Of this acreage, 1,567,827 acres are held in trust by the United States for the Crow, 369,901 acres are tribal, and 1,205,926 acres are individually allotted.

[42] Northern Cheyenne Research Project, *Second Annual Report,* (Lame Deer, Mont., August 1975) p. 3. There are an estimated 8 billion tons strippable on both the Northern Cheyenne and Crow Indian reservations, according to J. H. Rawlins, "Montana and Western Coal," *Coal Age* (April 1972) p. 117.

Table 3-2. Indian coal leases as of June 30, 1974, in Montana

Lessor	Lessee	Acreage	Competitive or negotiated	Initial lease date
Northern Cheyenne	Peabody Coal Co.	16,031	Competitive	Dec. 3, 1970[a]
Crow	Shell Oil Co.	30,247	Competitive	June 8, 1974
Crow	Westmoreland Coal	30,876	Competitive	June 14, 1972
Crow	AMAX	14,236	Competitive	Feb. 15, 1973

Source: James Dick, *Mineral Leasing on Indian Lands: Report to the Federal Trade Commission* (Washington, D.C., FTC, October 1975) (available from the National Technical Information Service, PB-246-568) p. 232.

ᵃ The Billings BIA Area Office treats this lease as six separate leases, all entered into on December 3, 1970. The approximate acreages of the six leases are 12,945; 479; 2,040; 248; 139; and 197. The original lease sale offered only two tracts, and a Peabody subsidiary (Sentry Royalty Co.) was the only bidder for both of them. After the bids were accepted, the tracts were first combined into one tract and then subdivided into six. Peabody is now attempting to re-unitize the six parts into a single tract.

serves at 4.5 to 6 billion tons in the eastern portion of the Crow Reservation.[43] Since 1968, the Crow tribe has granted exploration or mining leases to well-known energy development companies (table 3-2). Shell, Amax, and Westmoreland Resources held leases totaling 75,358 acres on the Crow Reservation. Coal mined by Westmoreland Resources is destined for midwestern utilities.

Between 1969 and 1971, the Northern Cheyenne auctioned prospecting permits for 52 percent of their reservation (243,000 acres). Six of these prospecting permits owned by Peabody Coal Company were converted to leases. The destinations of a portion of the mined coal were at least two coal gasification plants planned for construction near the reservation.[44] Another coal lease offer for 70,000 acres on the Northern Cheyenne Reservation which had more economically favorable terms led the tribe to question the prior leases. In 1974, the tribe formally petitioned the secretary of the interior to rescind their coal leases on grounds that the leases were a product of repeated procedural irregularities. In their petition, the tribe claimed that the Bureau of Indian Affairs (BIA) failed to enforce the diligence requirements set out in the Mineral Leasing Act and the bureau allowed coal mining permits to be issued to speculators rather than mining companies. In addition, they claimed that the royalty terms of their coal leases were, in the words of the petition, "unconscionable"

[43] Crow Impact Study Office, *A Social, Economic, and Cultural Study of the Crow Reservation: Implications for Energy Development Final Report,* a study for the Old West Regional Commission (Crow Agency, Mont., 1978) p. 4.

[44] The coal gasification projects have since been suspended.

and that the bureau disregarded the environmental impact of mining. In their petition, it is stated:

> This casual di.,regard by the trustee (BIA) toward environmental values operates to impose upon the inhabitants of the reservation . . . the risk that no actual environmental protection can be assured.[45]

The decision on their petition is pending, and the holder of the lease, Peabody, is not mining on the reservation. But, for all practical purposes, the lease appears dead given the secretary of the interior's action to rescind the Crow coal leases.

For many of the same reasons, and in particular, the very low royalty rates, the Crows also sought to have the existing coal leases voided in all but the case of the Westmoreland Coal Company. Former Secretary of the Interior Thomas Kleppe subsequently ruled that no energy company could have a lease for more than 2,560 acres of Crow land. Both Shell (with more than 30,000 acres under lease) and Amax (with more than 14,000 acres) have challenged this ruling in federal court. Only Westmoreland Resources is presently mining on the Crow-ceded area.

There are both internal and external pressures on the tribes to allow development of the coal resources. Since the recently lifted federally imposed moratorium on coal leasing did not affect the Indian lands, many energy companies turned their attention to Indian-owned coal. The tribes recognize the need for some type of economic development because of the high unemployment rates on the reservation, but they also have a deep concern that steps be taken to assure preservation of their cultural heritage and protection of environmental quality.[46] In fact, the Northern Cheyenne tribe formed the Northern Cheyenne Research Project, a group of experts whose purpose it is to assess the impacts of coal development on the land, air, and water. Whether coal development will take place on either reservation and the form it will take is difficult to predict, but we can say that if coal development takes the form of conversion, water depletion

---

[45] "Petition of the Northern Cheyenne Indian tribe to Rogers C. B. Morton, Secretary of the Interior, Concerning Coal Leases and Permits on Their Reservations," submitted January 7, 1973, by the firm of Ziontz, Pirtle, Morisset, Ernstoff, and Chestnut.

[46] The unemployment rate for family heads on the Crow Reservation was 43.7 percent in late 1976 and early 1977 and about 40 percent on the Northern Cheyenne Reservation. See Crow Impact Study Office, *Study of the Crow Reservation*, p. 33; and also Jean Nordstrom, James P. Boggs, Nancy Owens, and JoAnn Sooktis, *The Northern Cheyenne Tribe and Energy Development in Southeastern Montana, Volume I. Social, Cultural, and Economic Investigation* (Lame Deer, Mont., Northern Cheyenne Research Project, October 1977) p. 92.

will be associated with it. Therein lies the significance of Indian reserved water rights for coal development in the basin.

The aforementioned Winters Doctrine is the legal basis for the Indian reserved water rights. The U.S. Supreme Court held that when the Fort Belknap Indians ceded their land, they "had command of the lands and the waters—command of all beneficial use" whether for hunting, grazing livestock, or "agriculture and the arts of civilization."[47] The court concluded that without irrigation, their lands were almost useless. It is unclear, however, if the court's decision in the Winters case intended the reserved water to be used for purposes other than agriculture. Subsequent cases indicate that the reservation doctrine may apply to water withdrawals for other uses, however. For example, in *Conrad Investment Company v. U.S.* (also in 1908), the Court of Appeals held that the Indians retained "whatever water . . . may be reasonably necessary, not only for present uses, but for future requirements."[48] A similar opinion, that the federal government reserved rights to the use of water to meet present and future water requirements for Indian tribes, was held in the 1963 case of *Arizona v. California*.

The key problem with water rights claimed under the implied reservation doctrine is one of no clearly defined amounts or purposes. In *Arizona v. California* the court stated that, "the only feasible and fair way by which reserved water for the reservation can be measured is irrigable acreage."[49] Therefore, the case made it clear that when an Indian reservation has been established to provide an agricultural economy for the Indian tribe, the measure of the water right will include that amount of water needed to irrigate the practicably irrigable acreage and related uses.[50] The report of the special master of *Arizona v. California* concluded:

> The amount of water reserved for the five Reservations, and the water rights created thereby, are measured by the water needed for agricultural, stock and related domestic purposes. The reservations of water were made for the purpose of enabling the Indians to develop a viable agricultural economy; other uses, such as those for industry, which might

[47] 207 U.S. 564, 576 (1908). See also William H. Veeder, "Water Rights in the Coal Fields of the Yellowstone River Basin," *Law and Contemporary Problems* vol. 60 (Winter 1976) p. 77.

[48] 161 F. 829, 832 (9th Circuit, 1908).

[49] 373 U.S. 546 (1963). In *Arizona v. California,* the Supreme Court upheld an allocation of about one million acre-feet of Colorado River water for use on 135,000 irrigable acres of Indian reservation land. This represents an irrigation diversion rate of 7.4 acre-feet of water per acre.

[50] It is not altogether clear, however, what criterion is used to determine the extent of practicably irrigable acreage.

consume substantially more water than agricultural uses, were not contemplated at the time the reservations were created. Indeed, the United States asks only for enough water to satisfy future agricultural and related uses. This does not necessarily mean, however, that water reserved for Indian Reservations may not be used for purposes other than agricultural and related uses.[51]

The question naturally arises of how Indian reserved rights are defined if purposes other than agriculture were used to establish the reservation because not all Indian reservations are irrigable.[52] Neither Congress nor the U.S. Supreme Court has answered this question, although a few lower courts have held that Indian rights to water may be exercised for any "beneficial use."[53]

Unlike its decision on federal reserved water rights applied to national forests (*U.S. v. New Mexico* [1978]), the Supreme Court in its past consideration of reserved rights for Indian tribes considers the problem not to be one of finding an express intent, but rather one that poses the question of what the parties would have done if the problem had been considered (*Winters v. U.S.* [1908]). Recalling the Winters case, Justice McKenna wrote:

> The Indians had command of the lands and the waters—command of all their beneficial use, whether kept for hunting, "and grazing roving herds of stock," or turned to agriculture and the arts of civilization. Did they give up all this? Did they reduce the area of their occupation and give up the waters which made it valuable or adequate?[54]

He resolved the ambiguities in favor of the Indians. In *Arizona v. California,* Justice Black observed that the federal government must surely have known when it created the Indian reservations "that water from the river would be essential to the life of the Indian people and the animals they hunt and the crops they raised."[55]

In the Winters Doctrine, the court recognized that in laying aside their nomadic ways, Indians could turn both "to agriculture and the arts of civilization." It can be argued that the arts of civilization include industry

[51] Report of Special Master Rifkind at 265–266 (1960) in *Arizona v. California,* 373 U.S. 546 (1963). See also Harold A. Ranquist, "The Effect of Changes in Place and Nature of Use of Indian Rights to Water Reserved Under the 'Winters Doctrine'," *Natural Resources Lawyer* vol. 5, no. 1 (January 1972) p. 34.

[52] Not all Indian reservations were established with the intention of limiting development to irrigation only; some tribes depend on fishing to provide their sustenance.

[53] *U.S. v. Walker River Irrigation District,* 104 F.2d 334, 340 (9th Circuit, 1939).

[54] *Winters v. U.S.,* 207 U.S. at 576.

[55] 373 U.S. at 599.

as well as agriculture, and both require water. While agricultural uses predominate in the Colorado River Basin as shown in *Arizona v. California,* industrial uses related to coal development may be ultimately more relevant in the Yellowstone River Basin. However, in the two most recent cases dealing with federal reserved water rights, the court restricted the application of reserved rights to explicitly stated purposes in the originating legislation. It is conceivable that this precedent could be applied to Indian reserved water rights.

Uncertainty, therefore, pervades the quantification of Indian reserved rights in Montana. Will it be based on the restrictive criterion of "practicably irrigable acreage" or on the expansive criterion of all present and potential uses without reference to the purposes considered at the time the reservation was established due to changing economic conditions? State governments and some federal agencies (the Bureau of Reclamation)[56] argue that the restrictive criterion should be applied to Indian reserved water rights.[57] The Indians, on the other hand, contend that they are legally entitled to reserved rights based on the expansive criterion or the criterion of multipurpose use.

Besides the uncertainty about determining the purposes for which Indian reserved water rights can be applied, location of the rivers to which the tribes lay claim is also important. The reserved rights of the Northern Cheyenne apply to the Tongue River and Rosebud Creek—both of which traverse the heart of the coal country. The reserved rights of the Crow apply to Bighorn and Little Bighorn rivers and to the watershed of Rosebud Creek and the Tongue River. Moreover, the utilization of the reserved water rights of the Wind River Indians in Wyoming will affect the flow of the Bighorn River at the Wyoming-Montana border. Just as important is the priority of their reserved rights, which is determined by the date when the reservation was established.[58] More important, reserved rights are protected against divestiture by non-use. Therefore, the Crow reserved rights would date from 1851 and the Northern Cheyenne from 1884 on

[56] On November 6, 1979, the Bureau of Reclamation was renamed the Water and Power Resources Service.

[57] The Bureau of Reclamation in the past has asserted that Indian reserved rights should be limited to agricultural purposes. With respect to water storage projects, the bureau would then be able to allocate more water to other non-Indian users. Veeder contends this would free water for coal interests at the expense of the Indians (Veeder, "Water Rights," p. 90).

[58] Some advocates have argued that Indian reserved water rights date from time immemorial since they are the true natives of this country (Veeder, "Water Rights," p. 87).

some tributaries and 1900 on the Tongue River. Indian reserved water rights, however, do not have priority over state-granted water rights acquired prior to the date of the creation of the Indian reservation. Since state-granted water rights on the Tongue River for irrigation date back to 1886, the Northern Cheyenne would have priority only over those state water rights on the Tongue acquired after 1900.[59]

Aware of the studies that projected substantial amounts of water to be used for coal conversion facilities, the Northern Cheyenne and Crow tribes along with the federal government filed suit in federal court in 1975 to determine and adjudicate their reserved water rights. In *U.S. v. Tongue River Users Association et al.,*[60] the United States in its own right, and as fiduciary on behalf of the Northern Cheyenne and the Crow Indians, seeks a "declaration of water rights in and to the use of the waters of Rosebud Creek and of the Tongue River and their respective tributaries located in, on or adjacent to" the tribes' reservations in Montana. The Crow Indians claim rights to the use of the surface and ground water within the watershed of Rosebud Creek and the Tongue River, which were unappropriated on September 17, 1851. The Northern Cheyenne Tribe claims rights to the water of Rosebud Creek and tributaries located in or adjacent to the reservation, which were unappropriated on November 26, 1884, and to the use of the waters of the Tongue River and its tributaries, which were unappropriated on March 19, 1900.[61] The suit involves about 1,600 water users as defendants.

In addition, the Northern Cheyenne tribe itself filed suit in *The Northern Cheyenne Tribe of the Northern Cheyenne Indian Reservation v. Thomas Ralph Adsit* (hereafter referred to as *Northern Cheyenne Tribe v. Adsit*), for "quiet title" to water rights on the Tongue River and Rosebud Creek, except that the tribe asserts that the priority of its reserved rights dates "from time immemorial" or at least from the date of the treaty.[62] This action was subsequently combined with *U.S. v. Tongue River Users Association.*

[59] In a state court decision in 1914, the Northern Cheyenne tribe was given twenty-first place in a priority list of water users on the Tongue River. See Nordstrom and coauthors, *The Northern Cheyenne,* p. 9.

[60] *U.S. v. Tongue River Users Association et al.,* Civil No. CV-75-20-BLG (D. Mont., filed August 1, 1975).

[61] Besides their reserved rights, the Northern Cheyenne currently have a contract for 7,500 acre-feet of stored water from the state-owned Tongue River Reservoir. Laurence Siroky, Chief, Water Rights Bureau, to Constance Boris, June 20, 1978.

[62] *Northern Cheyenne Tribe v. Adsit,* No. CV-75-6-BLG (D. Mont., filed August 14, 1975).

In a suit dealing with the reserved rights of the Crow tribe, *U.S. v. Big Horn Low Line Canal,* the federal government, acting on its own behalf and as fiduciary on behalf of the Crow tribe, seeks a declaration of water rights on the Bighorn River, the Little Bighorn River, and several tributaries.[63] The action claims rights to the use of water in these rivers which were unappropriated as of September 17, 1851, for the present and future needs of the Indians, for the purposes for which the reservation was created. Such purposes include "municipal and domestic use, irrigation, stock watering and full utilization of the Reservation and its resources for the benefit of the Crow Indians."[64]

The Northern Cheyenne and Crow tribes adopted the expansive or multiple beneficial use criterion for quantifying their reserved water rights in the Tongue subbasin. In the amended complaint, the Indians lay claim to the waters which "are or will become reasonably necessary for the present and future needs of the Indians in fulfillment of the purposes for which the reservation was created. Such purposes include municipal and domestic use, irrigation and stock watering and full utilization of the reservation and its resources . . ."[65] for the benefit of the respective tribes. The Northern Cheyenne added environmental and aesthetic purposes to to their list of beneficial uses. Recently proposed rules by the Bureau of Indian Affairs define beneficial use of water as "any use of water, consumptive or otherwise, for agricultural, domestic, municipal, commercial, industrial, aesthetic, religious, or recreational purposes, or for the maintenance of adequate stream flows for fishery, environmental, or other beneficial purposes on an Indian reservation."[66] If the above definition of beneficial use of water is interpreted as an all-inclusive purpose for which the reservation was created, then quantification will not be tractable until the Indian claims of water rights are made known when the suit is brought

---

[63] *United States v. Big Horn Low Line Canal,* No. CV-75-34-BLG (D. Mont., filed August 29, 1975).

[64] Ibid., amended complaint at 18. In this same action the federal government claims reserved rights for use of water in the Custer National Forest (priority date 1906), Big Horn Canyon National Recreation Area (1966), Pryor Mountain Wild Horse Range (1968), and the Yellowtail Dam (1944). As discussed earlier, the *U.S. v. New Mexico* case severely limits the application of reserved rights in the national forests to timber supply and watershed protection. With the *U.S. v. New Mexico* and the *Cappaert v. U.S.* cases, there is a likelihood that the strict interpretation of reserved rights will be applied to other types of federal reservations.

[65] *U.S. v. Tongue River Users Association,* Civil No. CV-75-20-BLG (D. Mont., filed August 1, 1975), amended complaint at 12.

[66] 42 *Federal Register* 14885 (1977) [25 CFR Part 260].

to court. Understandably, the tribes refuse to comment on the amount of water they will request.

No explicit mention of the use of the waters for coal development on the reservations is made in the Crow and Northern Cheyenne briefs, although the initiation of the civil action reflects the Indians' deep concern that water for future off-reservation coal development will adversely affect the supply of water available to them, and hence the future economic development of the reservations. Whether or not Indian reserved water rights can be used for coal development remains unanswered, although it is worthy of note that in one pending case the United States in its fiduciary role claimed sufficient water to bring the coal to a marketable state on the Ute Mountain Ute and Southern Ute Indian reservations.[67] In chapters 5, 6, and 7, we estimate the range of reserved water right claims of the Crow and Northern Cheyenne using both the restrictive and the expansive criteria. This allows us to quantify the Indian reserved rights by economic function and thus enables us to evaluate the effects of legal constraints on water available for different economic functions, a subject that is discussed in chapter 9.

One final point is the jurisdictional issue over where the reserved and private claims to water will be adjudicated, whether in federal or state district court. Filing for adjudication of the Crow and Northern Cheyenne reserved rights in the U.S. District Court for the District of Montana led to a motion by Montana to dismiss the Indian water suits on the grounds

---

[67] *U.S. v. Akin,* 504 F.2d 115 (10th Circuit, 1974); reversed in part *sub nom. Colorado River Water Conservation District v. United States,* 424 U.S. 800 (1976). Also note that the Crow had at one time expressed an interest in siting a coal gasification plant on their reservation. If the pending litigation allows use of water for coal development on the Crow Reservation, then there arises the situation where coal development would have the most senior water right in the basin since the priority of reserved water rights for the Crow is 1851. One complicating and hitherto unanswered question, however, is whether the Indians (who lack the needed capital for coal combustion and conversion facilities) can transfer their reserved water rights to non-Indian coal developers since this would represent a change in the use of water, which is generally not allowed for in western water law. Some have also argued that Congress should provide for the leasing of reserved water rights for use off the Indian reservation since it appears that reserved water rights constitute the only major resource that Congress has not included within its leasing provisions on Indian reservations. See Bill Leaphart, "Sale and Lease of Indian Water Rights," *Montana Law Review* vol. 33, no. 2 (Summer 1972). On a related point, Harold Ranquist points out that there is no body of law or administrative procedure applicable to the issue of changes in the place or nature of use of water by Indian tribes. (Ranquist, "The Effect of Changes.")

that the state courts rather than federal courts are the proper forum for adjudicating water rights. The basis for the state's motion was the Mc-Carran Amendment of 1950 which allows for a general adjudication of all of the rights of various owners on a given watercourse in state courts. In a subsequent but related case, *Colorado River Water Conservation District v. U.S.* (1976), the Supreme Court held that the McCarran Amendment "provided consent to determine federal reserved water rights held on behalf of Indians in state court."[68] On November 26, 1979, the federal district court granted the state of Montana's motion to dismiss the Indian reserved rights suits on the basis of the above case and the policy of wise judicial administration.[69] As a consequence, the three pending suits of the Crow and Northern Cheyenne tribes were dismissed and later appealed. Specifically, the Northern Cheyenne tribe filed an appeal of the *Northern Cheyenne Tribe v. Adsit* case and both the Crow tribe and the United States filed notices of appeal of the *U.S. v. Tongue River Water Users Association* and *U.S. v. Big Horn Low Line Canal* cases.[70] Until the jurisdictional issue is resolved, there will be no determination of the Indian reserved water rights. This litigation appears to have stimulated interest

[68] 424 U.S. at 809.

[69] The principle of wise judicial administration is concerned with the "conservation of judicial resources and comprehensive disposition of litigation." The federal district court's decision for dismissal on this principle was largely based on Senate Bill 76 enacted by the Montana state legislature in May 1979, calling for a statewide adjudication of all existing rights (discussed in footnote 11, chapter 2). Section 16 of the bill provided that the Montana Supreme Court issue an order to file a statement of claim of an existing water right. The requirement to file a claim for existing rights to the use of water includes but is not limited to a "federal agency of the United States of America on its own behalf or as trustee for any Indian or Indian tribe asserting a claim to an existing right . . . prior to July 1, 1973." Since the general statewide adjudication was initiated by a recent order of the Montana Supreme Court, the federal district court concluded that: "it would seem that the greater wisdom lies in following *Colorado River* and on the basis of wise judicial administration, deferring to the comprehensive state proceedings." *The Northern Cheyenne Tribe of the Northern Cheyenne Indian Reservation v. Thomas Ralph Adsit*, Civil No. 75-6-BLG (D. Mont., Memorandum and Order filed November 29, 1979) at 6–7.

[70] The Northern Cheyenne tribe filed its appeal (appeal docketed, No. 79-4887, 9th Cir., December 26, 1979) to establish the principle that federal courts have exclusive jurisdiction in this state in adjudicating Indian reserved water rights. The U.S. attorney filed a notice of appeal of *U.S. v. Tongue River Water Users Association* (appeal docketed, No. 80-3042, 9th Cir., January 25, 1980) and *U.S. v. Big Horn Low Line Canal* (appeal docketed, No. 80-3063, 9th Cir., January 25, 1980). The Crow tribe filed its appeal of these two cases respectively (appeals docketed, No. 80-3041 and No. 80-3062, 9th Cir., January 28, 1980).

on the Wind River Reservation in Wyoming and among existing state water right holders.

WIND RIVER INDIAN RESERVATION—WYOMING

As mentioned in the beginning of this section, the application of reserved water rights of the Wind River Indian tribes will affect the inflow of the Bighorn River into Montana. The Wind River Indian Reservation in central Wyoming contains the headwaters of many of the tributaries of the Bighorn River, and therefore their reserved rights will affect downstream water right holders in both Wyoming and Montana. The 1,887,000-acre Wind River Reservation in west central Wyoming is the home of the Shoshone and the Arapahoe. In addition to grazing fees, farm rentals, and timber, oil and gas fields on the reservation produce substantial income. Roughly one-third of the irrigated farm land and nearly all the rangeland is used by tribal members.[71]

The interaction between the state and the Indian tribes over jurisdiction in adjudicating water rights in Montana has implications for the reserved water rights of the Wind River tribes in Wyoming. The jurisdictional issue again is whether the Indian reserved water rights are to be adjudicated in federal or state court. Filing of the Montana Indian tribal water suits in federal court stimulated defensive action in Wyoming. In January 1977, to head off potentially adverse consequences on state water appropriators and avoid a recurrence of requesting a transfer of suit regarding Indian water rights from federal to state court, Wyoming filed suit in state court for a general adjudication of water rights in the Bighorn subbasin.[72] The federal government, on behalf of the Wind River Indians, requested the suit be moved to federal court. A year later, a Wyoming federal district court judge held that the state has jurisdiction over the case.[73] The next step is to determine how to handle the logistical problem of having 20,000 individuals, including the Wind River tribes, defend their water rights in the Wyoming portion of the Bighorn River subbasin.

We do not feel competent to prejudge the results of the pending litigation; nor do we feel it would be appropriate for us to do so. We can only surmise that some difference will result in the amount of water that might

---

[71] U.S. Department of the Interior, *Indians of Montana-Wyoming,* p. 13.
[72] *Wyoming v. United States,* No. C77-039K (D. Wyo., May 31, 1977).
[73] Ibid. Order remanded to state court pursuant to 28 U.S.C. 1447 (1970).

be allocable to energy development, depending on the outcome of the adjudication suits. We will address the technicalities of these issues in subsequent chapters where we attempt to sort out the claims for water by economic function.

Before doing so, however, because the spatial and temporal variability of surface water flows can affect the choice and level of coal development in the Yellowstone River Basin, we turn to a description of the basin itself.

4 A Description of the Yellowstone River Basin and Water Resource Development

The hydrologic system itself, the Yellowstone River Basin, is the topic of discussion in this chapter. The variability of the system as well as the flow-regulating reservoirs, existing and proposed, are described. Because the interstate tributaries flow from Wyoming into Montana, it is necessary to discuss the legal claims on their flow: Wyoming's share of flow pursuant to the Yellowstone River Compact and the reserved water rights of Wyoming's Wind River Indian tribes.

Hydrologic Variability

The basin is itself a subbasin of the very large Missouri River Basin. As with its parent basin, the term "variable" probably best describes the Yellowstone Basin with respect to topography, temperature, precipitation, and flow (all of which in turn change with latitude and elevation). There are wide expanses of rolling hills, isolated flat-topped buttes and ridges, plains, and mountain ranges to the west intersected by the winding unimpeded Yellowstone and its tributaries. In June, the hiker climbing to the top of a ridge can observe snow and clouds and experience cold temperatures and strong winds while looking down on a placid, sunshine-filled valley below. Bounded by the rugged Rockies on the west and plains on the east, the basin drains a watershed of about 70,000 square miles with the total drainage area roughly split between Montana and Wyoming. In this study, we concentrate on the Montana portion of the Yellowstone River Basin, and more specifically on the subbasins containing the coal resources.

The Yellowstone River has its headwaters in the mountains of the country's first national park, Yellowstone, in northern Wyoming. From its

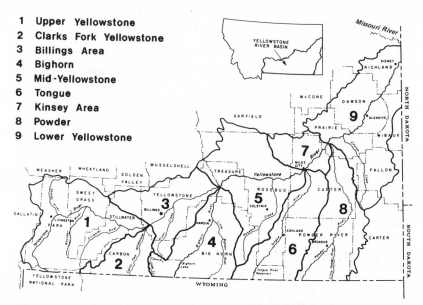

1   **Upper Yellowstone**
2   **Clarks Fork Yellowstone**
3   **Billings Area**
4   **Bighorn**
5   **Mid-Yellowstone**
6   **Tongue**
7   **Kinsey Area**
8   **Powder**
9   **Lower Yellowstone**

Figure 4-1.   The nine planning basins of the Yellowstone Basin   *Source:* Montana Department of Natural Resources and Conservation, Water Resources Division, *Which Way? The Future of Yellowstone Water* (Helena, Mont., 1976) p. 12

headwaters, the river flows unimpeded by dams in a northeasterly direction through southeastern Montana and a small bit of North Dakota where it joins the Missouri River (figure 4-1). The average annual flow of the Yellowstone River at the point of outflow from Montana (Sidney) over the period 1929 to 1975 was 8.45 million acre-feet (MMaf) of water when the annual flow estimates are adjusted to reflect the 1975 level of depletion.[1] But averages are misleading for seldom does "average" flow actually occur. Instead, flow tends to fluctuate widely around the annual averages, with the occurrence and the degree of the fluctuations being unpredictable. Therefore, the average annual flow has to be thought of as a statistical construct representing only the total flow over a period of time, divided by the number of years in the period.

Wide variations in seasonal temperatures, precipitation, and flow characterize the Yellowstone Basin as much as they do the larger Missouri Basin. Significant factors affecting the climate are the interior continental

[1] U.S. Department of the Interior, Bureau of Reclamation, *Yellowstone River Basin and Adjacent Coal Fields Depletion Study: 1975 Level of Development* (Billings, Mont., Upper Missouri Regional Office, November 1976).

location of the Yellowstone Basin and the absence of large inland water bodies. The north–south orientation of the Rocky Mountains along the basin's western edge restricts the flow of air masses from the Pacific Ocean, and, therefore, the air mass from the Gulf of Mexico is the major source of moisture into the basin. In midwinter, air flows from the gulf give rise to the so-called "chinooks," unseasonably warm winds that induce a thaw of winter snow which subsequently refreezes with the arrival of northern blasts of polar air from Canada. The frequent presence of cold continental polar air in the winter and warm continental air in the summer makes for a great range of temperature between winter and summer. There is also a large diurnal temperature variation, especially during the warmer months of the year.

In addition to the topography, precipitation patterns contribute to the characteristic hydrologic variability for which the parent Missouri Basin is noted. In crossing the expansive land area from the Gulf of Mexico, the air masses lose most of their moisture, contributing to the semiarid climate for the basin. In addition, the western barrier of mountains makes it difficult for moisture-laden air to penetrate the basin. As a consequence, rainfall is less than on the other side of the mountains. It also varies greatly from season to season and year to year. In the driest portion of the basin, the average annual precipitation over a sixteen-year period is 6.6 inches while the wettest portion has an average annual precipitation of 24 inches.[2] In the eastern section where the coal resources are located, average annual precipitation is roughly 14 inches, only half of which falls during the growing season.

Annual snowfall in the basin ranges from a low of 20 inches in the eastern plains to 300 inches in the mountainous areas, with most of the snowfall occurring from November to March.[3] The mountain snowpack is the primary source of water. It also constitutes much of the usable water in the mainstem reaches of the basin since the snowfall on the plains melts in early spring, sometimes before it can be applied by downstream irrigators.

The variation in the rate of runoff in the basin is accordingly quite large. The hydrologic variation on the mainstem is dominated by a seasonal pattern, reflecting the accumulation and melt of the snowpack. Surface runoff from the mountain snowmelt usually begins in April and reaches a peak in late May or early June at the height of the snowmelt.

[2] Montana Department of Natural Resources and Conservation, Water Resources Division, *Yellowstone River Basin Water Resources Situation Report* (1975).
[3] Ibid., p. 5.

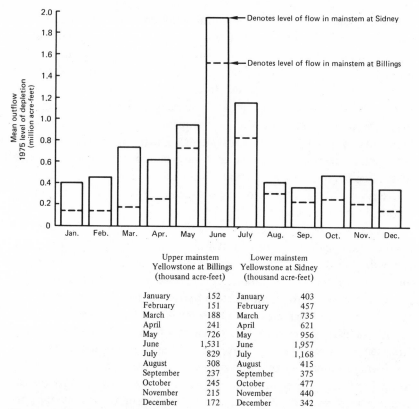

Upper mainstem Yellowstone at Billings (thousand acre-feet)		Lower mainstem Yellowstone at Sidney (thousand acre-feet)	
January	152	January	403
February	151	February	457
March	188	March	735
April	241	April	621
May	726	May	956
June	1,531	June	1,957
July	829	July	1,168
August	308	August	415
September	237	September	375
October	245	October	477
November	215	November	440
December	172	December	342

Figure 4-2. Mean monthly outflows of the Yellowstone at Billings and Sidney, reflecting the 1975 level of depletion

The pattern of flow in the mainstem itself varies with the location, the snowmelt pattern of the regulated and unregulated tributaries, and the pattern of irrigation return flow. For example, compare the pattern of flow in the Upper Yellowstone (Billings) with that of the Lower Yellowstone at its outflow point (Sidney) from Montana (figure 4-2). Two points are worthy of note: first, there is a fall peak in the Lower Yellowstone (this is probably caused by return flow from summer irrigation); second, the downstream flow is larger than the upstream flow because of the contributions of three major tributaries, two of which are regulated.

By autumn there is sometimes little or no flow on some of the tributaries in the eastern plains region of the basin (the Tongue and Powder sub-basins), causing serious problems for irrigators and for fish and wildlife. The low flows in the mainstem, on the other hand, occur during the months of December, January, and February. Low flows can seriously affect the native fish and wildlife resources and, of course, no flow will destroy the fishery. The latter situation occurred in May 1977 in a tributary of the Wind River in Wyoming, when an irrigation district in anticipation of the drought held the spring runoff from the Wind River mountains in an upstream reservoir. As a result, thousands of dead fish lay along a dry five-mile reach below the reservoir. The lowest flows of record for the mainstem at Sidney occurred in 1934 and 1961 when the annual flows were 3.9 and 4.2 million acre-feet respectively, about half of the average annual flow.

Low flow and its sometimes companion, drought, are not strangers to the Yellowstone Basin. Historical records of precipitation and runoff show that there have been short- and long-term droughts, localized, and widespread droughts. If one defines a drought as an extended period of deficient precipitation and runoff, then the extended drought from 1933 to 1937, when the five-year average precipitation over the Yellowstone Basin was 12.8 inches, is the most critical on record.[4] This long drought was associated with the dust storms of the 1930s.

Ice jams can cause low flows in winter. Then when they thaw, they cause high flows that upon reaching potential flood stage threaten the welfare of the region's residents. Hydrologic variability of this magnitude represents a serious limitation to water use, particularly as an industrial supply for coal conversion facilities where a dependable supply is needed every operating day of the year.

The nine subbasins of the Montana portion of the Yellowstone River Basin are illustrated in figure 4-1. There are many small and sometimes intermittent tributaries to the mainstem. Proceeding in a west to east direction, the major tributaries are the Boulder and Stillwater rivers in the uppermost reach of the Yellowstone Basin, the Clarks Fork Yellowstone, the Bighorn River, the Tongue River, and the Powder River. Of these major tributaries, the Bighorn is the largest contributor to the mainstem

[4] Missouri Basin Inter-Agency Committee, *Comprehensive Framework Study Missouri River Basin, Volume 1* (Washington, D.C., GPO, 1971) chapter 4, p. 60. Note that the term "drought" means various things to various people depending on their specific interest. Wayne Palmer in "Meteorological Drought," U.S. Department of Commerce, U.S. Weather Bureau Research Paper No. 45 (Washington, D.C., GPO, 1965) said: "To the farmer, drought means a shortage of moisture to the root zone of his crops. To the hydrologist, it suggests below average water levels in streams, lakes, reservoirs, and the like. To the economist, it means a water shortage which adversely affects the established economy."

flow, with a mean annual flow of 2.4 million acre-feet.[5] From the stand-point of coal development, a cursory glimpse at figure 1-3 in chapter 1 indicates that the Tongue and Powder tributaries wind through the rich coalfields while the larger volume Bighorn and the middle reach of the mainstem lie in relatively close proximity to the coal deposits. These four subbasins, Tongue, Powder, Bighorn, and Mid-Yellowstone, figure promi-nently in the prospective water supply for any new development in the basin.

The Powder River is located in the plains area of the basin and there-fore its high flows occur in early March or April, reflecting the earlier snowmelt pattern of the plains area. The same would be true for the Tongue River were it not regulated by the Tongue River Dam. Releases from the dam for irrigation usually occur in June. Both rivers have been known to run dry. From the historical records, flows very near zero were recorded in the 1938 and 1961 water years on the Tongue River at its mouth (Miles City). The historical record for the Powder also shows that very near to zero flows frequently occurred.[6]

At the 1975 level of depletion, the Tongue at its mouth has no flow or a flow approaching zero during the month of August for fourteen out of thirty-eight years of record. The unregulated Powder had no flow or a flow approaching zero during the month of September for thirteen out of thirty-seven years. Therefore, although the Tongue and Powder are sur-face water sources within the coalfields, any additional dependable supply could be made available only by building storage on the Powder or by adding storage in the Tongue subbasin.

Existing Water Uses and Reservoir Projects

Irrigation is, by far, the principal use of water in the Montana portion of the Yellowstone River Basin. Irrigation accounts for more than 95 percent of the total water withdrawals in the basin. Water rights to the Tongue

[5] Missouri Basin Inter-Agency Committee, *Comprehensive Framework Study.* The mean flow for the Bighorn River near Saint Xavier over the period 1935–75 corrected for the 1975 depletion level is 2.367 MMaf. See U.S. Department of the Interior, *Yellowstone River Basin and Adjacent Coal Fields.*

[6] Note that the seven-day, ten-year low flow for the Powder River (at Locate, Montana) is only one cubic foot per second (cfs). For the Tongue River (at Miles City, Montana) the seven-day, ten-year low flow is 3 cfs. (U.S. Geological Survey, *Water Resources Data for Montana Water Year 1975*; and Charles Riggs of the U.S. Geological Survey to Constance Boris, May 4, 1978).

River for irrigation by direct diversion date back to 1886. While strategically located in the coalfields near the large Decker mine, the state-constructed Tongue River Irrigation Reservoir, built in 1939, has long since had its yield preempted principally by irrigation use.

Both municipal and industrial use of water are minimal because of the ranching and rural character of the basin. Water is withdrawn from the Mid-Yellowstone subbasin and used for cooling in the two coal-fired power plants at Colstrip. Small additional amounts of water are withdrawn from the mainstem also for six smaller fossil-fueled power plants.

There are instream uses (for example, hydroelectric generation, recreation, and maintenance of fish and wildlife habitat) of the tributaries as well as of the mainstem, in addition to the withdrawals for irrigation, industrial, and municipal uses. There is some hydroelectric power generation at the Yellowtail Dam on the Bighorn River. Almost all of the flow of the Bighorn River is passed through the Yellowtail Dam which houses a hydroelectric power plant with a 250-megawatt (Mw) capacity at the site. The Yellowtail Dam, completed in 1967, produces about one billion kilowatt hours per year, assuming average flow (2.5 million acre-feet per year [af/yr]). Since the flow of the Bighorn is relatively large, timed releases from the Yellowtail Reservoir are reflected in the flow of the mainstem in the Mid-Yellowstone subbasin. The Yellowtail Reservoir area also supports water-based recreation, fish, and wildlife. The Yellowstone River itself west of Billings supports a cold-water trout fishery that is among the nation's finest and a diverse warm-water fishery to the east. In addition, the river bottoms and breaks sustain a variety of wildlife such as mule deer, white-tailed deer, and antelope, as well as waterfowl.

Presently, water resource developments in the Yellowstone Basin consist of seven reservoirs on tributaries to the mainstem. Five of the seven reservoirs are on small tributaries with total reservoir storage capacities ranging from 11,000 to 24,000 acre-feet (af). Of particular interest to the energy industry are the two remaining reservoirs, the very large Yellowtail Reservoir on the Bighorn River with a total storage capacity of 1,375,000 acre-feet and the smaller Tongue River Reservoir with a total storage capacity of about 68,000 acre-feet.

The only large reservoir in the Yellowstone Basin is the Yellowtail Reservoir on the Bighorn River, mentioned above, which until recently had a large portion of its storage reserved for industrial use through water option contracts initiated under the Bureau of Reclamation's Industrial Water Marketing Program. The energy companies' initial interest in stored Yellowtail water is indicated in table 4-1. The bureau executed option

Table 4-1. Industrial water option contracts for stored water from the federal Yellowtail Reservoir[a]—Bighorn subbasin
(acre-feet per year)

Holders of industrial water option contracts	Executed water option contracts[b]
Gulf Oil	50,000[b]
Exxon Oil	50,000[c]
Peabody Coal	40,000[c]
	40,000[c] (proposed for use on the Northern Cheyenne Reservation)
Shell Oil	28,000[c]
	20,000 (proposed for use on the Crow Reservation)
Westmoreland Resources	30,000[c] (proposed for use on the Crow Reservation)
Subtotal proposed for use in Montana as of October 1974	258,000
Subtotal as of March 1978	70,000

Sources: U.S. Department of the Interior, Water for Energy Management Team, *Report on Water for Energy in the Northern Great Plains Area with Emphasis on the Yellowstone River Basin* (1975) pp. III-9, III-11; Montana Energy Advisory Council, *Coal Development Information Packet* (Helena, Mont., Montana Energy Advisory Council, 1974) p. 45; Northern Great Plains Resource Program, *Report of the Work Group on Water* (Denver, Colo., NGPRP, December 1974) p. 21; E. R. Wilde, Acting Regional Director, Bureau of Reclamation, Billings, Montana, to Constance Boris, March 17 and 31, 1978.

[a] The Yellowtail Reservoir has a maximum storage capacity of 1,375,000 af and an active storage of 818,789 af assuming a thirty-year sediment deposition.

[b] The water option contract for Gulf Oil is expected to be used exclusively for coal development on the Crow ceded land. It was originally reserved for irrigation on the Crow Reservation.

[c] Water option contracts subsequently cancelled or expired.

contracts with energy companies for 258,000 acre-feet per year of stored Yellowtail water for use in Montana and 365,000 in Wyoming, yielding a total of 623,000 acre-feet per year in executed industrial water option contracts as of October 1974. In that same year, additional applications for water option contracts in Montana totaled 502,000 acre-feet per year, although no contracts based on these applications have been executed. Options were taken on 623,000 acre-feet of stored water at prices ranging from $9.00 to $11.00 per acre-foot when eventually used. Incidentally, although the reservoir is authorized for agriculture, little water has been applied to irrigation from the Yellowtail since its construction.

The states, farmers, ranchers, and Indian tribes affected by this program discovered the magnitude of the industrial water option contracts shortly after the *North Central Power Study*[7] was released. On October

[7] The *North Central Power Study* was the result of a joint effort by the Department of the Interior's Bureau of Reclamation and private and public electrical utilities. Its major conclusion was that the coalfields lying in the Colstrip–Gillette oval

16, 1973, the Environmental Defense Fund, joined by ranchers, farmers, irrigation companies, environmental groups, and later (1975) by the State of Montana, filed suit in *Environmental Defense Fund, Inc. v. Morton* (Civil No. 1220; D. Montana, Billings Division), against the Bureau of Reclamation challenging the reallocation of Yellowtail's water from primarily agricultural to industrial use. The federal district court granted summary judgment to the secretary of the interior holding that he had the power to make such a reallocation of the stored water without congressional approval. This decision was appealed in *Environmental Defense Fund v. Kleppe* (renamed Andrus) in October 1976 in the Ninth Circuit Court of Appeals. In *Environmental Defense Fund v. Kleppe,* the environmental and agricultural interests argued that the secretary of the interior acted outside his statutory authority by entering into arrangements to sell water for industrial uses from the Yellowtail Reservoir since Congress did not include industrial or municipal use of the impounded water in its authorization.[8] The environmental and agricultural groups contended that the Industrial Water Marketing Program and the individual water option contracts are "major federal actions significantly affecting the human environment" and are subject to the impact statement requirements of the National Environmental Policy Act. They further held that the bureau failed to consult with Montana state officials on the effects of the consumptive industrial diversion of water on downstream fish and wildlife, violating the Fish and Wildlife Coordination Act of 1964, and that the secretary determined the availability of water for industry on the basis of projected irrigated acreage far below the amount intended by Congress.[9]

On the other hand, the Department of the Interior argued that the Yellowtail Dam authorization provided for water for industrial use among

---

were the most economic for mine-mouth electrical generation. Of the forty-two proposed mine-mouth coal-fired power plants, twenty-one were located in Montana— thirteen of which (or 63,000 megawatts [Mw] of production capacity) were located in the basin. Over one million acre-feet of water were projected to be needed to supply the production of 63,000 Mw annually. See North Central Power Study, Coordinating Committee, *North Central Power Study, Report of Phase I, Volume I; Study of Mine-Mouth Thermal Powerplants with Extra-High Voltage Transmission for Delivery of Power to Load Centers* (October 1971), under the direction of Assistant Secretary of the Interior James R. Smith.

[8] The allocation of the stored water to industrial use in the Boysen Reservoir on the Wind River in Wyoming, a tributary to the Bighorn River, is also challenged in this case. See *Environmental Defense Fund v. Kleppe* (appeal docketed, No. 76-3133, 9th Cir., October 4, 1976).

[9] *Environmental Law Review* vol. 7, no. 6 (June 1977) p. 65,457.

the other purposes. It contended that the fact that the reservoir was given certain primary purposes has not foreclosed modification of those purposes when desirable or necessary. In addition, the Fish and Wildlife Coordination Act amendments of 1964 were held not to be applicable to projects already constructed or under construction.[10] Moreover, Interior contended that the secretary adequately considered whether the industrial use of water would impair the efficiency of the project for irrigation purposes.

The district court ruled against the Environmental Defense Fund, which appealed the decision. As a result of the suit, the Department of the Interior imposed a moratorium on sales of water option contracts for the stored Bighorn water in the Yellowtail Reservoir until the matter was resolved.

In early June, 1979, the federal appellate court in its revised opinion upheld the Environmental Defense Fund's arguments with respect to the National Environmental Policy Act and the Fish and Wildlife Coordination Act. As a result, the Bureau of Reclamation has been ordered to prepare a programmatic environmental impact statement on the Industrial Water Marketing Program before it can proceed with the program. In addition, for each water option contract application, the bureau is to prepare a site-specific environmental impact statement. However, the appeals court agreed with the district court finding that industrial use of project water had been authorized. This was subject to the condition that:

> marketing of water for such purposes must be done in accordance with federal reclamation law and, under this law, the Secretary of the Interior had authority to sell water for industrial use only if "it will not impair the efficiency of the project for irrigation purposes."[11]

Since some of the industrial water option contracts were initiated in 1967, their ten-year terms are up for renewal. Four companies (Exxon, Peabody, Shell, and Westmoreland) have either cancelled or let their options expire. The initial extent of the bureau's Industrial Water Marketing Program of 258,000 acre-feet per year in industrial contracts dwindled to 70,000 in early 1978.[12] (See table 4-1.) Cancellations of the option

---

[10] Construction on the Yellowtail Dam began in 1960.

[11] *Environmental Defense Fund v. Andrus,* no. 76-3133 and no. 76-3506 (9th Circuit, filed June 1, 1979) at 3.

[12] Incidentally, of the 365,000 acre-feet per year of water option contracts for Yellowtail Dam water proposed for use in Wyoming, Kerr-McGee, Panhandle Eastern, John Wold, and Colorado Interstate Gas cancelled their option contracts totalling 160,000 acre-feet per year.

contracts for use on the Indian reservations can be partially attributed to the Northern Cheyenne and Crow lawsuits requesting the voiding of their coal leases with Peabody and with Shell and Westmoreland, respectively, a request with which Interior essentially acquiesced.

Potential Reservoir Development

At the present time, there are no impoundments on the mainstem of the Yellowstone. Although several potential storage sites have been identified in the basin, sentiment remains strongly against impoundment of the mainstem. The proposed Allenspur site on the upper mainstem near Livingston, reputed to be the best remaining damsite in Montana, is a case in point. It has a potential storage capacity of 1.7 million acre-feet that could be made available to downstream uses such as irrigation or coal conversion. However, the proposed site lies in the middle of a 95-mile blue-ribbon reach of the Yellowstone River, renowned for its aesthetic value and its native trout fishery. Vigorous and widespread opposition led to a joint resolution passed by the Montana Legislature in 1973 declaring that construction of the Allenspur Dam would be contrary to state goals and objectives. Strong public pressure to preserve the free-flowing characteristics of the mainstem still persists. In comments received in the 1977 state hearings on the water reservation requests, the point was made that the free-flowing Yellowstone is a unique and valued resource for Montana. Both events then would suggest it is highly unlikely that storage on the mainstem would be built, at least given present public sentiment.

Developing offstream storage, however, has a greater chance of political acceptance, and in fact has been proposed as an alternative to storage at the Allenspur site. For example, water for the Buffalo Creek Reservoir on Buffalo Creek would be pumped from the Yellowstone during high flows and released to the mainstem during low flows to firm up the water supply for diversion to the coalfields. Two other offstream reservoirs, Sunday Creek and Cedar Ridge, would further supplement the Buffalo Creek Reservoir.[13] In fact, the Bureau of Reclamation has applied to the state for water reservations for four offstream storage sites (table 4-2). Incidentally, these are the same sites identified as potential water sources for

13 Montana Department of Natural Resources and Conservation, Water Resources Division, *Draft Addendum Environmental Impact Statement for Water Reservation Applications in the Yellowstone River Basin* (Helena, Mont., DNRC, June 1977).

Table 4-2. Water reservation requests for proposed multipurpose storage[a]

Subbasins	Applicant	Reservation request (acre-feet/yr)
Onstream storage		
Bighorn	Bureau of Reclamation	131,700
Tongue	Montana Dept. of Natural Resources and Conservation	450,000
Offstream storage		
Billings Area		
Buffalo Creek	Bureau of Reclamation	68,700
Mid-Yellowstone		
Cedar Ridge	Bureau of Reclamation	121,800
Kinsey Area		
Sunday Creek	Bureau of Reclamation	539,000

Source: Montana Department of Natural Resources and Conservation, Water Resources Division, *Draft Addendum Environmental Impact Statement for Water Reservation Applications in the Yellowstone River Basin* (Helena, Mont., DNRC, June 1977) pp. 3, 5, 32.

[a] The purposes for water stored in offstream reservoirs as stated in the Bureau of Reclamation's applications are: municipal, industrial, recreation, and fish and wildlife.

coal development in the *North Central Power Study*. Surplus flow from the mainstem would be diverted to these offstream storage sites for municipal, industrial, and fish and wildlife uses during low flow periods. The bureau also requested a reservation of 131,700 acre-feet of water per year to be diverted from the existing Yellowtail Reservoir on the Bighorn River for full-service irrigation of 42,000 acres and a supplementary water supply to 950 acres.[14]

As mentioned in the beginning of the previous section, the Tongue River Reservoir is the only other existing reservoir with a storage capacity greater than 24,000 acre-feet. It was built in 1939 by the Montana State Water Conservation Board. Its maximum capacity of 68,000 acre-feet is small in comparison to Yellowtail. Irrigation has been the major use of water from the Tongue, with rights dating back to 1886. Consequently, it

---

[14] As an alternative to adding reservoir capacity, the Bureau of Reclamation had earlier proposed pipeline diversions from existing reservoirs. The two pipeline diversions for conveying a portion of Wyoming's compact share from the Bighorn River for industrial use in Gillette, Wyoming, that have been proposed are: (a) a 180-mile pipeline that would convey 416,000 acre-feet per year to Gillette, Wyoming, diverted from the Bighorn River downstream from the Yellowtail Dam in Montana; (b) a 202-mile-long pipeline conveying from 175,000 to 382,000 acre-feet per year from Bighorn Lake behind Yellowtail Dam to Gillette, Wyoming. See U.S. Department of the Interior, Bureau of Reclamation, *Appraisal Report on Montana-Wyoming Aqueducts* (April 1972).

Table 4-3. Significant existing reservoir storage in the Yellowstone River Basin.

Subbasin/reservoir	Maximum storage	Minimum storage	Active reservoir storage	Reservoir surface area (acres)
	(	acre-feet	)	
Bighorn				
Yellowtail Reservoir[a]	1,375,000	502,000	614,000	17,298
Tongue				
Tongue River Reservoir (storage elevation 3,424.4 ft.)[b]	68,000	n.a.	n.a.	3,300

Note: n.a. = not available.

[a] Data on the existing Yellowtail Reservoir are based on information provided by the U.S. Bureau of Reclamation in Billings, Montana (Wilde to Boris, December 6, 1977). The active storage suggested here is less than that used in the simulation model runs in chapter 9, as the Bureau of Reclamation's data are based on an allocation of storage for an 86-year accumulation of sediment. Since some activities can be undertaken with a 30-year life cycle in which the additional storage representing the difference between 30 and 86 years of sediment accumulation could be considered for active use, we use the larger active storage possibilities consistent with 30-year sediment accumulation.

[b] For information on the Tongue River Reservoir, see R. C. Harlan and Associates, *Tongue River Project Modification Feasibility Study* (San Francisco, Calif., R. C. Harlan and Associates, October 1976). The firm annual yield of the reservoir is 42,000 acre-feet.

is also the primary use of water in the Tongue River Reservoir. The Tongue River Reservoir has its storage completely obligated, principally to irrigation.

Much interest has been shown in developing new or expanded onstream storage in the Tongue and Powder subbasins since these are the subbasins that also have extensive coal deposits. The storage possibilities on the Tongue River consist of raising the existing Tongue Dam to three alternate elevations, constructing a new reservoir called the New High Tongue Dam, and constructing the New High Tongue Reservoir together with raising the existing Tongue River Dam. (For storage capacities and each alternative, see tables 4-3 and 4-4).[15] On the Powder River, studies have been made for developing the upstream Moorhead site. Construction of the Moorhead Dam has been proposed since the late 1940s. It would lie astride the Montana–Wyoming state line. The existence of coal deposits in the Powder subbasin has made the construction of the potential Moorhead Reservoir more appealing than in the past, since it lies just upstream from the coalfields in Montana and could serve as an initial-stage source of water. The Moorhead Reservoir is expected to have a maximum stor-

[15] Feasibility studies for increasing the storage capacity on the Tongue River have been done for the state by Bechtel, Inc. (1967–69) and R. C. Harlan and Associates (1976–77).

Table 4-4. Selected potential reservoir storage in the Yellowstone River Basin

Subbasin/reservoir	Maximum storage	Minimum storage	Active reservoir storage	Reservoir surface area (acres)
	(	acre-feet	)	
Powder				
Moorhead Reservoir[a]	1,150,000	493,000	657,000	18,500
Tongue				
Tongue River Reservoir[b]				
a. Raise existing reservoir (elevation of 3,424 ft.) to storage elevation 3,438 ft.	130,000	n.a.	n.a.	5,000
b. Raise existing reservoir to storage elevation of 3,465 ft.	320,000	n.a.	n.a.	8,400
c. Construct New High Tongue River Dam (storage elevation of 3,438 ft.)	320,000	n.a.	n.a.	7,700
d. Raise existing reservoir to storage elevation of 3,438 ft. and construct New High Tongue Dam	450,000	n.a.	n.a.	10,000

Note: n.a. = not available.

[a] Data on the proposed Moorhead Reservoir are from U.S. Department of the Interior, Bureau of Reclamation, *Reconnaissance Report on Moorhead Unit Montana-Wyoming* (Great Falls, Mont., October 1969). The Bureau of Reclamation's data are adjusted to reflect a 30-year sediment storage accumulation rather than the bureau's 77-year sediment accumulation. The minimum storage of 493,000 acre-feet is based on a 243,000 acre-foot allocation for 30-years sediment storage and dead storage and a 250,000 acre-foot allocation for flood control. In turn, the 657,000 acre-foot estimate is the active storage after a 30-year project life. Note that the Intake Water Company is proposing a smaller 564,400 acre-foot capacity storage reservoir at the Moorhead site as an alternative.

[b] For statistics on alternative reservoir capacities on the Tongue River, see R. C. Harlan and Associates, *Tongue River Project Modification Feasibility Study* (San Francisco, Calif., R. C. Harlan and Associates, October 1976).

age capacity of 1.15 million acre-feet. However, because of the heavy sediment load on the Powder River, siltation would become a problem and storage capacity would decrease with time to an estimated 730,000 acre-feet about twenty years hence.

The state seriously considered developing storage on both the Tongue and Powder rivers. The DNRC applied for a 450,000-acre-foot water reservation on the Tongue River and a 1,150,000-acre-foot reservation on the Powder River as storage for irrigation, industrial, and instream uses. However, its application for storage on the Powder River was subsequently withdrawn when feasibility studies indicated that water quality problems might result from such construction. State officials hoped that the federal government would construct the Moorhead Reservoir for irrigation, industrial, and instream uses. However, one private energy-associated company, Intake Water Company, already has a water right application for Powder River storage pending expiration of the Yellowstone moratorium.[16] Specifically, Intake Water Company is proposing a smaller 564,000-acre-foot capacity reservoir at the Moorhead site.

Because of the interest shown, both by government and industry, in increasing storage on the Tongue and in adding storage on the Powder, these potential storage alternatives as well as the existing reservoirs will be included in our analysis of storage possibilities for augmenting water available for competing uses in chapter 9.

While an increase in stable water yield in the basin would result from such reservoirs, account must be taken of increased upstream water usage in Wyoming. In the next two sections, we estimate Wyoming's likely use of its share of Yellowstone River Compact water as well as the range of reserved water right claims of Wyoming's Wind River Indian tribes. Specifically, the increase in depletion owing to upstream users should be reflected in reduced flows of the tributaries from Wyoming into Montana, since that becomes the amount available to users in Montana.

Allocation of Water Under the Yellowstone River Compact

As mentioned in chapter 2, the Yellowstone River Compact allocates the surplus flow (average annual flow less existing water rights as of 1950 and supplemental water for the 1950 water rights) of the four interstate tributaries on a percentage basis between Montana and Wyoming. The state of Wyoming has independently estimated its share of the surplus flow, assuming average annual flow conditions. This is shown in table 4-5. In the critical low flow period, Wyoming's approximate share of the flow from the four interstate tributaries could be reduced to 1.4 million acre-feet while Montana's share would be .6[17] However, Wyoming would be

---

[16] Also, prior to the 1973 Water Use Act, Intake filed for the use of 111 cubic feet per second from the lower Yellowstone. Utah International, Inc., investigated a 106,730-acre-foot capacity reservoir on a tributary of the Tongue in Wyoming, intending to use that water in Montana.

[17] Montana does not necessarily agree with Wyoming in estimates of each state's share of the flow of the interstate tributaries. Little has been done to resolve these conflicts in the twenty-nine year history of the compact. Therefore, it is not known how much flow is actually available for further appropriation in Montana.

Table 4-5. Wyoming's estimate of each state's share of surplus flow under the Yellowstone River Compact

(acre-feet)

Interstate tributary	Wyoming	Montana
Clarks Fork Yellowstone	429,000	285,000
Bighorn	1,800,000	400,000
Tongue	96,400	144,700
Powder	120,700	166,600
Total	2,446,100	996,300

Note: Since Montana does not necessarily agree with these estimates, it has decided to calculate independently its share of the surplus flow of the interstate tributaries.

Source: Wyoming State Engineer's Office, *Wyoming Framework Water Plan* (Cheyenne, Wyoming, May 1973) p. 35.

able to capture its full share of the compact allocation on a firm basis only if additional reservoir storage capacity were built. At present, it does not appear to be economic to build reservoirs for irrigation only, although this is probably not the case for industrial (energy development) use. Since the Clarks Fork Yellowstone is too distant to be used in the coalfields, we estimated Wyoming's projected depletions for the Bighorn, Tongue, and Powder rivers. We begin first with the Tongue and Powder rivers.

Wyoming estimates that the average unused and unappropriated water in the Tongue River under the Yellowstone Compact is 241,000 acre-feet per year. Wyoming's share of the Tongue River under the Yellowstone River Compact is 40 percent or 96,400 acre-feet per year, given average flow conditions, while in the Powder subbasin, Wyoming was allocated 42 percent of the average annual unused and unappropriated water supply of 120,700 acre-feet per year. Storage is needed to capture Wyoming's share of the surplus flow of the Tongue River. In a year of extreme low flow, such as 1961, little if any compact water would be available without reservoirs, since providing supplemental water supplies to the pre-1950 rights would preempt the total available water supply.

The projected depletion in Wyoming's portion of the Tongue and Powder subbasins is of particular importance because of their proximity to substantial coalfields. Currently, about 80 percent of the water in the Tongue and Powder subbasins in Wyoming is used for irrigation, and the present consumptive use of water for irrigation is estimated to be 158,400 acre-feet per year. However, late season shortages are common. The *Wyoming Framework Water Plan* estimates an annual shortage of 72,480 acre-feet of consumptive use for irrigation alone. Future projects to develop large acreages of new irrigation appear quite unlikely (table 4-6),

Table 4-6. Projected water depletion in Wyoming's portion of the Tongue and Powder subbasins
(acre-feet)

Water uses	Present	Year 2000	Year 2020
Irrigation	158,000	158,000	158,000
Industry	21,000	240,000	477,000
Municipal, domestic, and stock	14,000	19,000	22,000

Source: Wyoming Framework Water Plan, p. 164.

although five projects have been identified as having a potential to supply supplemental water for irrigation.

As is evident from table 4-6, no increase in irrigated acreage is projected. Moveover, in 1973, it was estimated that at least 12,000 acres of irrigated land in Wyoming were to be purchased by industry. The water rights on these lands will eventually be converted from agricultural uses to industrial uses. It is assumed, however, in the *Wyoming Framework Water Plan* that water spreading[18] developments will offset these losses to industry, and therefore the total irrigated acreage is projected to remain nearly constant. Storage in both the Tongue and Powder subbasins would be required for industrial projects.

Since no new irrigation is projected in the Tongue River subbasin, only water for potential industrial developments is considered in our analysis. An increase in consumptive use of water of 219,000 acre-feet per year for industry (from the present to the year 2000) is projected in the Powder and Tongue subbasins together. However, because this estimate is for both subbasins, it is not possible to separate the estimate for each. There are three proposed industrial water storage projects for the Wyoming portion of the Tongue, but we have taken as a working assumption that only one, the Upper State Line Dam, would be built. This proposed reservoir would improve water supply only for Wyoming and would provide a firm water supply of 86,000 acre-feet per year.[19] Of the other two, the dam on the Lower State Line site would develop water for both Montana and Wyoming, and the Rockwood Dam is not compatible with the

---

[18] Water spreading is akin to flood irrigation. Water is diverted onto the land from intermittent streams during periods of spring runoff or high-intensity storms. The water is generally available only for short periods of time with one irrigation application or less expected in a normal year. This once-a-year irrigation application is prevalent in the Powder subbasin.

[19] Wyoming State Engineer's Office, *Wyoming Framework Water Plan* (Cheyenne, Wyoming, May 1973) p. 166.

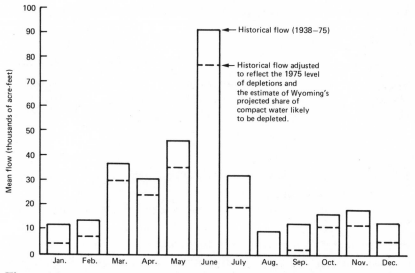

Figure 4-3.   Mean monthly outflows for the Tongue River subbasin

Upper Tongue's designation as a scenic river. Moreover we use the working assumption that there would be an industrial water depletion equivalent to the total firm annual water supply of the proposed Upper State Line Dam.

Looking next to the Powder subbasin, only industrial use is projected for this subbasin. However, no future industrial water supply would be available without storage. The Reynolds Mining Corporation has water permits for approximately 55,000 acre-feet per year that would come from Wyoming's compact share.[20] Because it is likely these permits will justify construction of storage capacity, we estimate Wyoming's share of surplus flow of the Powder River based on the industrial use of 55,000 acre-feet of water per year, or approximately 4,600 acre-feet per month—all of which is assumed to be depleted.

To reiterate, the purpose of reviewing the depletion of flows occurring in Wyoming is to help assess the inflow to Montana and hence the water available for competing users. Figures 4-3 and 4-4 illustrate the mean historical flow for the Tongue and Powder subbasins respectively, adjusted for the present level of depletions and adjusted for Wyoming's estimated share under the Yellowstone River Compact. As is evident in

[20] Ibid.

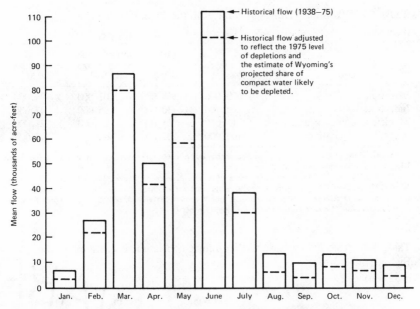

Figure 4-4. Mean monthly outflows for the Powder River subbasin

figure 4-3, projected depletions in the Tongue River could not be accommodated without additional storage.

In the case of the Bighorn River, Wyoming is entitled to 80 percent of the unused and unappropriated flow. Assuming average flow conditions and adjusting for pre-1950 water rights, Wyoming estimates that the annual surplus flow is about 2.1 to 2.3 million acre-feet. Accordingly, under the 80 percent allocation for the Bighorn River, Wyoming would be entitled to 1.8 million acre-feet per year. However, use of all of Wyoming's compact allocation would require the construction of additional storage, and at least a portion of the water supply would have to be diverted from the Yellowtail Reservoir or from the river system below Yellowtail Dam. Storage would be required to impound spring runoff for release during the peak consumptive use period of July and August. Since additional reservoir storage on the Bighorn (Wind River in Wyoming) does not appear economic, for analytical purposes in chapter 9, we simulate the case which represents Wyoming's share of surplus flow of the interstate tributaries likely to be depleted in the future. Based on data from the state engineer's office, tables 4-7 and 4-8 represent annual estimates of Wyoming's present and future water depletion by use.

Table 4-7. Wyoming's consumptive uses in the Bighorn subbasin
(acre-feet)

Use	Annual consumption use			
	Present	1980	2000	2020
Irrigation	1,029,000	1,160,000	1,302,000	1,398,000
Industrial	28,000	30,000	56,000	47,000
Municipal, domestic, and stock	13,000	15,000	21,000	27,000
Reservoir evaporation	105,000	105,000	n.a.	145,000

Notes: These estimates include groundwater use, but not the reserved water right claims of the Wind River Indian tribes. n.a. = not available.

Sources: Wyoming State Engineer's Office, *Wyoming Framework Water Plan*, (Cheyenne, Wyoming May 1973) pp. 140, 149. See also Wyoming State Engineer's Office, *Wyoming Water Planning Reports* no. 10 and no. 11 (Cheyenne, Wyoming 1972); and Wyoming State Engineer's Office, *A Water Development Program for Wyoming*, (Cheyenne, Wyoming, October 1974).

Table 4-8. Projected increase in Wyoming's consumptive water use in the Bighorn subbasin
(acre-feet)

Use	Present to 1980	Present to 2000	Present to 2020
Irrigation	131,000	273,000	369,000
Industrial	2,000	28,000	19,000
Municipal, domestic, and stock	2,000	8,000	14,000
Reservoir evaporation	n.a.	n.a.	40,000
Transbasin diversion to Powder and Tongue subbasins	7,500	7,500	7,500
Total	142,500	316,500	449,500

Note: n.a. = not available.

Table 4-9. Percentage distribution of water depletion for irrigation in the Bighorn subbasin in Wyoming

Month	Percentage of total water depletion for irrigation
April	1
May	13
June	17
July	25
August	32
September	11
October	1

Note: This distribution for monthly water depletion is based on the depletion rates for hay (alfalfa) in the U.S. Department of Agriculture subarea 1008 in Wyoming.

Source: U.S. Department of Agriculture, Soil Conservation Service, *Crop Consumptive Irrigation Requirements and Irrigation Efficiency Coefficients for the United States* (June 1976).

To derive monthly water depletion estimates from the annual estimates, we employed a working assumption (good to a first approximation), according to which monthly industrial and municipal water use remains constant, but irrigation use varies according to the distribution shown in table 4-9.

The monthly water depletion estimates resulting from irrigation were derived by applying the percentages in table 4-9 to the projected increase in consumptive use for expanded irrigation—131,000 acre-feet for 1980 and 273,000 for 2000. Calculating the increase in water depletion from the present to the years 1980 and 2000 for the remaining water uses, we have the following:

1980

$$\frac{\text{industrial}}{\text{depletion}} + \frac{\text{municipal}}{\text{depletion}} + \frac{\text{transbasin}}{\text{transfer}} = \frac{\text{water}}{\text{depletion for}}$$
$$\text{nonagricultural uses}$$

$$2{,}000 \text{ af/yr} + 2{,}000 \text{ af/yr} + 7{,}500 \text{ af/yr} = 11{,}500 \text{ af/yr, or}$$
$$960 \text{ af/mo}$$

2000

$$\frac{\text{industrial}}{\text{depletion}} + \frac{\text{municipal}}{\text{depletion}} + \frac{\text{transbasin}}{\text{transfer}} = \frac{\text{water}}{\text{depletion for}}$$
$$\text{nonagricultural uses}$$

$$28{,}000 \text{ af/yr} + 8{,}000 \text{ af/yr} + 7{,}500 \text{ af/yr} = 43{,}500 \text{ af, or}$$
$$3{,}625 \text{ af/mo}$$

In our analysis, the sum of the projected increase in monthly water depletion for irrigation and the monthly depletion for the nonirrigation water uses for either the year 1980 or the year 2000 represents the range of likely depletion of Wyoming's share of the Bighorn River. Either option can be simulated in the RFF/Montana Yellowstone River Basin simulation model (described in chapter 8) through a subroutine (appropriately named DEPLET) that reflects the depleted inflow to Montana as a result of upstream use in Wyoming. It should be emphasized that these values are only estimates of what the inflow to Montana would be if Wyoming's probable depletions resulting from application of its compact share were fulfilled.

However, it should be emphasized that all compact-derived appropria-tions from the Bighorn River and the Tongue which contemplate the diversion of water on, adjacent to, or running through, Indian reservations are subject to Indian reserved water rights. Article X of the compact ex-pressly protects Indian reserved water rights from preemption by compact-derived appropriations. Therefore, for purposes of the analysis, we should consider an additional source of water depletion in the flow of the Bighorn River before it enters Montana, that is, the reserved water rights of the Wind River Indian tribes. We have already alluded to this topic and now proceed to quantify our earlier discussion.

Reserved Water Rights of the Wind River Indian Tribes in Wyoming

The Wind River Reservation is the home of the Arapahoe and Shoshone Indian tribes in north central Wyoming. The reservation was originally established for the Shoshone tribe by the Fort Laramie Treaty in 1868. The Arapahoe tribe was temporarily placed on the Shoshone Reservation in 1878. In 1897, Congress purchased a portion of the Shoshone Reserva-tion for the Arapahoe. The Wind River, the uppermost reach of the Bighorn River, cuts across the expansive 2,268,000-acre reservation.[21]

Because of the early priority date of the reserved rights, the consump-tive use by the Wind River tribes of reserved water rights will affect the flow of the Bighorn River available to users in Montana. As mentioned in chapter 3, adjudication of the Wind River Indian reserved water rights will take place in state court. The immediate goal of the Wind River tribes is to protect their joint reserved water rights, since some types of economic activity are tied to the availability of water. Ultimate adjudication of all water rights in the Bighorn River basin of Wyoming is expected to take several years, perhaps a decade. Since we cannot predict the judicial out-come of the joint reserved rights of the two tribes, we relied on case law to estimate the range of reserved rights using both the restrictive in-terpretation and the expansive interpretation of the term "beneficial use." Therefore, we will consider first the present economic activities on the reservation.

[21] About 1,761,000 acres are tribal land, 127,000 acres are Indian allotted lands, and the rest is nontrust land. Wind River Economic Development Planning Pro-gram, *Overall Economic Development Program* (Fort Washakie, Wyoming, June 1976) p. 5.

Oil and gas production and cattle grazing are the two major activities on the Wind River Reservation. The reservation is considered rich in minerals such as oil, gas, uranium, gypsum, and phosphate. Royalty income from oil and gas production provided the largest source of tribal income in past years. However, declining yields from the oil and gas wells have reduced revenue in the recent past, and the tribe is considering the development of gypsum and uranium reserves. Subbituminous and lignite coal reserves are estimated to be in the 50 to 100 million ton range. Although coal has been produced in the past, there is currently no coal production on the reservation. It appears that coal development may be less attractive than elsewhere because the seams lie further below the surface than is the case on Indian reservations in the Montana portion of the basin.[22]

Besides minerals, there are about 258,000 acres of commercial timberland, and commercial logging was done on the reservation between 1965 and 1972. In 1972, the Arapahoe and Shoshone tribal councils took action to stop timber cutting in the Roadless Area for an indefinite period of time. The Roadless Area comprises about 90 percent of the commercial forest land on the reservation.

Because of the large land base of the reservation, about 1,612,000 acres are in use as cattle rangeland.[23] About 85 percent of the presently irrigated land is in hay production for horse and cattle feed. However, many of the farm and ranch operations on the reservation are leased to non-Indians because the majority of Indians lack the capital to secure the loans needed to put the land under irrigation. The major non-Indian operations are in the eastern part of the reservation in Riverton Withdrawal Area, and some non-Indian agricultural developments are in the Le Clair-Riverton and Riverton Valley projects. Stored water for these irrigation projects is available from the Boysen Reservoir. However, future Indian irrigation development will require additional storage. The two tribes are presently investigating the development of 15,000 acres of sprinkler irrigation on trust lands in the Riverton area, but storage would be needed before the proposed project could be developed to its capacity.

The Bureau of Indian Affairs (BIA) estimated that about 200,000 additional acres could be feasibly irrigated if storage reservoirs were built

[22] However, the Peabody Coal Company has on several occasions requested the tribes to let coal leases. Also, Cameron Engineers forecasted two 1,000-megawatt coal-fired power plants for the Wind River region for the year 2000 that may possibly utilize Indian water resources.

[23] See Wind River Economic Development Planning Program, *Overall Economic Development Program*, p. 14.

and newer irrigation practices such as sprinklers were employed.[24] The Bureau of Reclamation, on the other hand, estimated that no more than 50,000 additional acres could be irrigated feasibly. Their finding was based on the use of a more conservative feasibility standard—that the soil must be permeable to a depth of eight feet. The BIA feels that such a standard is meaningless because of newer irrigation methods such as sprinklers.[25] Therefore, the standard used to estimate feasible irrigable acreage will be a major determinant of Indian reserved water rights .

Finally, recreation-oriented industry is another possible economic activity. Two major tourist routes to Yellowstone and Grand Teton national parks pass through the reservation, which is surrounded by scenic mountains and encompasses large uninhabited areas. In addition, there are reaches of blue ribbon trout fishing on the Wind River and its tributaries which represent a valuable resource. Currently, fishing and hunting are prohibited to nonenrolled tribal members. The Indians are considering a fish hatchery, although there is reluctance to open the reservation to tourists.[26]

According to the joint tribes' *Overall Economic Development Program,* other alternatives being considered are a feedlot and meat-processing plant, a shopping center at Riverton, and developing a water utility for irrigation, municipal use, and industrial use. From the standpoint of estimating a range of Indian reserved water rights for the two tribes, however, these developments are problematic. What we do, as a working assumption for the purposes of our study, is to adopt the BIA's estimate of feasible irrigable acreage and to assume a minimum instream flow needed to maintain a wild trout fishery, since reserved water rights can be estimated by the amount of irrigable acreage under the restrictive criterion and moves have been made to include minimum instream flow for fish and wildlife resources under the expansive criterion (see March 17, 1977, BIA proposed rules on the definition of beneficial use[27]). The simulation planning model can accommodate data appropriate to other assumptions equally readily, but we have too little information to do any more productively.

Using the Bureau of Indian Affairs estimate, we take the irrigable acreage on the reservation to be capable of being increased by 200,000 acres.[28] Much of the presently irrigated land is in hay production for horse

[24] Ibid., p. 69.
[25] Ibid., p. 49.
[26] Ibid., p. 72.
[27] Proposed Rules, 42 *Federal Register,* 14885 (1977) [25 CFR Part 260].
[28] Ibid., p. 69.

Table 4-10. Estimates of monthly water depletion for increased irrigation on the Wind River Indian Reservation in the Bighorn subbasin in Wyoming (acre-feet)

Month	Increase in water depletion
April	4,800
May	62,400
June	81,600
July	120,000
August	153,600
September	52,800
October	4,800

and cattle feed. In estimating the increase in net water depletion resulting from an expansion in economically feasible irrigable acreage on the reservation, we will use the water withdrawal and depletion requirements for hay (alfalfa). This is because hay has the highest consumptive water requirement of all crops grown in the area in which the reservation is located, and also because hay is a good indicator of relative water use. The water depletion requirement for hay (alfalfa) is estimated at 2.4 acre-feet of water per acre planted.[29] Therefore, an additional 200,000 acres placed into irrigation would deplete roughly 480,000 acre-feet of water per year for subarea 1008 in which the reservation is located. Using the percentage distribution for monthly depletions given in table 4-9, the estimated monthly water depletions for irrigating an additional 200,000 acres on the Wind River Reservation are shown in table 4-10.

The other component needed for estimating the range of the Wind River Indian reserved right claims is an instream flow reservation for the maintenance of a wild trout fishery. No estimation of instream flows has yet been made for reaches of the Wind River on the reservation. However, several methods have been proposed for estimating instream flows for fish

[29] The crop consumptive irrigation requirement for hay (alfalfa) in the study area is 2.0 af/acre based on 1975 data. A water conveyance efficiency from the source to the farm of 59 percent and an onfarm water application efficiency of 39 percent yield an irrigation system efficiency of 23 percent. Dividing the hay consumptive irrigation requirement by the system efficiency gives a gross diversion requirement of 8.7 af/acre. Again using 1975 data, the return flow is estimated to be 72 percent of the gross diversion requirement or 6.26 af/acre. Subtracting the return flow from the gross diversion yields a water depletion rate of 2.44 af/acre planted. (Data from U.S. Department of Agriculture, Soil Conservation Service, *Crop Consumptive Irrigation Requirements and Irrigation Efficiency Coefficients for the United States* [June 1976] pp. 15, 115.)

and wildlife maintenance. For example, Tennant suggested a minimum instantaneous flow of 30 percent of the average annual flow from October through March and 50 percent from April through September for a class II (excellent) fishery.[30] An alternative method was proposed by Robinson that is similar to Tennant's except that the monthly flows are determined in relation to the historic median flow for June, as this flow represents maximum fishery values in most areas.[31] The Instream Needs Subgroup of the Work Group on Water for the Northern Great Plains Resources Program recommended a flow for each month that was equalled or exceeded 90 percent of the time as determined from the flow duration curves for each month of the year.[32]

Application of the methods to the problem of quantifying the instream flow requirements for a natural trout fishery is not necessary in this study because the maintenance of a minimum instream flow would not deplete inflow to Montana, although it would have a severe effect on the irrigation of 102,000 acres near Kinnear, Wyoming. Assuming that the Wind River Indian reserved water rights will be based on agricultural and fishery uses, the flow of the Wind River (Bighorn River) was assumed to be depleted by the amount reflecting the projected increase in irrigation. Since the instream flow needed for the maintenance of a native trout fishery is not a consumptive use, there was no adjustment of stream flow into Montana for this use.

Summing both the plausible development of Wyoming's share of the Bighorn River water allocated by the Yellowstone Compact and the development of the reserved water rights of the Wind River Indian tribes, the flow of the Bighorn River into Montana would be depleted by the amounts given in table 4-11.

Other Potential Sources of Water

This chapter would not be complete without mentioning groundwater as a potential source for irrigation, coal conversion, and slurry transport. Knowledge of groundwater systems in the basin is not very adequate although research efforts are under way on the shallow and the deep

[30] C. B. Stalnaker and J. L. Arnette, *Methodologies for the Determination of Stream Resource Flow Requirements: An Assessment* (Logan, Utah, Utah State University for the U.S. Fish and Wildlife Service, 1976) pp. 89–90.

[31] Ibid., p. 91.

[32] Northern Great Plains Resources Program, *Report of the Work Group on Water* (Denver, Colo., NGPRP, December 1974).

Table 4-11. Total projected increase in water depletion for the Bighorn subbasin in Wyoming
(acre-feet)

Month	Increase in water depletion	
	1980	2000
October	7,070	11,155
November	960	3,625
December	960	3,625
January	960	3,625
February	960	3,625
March	960	3,625
April	7,070	11,155
May	80,390	101,515
June	104,830	131,635
July	153,710	191,875
August	196,480	244,585
September	68,170	86,455

Note: The total projected increase in water depletion is the sum of (1) Wyoming's share of Yellowstone River Compact water likely to be depleted and (2) estimated reserved water right claims of the Wind River Indian tribes.

groundwater sources. The deep groundwater source is the Madison Limestone Formation which has been suggested as a source of water for coal slurry transport. The shallow groundwater sources are the coalbeds themselves which double as aquifers.

The Madison Formation is an aquifer composed of limestone and dolomite that underlies southeastern Montana, northeastern Wyoming, western North and South Dakota, and northwestern Nebraska. Water has been produced from the formation since 1917 with the drilling of the Tisdale well in Wyoming which yielded more than 4,000 gallons per minute (GPM).[33]

It is unclear if the Madison Limestone Formation is one single continuous aquifer or several discontinuous hydrologically isolated aquifers. Its thickness ranges from about 200 feet near the south end of the basin in Wyoming to 800 feet near the Montana-Wyoming border and is about 1,400 feet thick near the Yellowstone River.[34] In the area of the coalfields in the Tongue and Powder subbasins, the Madison is roughly 100 to 500

[33] Frank Swenson, *Possible Development of Water from Madison Group and Associated Rock in Powder River Basin, Montana–Wyoming* (Denver, Colo., Northern Great Plains Resources Program, July 1, 1974).

[34] U.S. Congress, Office of Technology Assessment, *A Technology Assessment of Coal Slurry Pipelines* (Washington, D.C., GPO, March 1978) p. 92.

feet thick and about 3,000 to 4,000 feet below the land surface.[35] Small-well yields may be expected in areas where the Madison is thin and larger yields from the thicker sections of the aquifer. The water-bearing and transmitting capability of the Madison is highly variable because it is limestone, which has karst or solution-cavity features. Water is stored in and transmitted through fractures and solution cavities. The occurrence of these is quite variable, which may explain the wide range in well yields from 8 to 5,000 gallons per minute (GPM).[36] According to the Wyoming state engineer's office, limestone can rank among the most productive aquifers or can be as unproductive as shale.[37]

Water quality in the Madison also varies from one area to another. Along the flanks of the Black Hills, water samples indicate a dissolved solids concentration of less than 1,000 milligrams per liter. In the coal area of Montana and Wyoming, samples of water in the deep aquifers indicate a dissolved solids concentration of about 2,000 milligrams per liter.[38] As a general statement based on still inadequate information on the Madison Formation, the water is marginal-to-unsatisfactory for use in irrigation and other uses demanding water of relatively good quality.[39]

It is also expected that increased pumping in any one area of the Madison will likely have a measurable effect upon the potentiometric surface (the level to which nonflowing water would rise in a well) at distances up to 10 to 20 miles, creating a need for greater pumping to maintain flows in other wells. Presently, however, existing data are inadequate to predict the quantity and quality of water the aquifer will yield and the effects of development on the system.

Shallow groundwater is found in those coalbeds that are also aquifers. Coalbeds currently mined in the Colstrip and Decker areas of the basin are aquifers. The coalbed aquifer mined near Decker is an important source of groundwater for stock and domestic uses. This is also true of the Rosebud coal seam at Colstrip. It is estimated that the Rosebud coalbed and the underlying McKay coalbed transmit about 9,900 acre-feet of

---

[35] Swenson, *Possible Development*, p. 1.

[36] State of Wyoming, State Engineer's Office, *Investigation of Recharge to Ground Water Reservoirs of Northeastern Wyoming (The Powder River Basin)* (June 1976).

[37] U.S. Congress, Office of Technology Assessment, *Technology Assessment*, p. 93.

[38] Swenson, *Possible Development*, p. 2.

[39] Ibid., p. 1. Much of the test-well data on the Madison indicates that the water has too high a percentage of sodium for use in irrigation.

water per day across areas likely to be mined.[40] Since 1974, observations at a site where both the Rosebud and McKay seams are being mined have indicated a decline of one foot or more in water level measurements for a distance of 1.5 miles west of the mine.[41] Water level declines have also been observed after one year of mining the coalbed near Decker. It is believed that wells very close to the final mine cut will become nonproductive and water will have to be obtained from deeper aquifers. Being so near the Tongue River, it is estimated that the mine near Decker intercepts about 40,000 gallons per day (.12 acre-feet per day) that previously discharged into the Tongue River.[42]

Just as in the case of the Madison aquifer, groundwater quality of the shallow coalbeds varies widely. Near Colstrip, dissolved solids concentrations range between 400 to 6,000 milligrams per liter, with the highest concentrations generally being in water from the oldest mine spoils. Limited research results indicate that the leaching of soluble salts from mine spoils and their eventual transport to surface or groundwater is probably one of the major water quality problems expected from mining.[43]

It appears to be difficult, however, to extrapolate the water quality relationship to mining near Colstrip to that near Decker. That is, dissolved solids, bicarbonate, sodium, and sulfite concentrations in the Decker mine effluent have decreased rather than increased by approximately 40 percent since mining.[44] These results are not yet explainable, though they may be partially attributable to the reduced rate of flow entering the mine from coalbed and overburden aquifers relative to the rate of inflow from the

[40] Wayne Van Voast, Robert B. Hedges, and John J. McDermott, *Hydrogeologic Conditions and Projections Related to Mining near Colstrip Southeastern Montana,* Bulletin 102 (Butte, Mont., Montana College of Mineral Science and Technology, June 1977). Transmissivity is defined as the flow of water in a volume measurement per day through a section of aquifer one foot wide under a hydraulic gradient of one foot per foot.

[41] Ibid., p. 1.

[42] Wayne Van Voast, *Hydrologic Effects of Strip Coal Mining in Southeastern Montana—Emphasis: One Year of Mining near Decker,* Bulletin 93 (Butte, Mont., Montana College of Mineral Science and Technology, June 1974) p. 1.

[43] Of additional concern are the potential adverse effects of mining on alluvial valley floors. These unconsolidated deposits often exist in a state of delicate hydrologic balance which, if mined, could preclude future use of the area for agriculture and could result in deterioration of surface and ground water quality.

[44] Wayne Van Voast and Robert B. Hedges, *Hydrogeologic Aspects of Existing and Proposed Strip Coal Mines near Decker, Southeastern Montana,* Bulletin 97 (Butte, Mont., Montana College of Mineral Science and Technology, December 1975).

Tongue River Reservoir and alluvium. These chemical differences may indicate that groundwater discharge from the coalbed to the mine may have decreased by as much as 40 percent.

Chemical analyses of water samples from wells and springs in the Tongue and Powder subbasins (northern Powder River coal basin) indicated total dissolved solids concentrations in the 1,000 to 3,000 milligrams per liter range with several samples having a total dissolved solids concentration of over 6,000 milligrams per liter.[45] Summarizing, the shallow groundwaters intercepted by the mine cut are waters that might have discharged naturally into the river. On the other hand, except at its outcroppings, the Madison Formation is too deep to affect surface water flow. Even though groundwater, particularly the Madison Formation, may be important as an alternative source of water, this study is concerned with surface water as the source for consumptive and nonconsumptive use. Information regarding the Madison Formation groundwater quantity and quality is too limited at this stage and is in any event hydrologically independent of surface flows with which we deal. Therefore, while our simulation model does incorporate general relationships between surface and shallow groundwater movements, the surface waters are alone being considered for meeting competing uses of water for various purposes in the Yellowstone River Basin.

Summary and Conclusions

Wide fluctuations in flow dominated by seasonal variations characterize the Yellowstone River Basin. High flows on the eastern tributaries occur in early spring while the mainstem flood flows follow about two months later. Similarly, at times, little or no flow occurs in late summer or autumn in the Tongue and Powder subbasins while low flows in the mainstem occur in the winter months. Hydrologic variability of this nature represents a serious limitation on the usability of the water in the Basin.

A major portion of the Fort Union Formation underlies the less water-abundant Tongue and Powder subbasins. There is the existing small Tongue River Irrigation Reservoir, which is strategically located near the large Decker coal mine, but its yield has long since been preempted by

[45] Roger W. Lee, "Ground-Water-Quality Data from the Northern Powder River Basin, Southeastern Montana," U.S. Department of the Interior, U.S. Geological Survey, Water-Resources Investigations, Open-File Report 79-1311, Helena, Montana (October 1979).

irrigation uses. The only existing major reservoir in the basin is the 1.375-million-acre-foot Yellowtail Reservoir on the Bighorn River. Lying in relatively close proximity to the coalfields, a large portion of its stored water (258,000 acre-feet), representing Montana's share, had been reserved for use by major energy companies. However, cancellations and expiration of water option contracts approach 190,000 acre-feet, thus leaving only 70,000 acre-feet for which executable options exist at the present time.

Proposed storage in the coal-bearing subbasins consist of the new High Tongue Dam, the Moorhead Reservoir on the Powder River, and three proposed storages offstream in the mainstem Yellowstone Basin. Both of the proposed reservoirs on the Powder and on the Tongue rivers have sizable storage capacities. Because of the interest shown, both by the federal government and by industrial interests, a selective set of these potential reservoirs will be included in our analysis of possibilities for augmenting usable water supplies (chapter 9). While an increase in stable water yield would result from such reservoirs, account must also be taken of the water that is legally subject to depletion by upstream uses in Wyoming under the Yellowstone River Compact and the Indian reserved water rights doctrine.

Wyoming's share of Yellowstone Compact water was estimated for the Bighorn, Tongue, and Powder subbasins since the increase in depletion would reduce the flow that would be available to Montana and this needs to be accounted for, particularly in the coal-bearing subbasins. The monthly inflow reductions associated with upstream depletions in Wyoming are illustrated in figures 4-3 and 4-4 for the Tongue and Powder subbasins respectively. In similar fashion, full utilization of the reserved rights of the Wind River Indian Reservation (upper Bighorn River) will reduce the flow available for use in Montana.

Finally, we note in passing, a potential source of water from deep aquifers, but as these are hydrologically independent of surface water, we will confine our analysis to surface flows on which economic demands will be made.

This chapter has detailed the various sources of water potentially available for energy development, but there are competing demands and legal claims on the physically available supplies. Without reviewing the possibility that water supplies may be preempted for other purposes, it is not possible to evaluate whether the availability of water will pose a constraint on the development of energy sources in the eastern Montana portion of the Fort Union Formation. Accordingly, in the next three chapters we address the potential levels and nature of the claims on the water physically available in the Yellowstone Basin. In chapter 5, we look at the quantity of water technically necessary to extract, transport, and convert the coal to other energy forms. In chapter 6, we address other withdrawal uses of water such as irrigation agriculture and municipal use. Finally, in chapter 7 we look at the implications of the steadily growing attention being given to instream uses that would prevent the diversion of water for withdrawal uses. These chapters will provide the background for our "data file" that will be used in conjunction with our hydrologic simulator described in chapter 8. The simulator provides a mechanism by which to evaluate quantitatively the implications of different policy options, outcomes of current litigation, and related imponderables that need to be considered before drawing conclusions about the supply of water for, or its potential constraint on, the development of energy resources in the Yellowstone River Basin.

5 Water Withdrawal Estimates for Energy Development Activities

We begin this chapter with a careful investigation of the rates of water withdrawal and depletion associated with each of the possible activities—extraction, transportation, coal-fired electrical generation and coal conversion—that may possibly occur in the Tongue, Powder, Bighorn, and Mid-Yellowstone subbasins. These activities range from the extraction and export of coal for uses outside the state (except for relatively small demands for instate consumption), through various transport modes which may have implications for water depletion from the basin, and finally to activities involving the combustion and conversion of coal (figure 5-1).

It should be noted that in the "water for energy" literature, one often encounters the terms "water demand," "water requirement," or "water usage" for a given coal-fired electrical generating plant or coal conversion facility. These terms are often not defined. As a consequence, it is not clear whether water withdrawal or water depletion is being discussed. "Water requirement" usually implies a fixed need for water, assuming that the technology for a given conversion facility is fixed. In contrast, "water demand" is a specialized term used by economists to express the relationship between the quantity of water used at various prices. In our analysis, we are compelled to work with estimates of requirements since there is no information regarding price elasticity of water for the processes we examine.

We begin then with a "normalized" requirement of water per unit of coal mined. This involves use of water for various dust suppression activities and for domestic and sanitary uses of mine personnel for a standard-size, 10-million-ton-per-year coal mine.[1] Next we discuss the water re-

---

[1] We chose the annual production rate of 10 million tons for the hypothetical coal mine since this is roughly the amount that would be needed as feedstock for a 2,600-Mw coal-fired power plant operating at an 80 percent plant factor. A 1,300 Mw steam electric unit operating at an 80 percent factor is equivalent to a 1,000 Mw coal-fired power plant operating continuously.

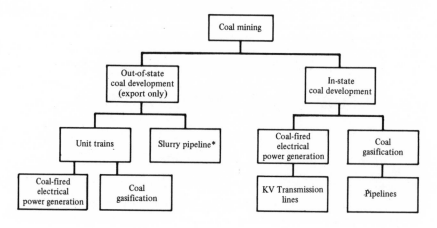

* Since current legislation in Montana expressly forbids the use of any water (surface or subsurface) for coal slurry transport, the policy of mining coal for export only could be better characterized as mining coal for export by rail only. The reluctance of Montanans to see the state's water transported elsewhere is expressed in section 3 of the 1973 Montana Water Use Act, which states that the "use of water for slurry to export coal from Montana is not a beneficial use." Unless the act is amended, coal slurry pipelines could not be used to export coal from the state. Accordingly, we assume that the level of mined coal represented in the alternative coal development strategies is exported only by rail, although we can also examine the implications of slurry transport of coal on the availability of water for other uses, as discussed in chapter 9.

Figure 5-1. Alternative ways to develop coal in Montana

quirements for boiler feed, flue gas scrubbing, cooling, and other process water uses associated with coal-fired electrical generation. Coal gasification is taken up in turn, and finally we look at coal slurry pipeline transport only for comparative purposes, since water used for coal slurry transport is not considered a beneficial use under present state legislation.

Coal Mining

Underlying the Yellowstone Basin is the large Fort Union Formation estimated to have some 50 billion tons of strippable subbituminous coal and lignite in southeastern Montana alone.[2] That portion of the Fort Union coal region lying in the eastern portion of the basin is of particular interest to coal producers because it is known to contain the highest ranked coal

[2] See Robert Matson, "Adequacy of Coal Resource Data, Fort Union Formation, Eastern Montana" in Montana Academy of Sciences, *Proceedings of the Fort Union Coal Field Symposium, Volume 1* (Billings, Mont., April 1975) p. 69.

(subbituminous) in the formation that is readily available by strip mining methods. In 1975, 20.8 million tons of coal were mined in the state, almost entirely for export. A year later, production rose to 26.1 million tons. By 1977, 29.3 million tons were reported mined.[3]

Much of the present coal mining in the basin is occurring in the Mid-Yellowstone and Tongue River subbasins (see figure 5-2).[4] In the northern Big Horn county section of the Mid-Yellowstone subbasin, the mining activity is centered in the Sarpy Creek area (Westmoreland Resources) while in the southern part of the Tongue subbasin, large-scale mining is taking place at Decker (Decker Coal Company). The Westmoreland Mine is part of a 31,000-acre tract in the Crow Ceded Area leased in 1970. Westmoreland has contracted to supply four midwestern utility companies with 77 million tons of coal over a twenty-year period.[5] Production is expected to reach 6.5 million tons of coal a year by 1980. The Decker mine is approximately 10 miles east of the Crow Reservation. It has been in operation since 1972 and produced about 10 million tons of coal in 1977. Approximately 20 million tons annual production is projected for the entire Decker 17,530-acre leasehold by 1980.[6]

There are four major coal beds in the Decker area. At the Decker mine, the Anderson coal bed merges with the Dietz No. 1 bed for a combined thickness of more than 50 feet. West of the mine, these two beds combine with a third for a thickness of 80 feet.[7] The Anderson bed in the Decker coal field runs about 8,705 to 9,850 British thermal units per pound (Btu/lb); it has a sulfur content of 0.2 to 0.6 percent, a moisture content of 20.59 percent to 25.79 percent, and an ash content of 2.9 to 6.5 percent on an "as received" basis.[8]

In Rosebud County, the Rosebud coalbed is of special significance because of large-scale mining by both the Western Energy Company and the Peabody Coal Company. The principal coal beds in the Colstrip area

[3] All coal production estimates are in short tons. The sources of estimates are the U.S. Department of Energy, Energy Information Agency, *Energy Data Reports, Weekly Coal Report,* and *Minerals Yearbook* (various dates in 1978).

[4] The Mid-Yellowstone subbasin encompasses all of Big Horn County and about 70 percent of Rosebud County. The Tongue subbasin is comprised of about 30 percent Rosebud County, 10 percent Big Horn County, and 20 percent Custer County.

[5] See *Cody v. Morton,* 527 F 2d 786 (9th Cir., 1975).

[6] U.S. Department of Interior, Geological Survey, *Final Environmental Impact Statement, East Decker and North Extension Mine* (1976) (FES 74-12).

[7] Robert E. Matson and John W. Blumer, *Quality and Reserves of Strippable Coal, Selected Deposits, Southeastern Montana,* Montana Bureau of Mines and Geology, Bulletin #91 (December 1973), p. 14.

[8] Ibid., pp. 14, 20.

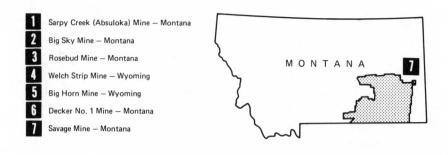

1 Sarpy Creek (Absuloka) Mine — Montana

2 Big Sky Mine — Montana

3 Rosebud Mine — Montana

4 Welch Strip Mine — Wyoming

5 Big Horn Mine — Wyoming

6 Decker No. 1 Mine — Montana

7 Savage Mine — Montana

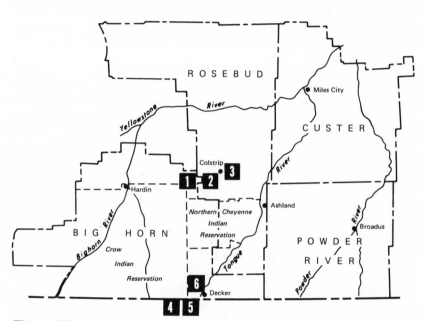

Figure 5-2. Existing strip mines in the Fort Union coal region of southeastern Montana   *Source:* U.S. Environmental Protection Agency, *Surface Coal Mining in the Northern Great Plains of Western United States* (June 1976)

are the Rosebud and McKay beds. The Rosebud coal averages 25 feet in thickness in the Colstrip coal deposit, beneath which lies the 8-foot thick McKay coal seam. Rosebud coal averages about 7,810 to 9,090 Btu/lb, with a sulfur content of 0.5 percent to 1.1 percent, an ash content of 8.8 percent to 12.6 percent, and a moisture content of 20.24 percent to 23.88 percent.[9]

Core samples analyzed from the Peabody Big Sky Mine had slightly higher values for the coal quality characteristics: a heating value of 8,568 Btu/lb of coal, 24.7 percent moisture, 1.2 percent sulfur, and 10.1 percent ash.[10] For the purposes of this study, we will use the typical coal quality characteristics for Rosebud coal, namely, 8,500 Btu/lb of Rosebud coal, 25 percent moisture content, 8 percent sulfur, and 10 percent ash. Consideration of the coal quality characteristics is relevant when the moisture content of the coal is a factor in estimating the rate of water withdrawal for the coal gasification process.

THE COAL MINING PROCESS

In this section, we derive an estimate of the monthly rate of water depletion for a 10-million-ton-per-year coal mine. In order to place the uses of water associated with coal mining into perspective, we begin by outlining the sequence of steps that precedes commercial coal production. Prior to a coal mine opening, entry rights are acquired and exploratory drilling is done to define the coal resource and its surroundings in order to reduce the risks involved in development. The surface mining process is often initiated on a new lease area by extracting coal from a small pit for a test burn at a power plant. Access and haul roads are constructed for delivery of mining equipment and eventual transport of coal. A rail spur may also be constructed if rail transport of coal is planned. Coal storage silos, a coal loading facility, and water supply and pumping facilities are also constructed.

The first activity at a surface mine is the removal of topsoil in order to reach the overburden and the coal seam. The soil is saved for later use in reclamation of the mined area. If the nature of the overburden is hard, it is blasted using ammonium nitrate and fuel oil. The overburden is removed either with a dragline or large shovels. The dragline is a huge piece

---

[9] Ibid., p. 78. (Proximate analyses of nineteen coal core samples obtained on the Colstrip drilling project were analyzed by the U.S. Bureau of Mines.)

[10] U.S. Department of the Interior, *Environmental Impact Statement—Big Sky Mine*, vol. 1 (1975) p. 70. Typical coal quality characteristics of nine drill hole samples are from the Big Sky Mine.

of equipment which is generally constructed on the site and takes almost a year to complete. The newest draglines are "walking" ones.[11]

There is an increasing tendency for surface coal mining operations in the Northern Great Plains states to move toward "truck and shovel" operations. Just as the phrase implies, small shovels remove the overburden and load it into trucks for hauling to dump sites. Large equipment requires long delivery times. The use of smaller equipment allows for a shorter start-up time than is possible with draglines and also allows greater flexibility in segregating topsoil from the remaining overburden. Almost every major mine has road construction equipment, such as scrapers and dozers, which are used to remove in-place soils and to rehandle spoil after dumping by dragline or shovel.

Moderate size shovels are used to remove the coal from the seam and load bottom-dump trucks with capacities ranging up to 200 tons.[12] The coal is then hauled to a crusher and delivered by a conveyor system to silos or other storage facilities. This type of storage facilitates the semiautomatic loading of unit trains. Let us now consider water use at the 10-million-ton-per-year coal mine.

WATER USE ESTIMATES

Generally speaking, very little water is used in the stripping of coal in southeastern Montana. Water use at a mine is roughly only one percent as great as that used at a coal-fired power plant. The water that is used at a surface mine is for: dust suppression on haul roads, dust suppression at the coal loader, mine personnel use (domestic and sanitary), service water (equipment washing and fire quenching), and irrigation of reclaimed mined land.

We will estimate the water that would be "depleted" for each of these mine uses for our model surface coal mine which has an annual coal production rate of 10 million tons per year and operates 250 days per year. We assume a 95-percent coal recovery rate from an average of 24-foot thick coal seams and 1,730 tons of coal per acre-foot (af) of coal deposit.[13]

[11] The walking mechanism consists of a shaft, cam, and elongated shoe which moves vertically. The dragline is supported by the camjack as it moves.

[12] U.S. Environmental Protection Agency, *Surface Coal Mining in the Northern Great Plains of the Western United States* (June, 1976) p. 14.

[13] The coal volume estimate is from the Montana Department of State Lands and does not include other mine disturbances such as access roads, railroad loops, initial spoil placement, or maintenance facilities. See Montana Energy Advisory

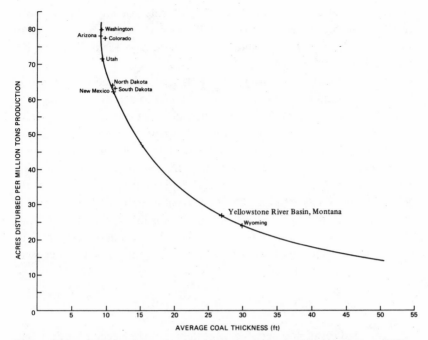

Figure 5-3. Relationship of coal thickness to acres disturbed per million tons production, assuming 1,750 tons per acre-foot and 80 percent recovery   *Source:* Adapted from National Academy of Sciences, *Rehabilitation Potential of Western Coal Lands* (Cambridge, Mass., Ballinger, 1974) p. 32

The assumptions describing the character of our model mine indicate that about 250 acres per mine of 10 million tons annual output would be disturbed for each year of operation (see figure 5-3).[14] This estimate does not include the land needed for topsoil storage, clinker removal and storage, and overburden placement. The total land disturbance would likely be double the annual acreage disturbed by the mining alone.

Operating mines in the study area that are on the production scale of our model mine are the Decker mine at Decker, Montana, and the Western

---

Council, *Coal Development Information Packet* (Helena, Mont., December 1974) p. 51. For comparative purposes, the National Academy of Sciences report, *Rehabilitation Potential of Western Coal Lands* (Cambridge, Mass., Ballinger, 1974) assumed 1,750 tons of coal per acre-foot of coal deposit.

[14] The calculation for acreage disturbance caused by the coal mining alone is:

$$\frac{10,000,000 \text{ tons/yr}}{(1,730 \text{ tons/acre-foot of coal deposit}) \ (.95) \ (24\text{ft})} = 253 \text{ acres/yr}$$

Energy Mine at Colstrip, Montana. At this scale, roughly 10 to 15 miles of 50- to 80-foot-wide haul roads will traverse the mine area.[15] Bench areas are not wet down as a rule except as a safety precaution during dry and windy conditions.

The amount of water used for dust suppression, the largest use of water at coal mines in the study area, is difficult to quantify because it depends on the water evaporation rate, the mode of operation at the mine (whether water is sprayed only during dry spells or all the time the mine is in operation), and the proximity of the mine to local communities downwind. One estimate of water use for dust suppression on unpaved areas is based on the assumption that an annual deposition of water equal to the net annual pond evaporation rate is sufficient to keep the fugitive dust at the mine under control.[16] Using this as a working hypothesis and assuming 10 miles of 80-foot-wide haul roads (4,200,000 square feet) and an annual pond evaporation rate of 49 inches per year, or 4 feet per year, then we calculate that

$$(4.2 \cdot 10^6 \text{ft}^2)(4 \text{ ft/yr})(\text{af}/43{,}560 \text{ ft}^2) = 385 \text{ af/yr}$$

or in rounded form, 400 acre-feet of water would be needed for dust suppression for a 10-million-ton-per-year coal mine.

The theoretical estimate of 400 acre-feet per year (af/yr) of water for dust suppression on haul roads appears to compare well with the amount applied at operational mines. At the 10.2-million-ton-per-year Decker coal mine, about 40,000 gallons per hour of water is used every hour for 16 hours per day, or 1.96 acre-feet per day. Assuming the mine operates 250 days per year and adjusting for the time when the water cannot be applied because of temperatures at or below freezing (68 percent of the time), then

$$(1.96 \text{ af/day})(250 \text{ days/yr})(.68) = 333 \text{ af/yr} \approx 330 \text{ af/yr rounded}$$

At the Western Energy Mine, mining personnel estimate that water for dust suppression on the haul roads is roughly one million gallons per day

[15] David Jennings of the Decker Mine and Rick Dale of the Western Energy Mine to Constance Boris, August 30, 1977 and August 31, 1977 respectively.

[16] Water Purification Associates, *An Assessment of Minimum Water Requirements for Steam Electric Power Generation and Synthetic Fuel Plants in the Western United States,* a report prepared for the Science and Public Policy Program of the University of Oklahoma (Cambridge, Mass., Water Purification Associates, August 24, 1976).

Table 5-1. Estimates of coal mine water use for dust suppression
(acre-feet per year)

Coal mine of 10 million tons/yr	Water for dust suppression
Decker	330
Western Energy	380
Theoretical	385

(MGD) and water is applied about 125 days of the year, or 380 acre-feet per year.[17] The range of water use estimates for mine dust suppression is shown in table 5-1.

The range of estimates is reassuringly close despite the reasons for variability cited earlier. For the purposes of this study, we will use the rounded estimate of water use for dust control of 400 acre-feet per year.

The next use of water in a mine is for dust suppression at the coal loaders. Once again, the mode of operation is important in estimating water use for this purpose. At the Decker Mine, roughly 120 gallons per minute (GPM) are used at the tipple when a unit train is loaded.[18] Assuming that it takes three hours to load a unit train (10,000 ton capacity) and that the coal is loaded an average of three times a day for every day of the year, then

$$(120 \text{ gal/min})(1,440 \text{ min/day})(1/3)(365 \text{ days/yr})(\text{af}/325,900 \text{ gal})$$

$$= 64 \text{ af/yr} \approx 60 \text{ af/yr rounded}$$

In contrast, at the Western Energy Mine, dust suppression at the coal loader is negligible. We use for this study upper bound estimates of water depletion in order to avoid underestimating water use. Accordingly, we will use Decker's 60 af/yr estimate for dust suppression at the coal loader.

Incidentally, none of the water used for dust suppression at the operating mines is directly withdrawn from surface water sources. Operating mines use the seepage from the coal seam and from runoff into the mine pit for dust suppression. This also provides a means of disposing of the

[17] Tim Wood, mining engineer, Western Energy Mine, to Constance Boris, September 2, 1977.

[18] David Jennings, mining engineer, Decker coal mine, to Constance Boris, September 2, 1977.

water obtained from dewatering the pit. Accordingly, while an estimate of 460 acre-feet of water annually is used for dust suppression at the mine, it should be noted that no surface water is directly withdrawn.[19]

Unlike dust suppression, the water used for domestic and sanitary use by mine personnel must be of high quality. Groundwater is the usual source of water for use by mine personnel. Since wastewater is not recovered, water withdrawal for mine personnel use is equal to depletion. At the Decker and Western Energy mines, no estimates of water for mine personnel use are available. Theoretically, it can be estimated by the product of the per capita daily usage and the number of workers at the mine. Assuming 250 workers at our model mine and a per capita daily usage rate of 50 gallons per capita per day, then

$$(50 \text{ gal}/\text{capita}/\text{day})(250 \text{ men})(250 \text{ day}/\text{yr})(af/325,900 \text{ gal})$$

$$= 9 \text{ af}/\text{yr, or in rounded form, } 10 \text{ af}/\text{yr}$$

Service water for equipment washing, maintenance, and fire quenching is another difficult quantity to estimate. Based on an analysis of several mine designs, Water Purification Associates estimates the service water quantity to be 1.5 times the quantity used by mine personnel.[20] Using this rule of thumb, service water would be in the range of 15 acre-feet per year.[21] The source of this water is usually mine seepage, and once it is used, it is not recoverable.

The final use of water at the mine that we shall consider is irrigation of reclaimed land. Except for the application of water after initial seeding, irrigation of reclaimed land is not practiced at the operating coal mines in the study area because the state strip mining law requires that the land be returned to self-sustaining "native" (mixed prairie grass) vegetation. In addition, the mean annual precipitation of 12 to 16 inches on the surface minable lands in the study area appears adequate, according to a National

[19] There are occasions at the Western Energy Mine when there is not enough mine seepage water for dust suppression on haul roads. Other alternatives for obtaining water are the flush pond or possibly the service pond for the power plant units, Colstrip I and II, the source of which is the Yellowstone River.

[20] Water Purification Associates, *An Assessment,* p. 143.

[21] For comparison, mine personnel at Western Energy estimate 12 GPM or (12 gal/min) (1,400 min/day) (250 day/yr) (af/325,900 gal) = 13.26 or 13 af/yr of water for both mine personnel use and service water. This corresponds closely enough to our estimate for both uses of water at 25 af/yr.

Table 5-2. Water depletion estimates for a 10-million-ton-per-year coal mine in the Yellowstone Basin, by use
(acre-feet per year)

Use	Estimate
Dust control	
Unpaved areas	400
Coal loader	60
Mine personnel	10
Service water	15
Irrigation of reclaimed land	0
Total	485
In rounded form	500

Academy of Sciences (NAS) report, so that supplemental irrigation would only be needed in drought years in the early stages of establishing cover.[22]

It would be appropriate to present a range of estimates for each water use at the mine to account for variable conditions. However, to satisfy data input requirements and minimize costs for the hydrologic simulation model, we use one value (monthly estimate) rather than a range of estimates. Therefore, we summarize the water depletion estimates for uses at the mine that will be used in further analysis in table 5-2.[23]

Actually, since the source of water for all of the above uses is almost entirely from mine dewatering, the estimated 500 acre-feet per year for mine use in this area probably would not be withdrawn from surface water sources.[24] The value of the estimate lies in the possibility that shallow

[22] The National Academy of Sciences report, *Rehabilitation Potential,* found that "those areas receiving ten inches or more of annual rainfall can usually be rehabilitated provided that evapotranspiration is not excessive, landscapes are properly shaped, and techniques demonstrated to be successful in rehabilitating disturbed rangeland are applied" (p. 2). The committee hastened to add, however, that this belief is not based on long-term, extensive, and controlled experiments on surface mined land.

[23] There are indirect uses at the mine that result in water depletion such as evaporation from diversion and siltation dams on the mine site. The amount of evaporation is difficult to estimate without measuring the surface area of the dams on a monthly basis, and so the indirect uses of water are ignored in the study.

[24] Strictly speaking from a hydrologic point of view, however, shallow groundwater and surface water sources are intimately linked. For example, at the East Decker mine, water is drawn from alluvium and the coal seams. The maximum inflow to mine cuts would occur when the Tongue River Reservoir storage is at the spillway elevation, and less when the reservoir level is lower. See Montana Bureau of Mines and Geology, *Hydrogeologic Aspects of Existing and Proposed Strip Coal Mines near Decker, Southeastern Montana* Bulletin 97 (December 1975) p. 22.

ground and surface water in the study area are interrelated. Thus, this amount would represent an upper bound for annual surface water withdrawal and depletion for mine uses. The monthly water depletion is approximately 40 acre-feet per month, a negligible amount. We will, however, reflect this value in our total water depletion estimates for coal development in keeping with our philosophy of being conservative in evaluating water withdrawal and availability.

Electrical Generation

Careful analysis of water use is required in electrical generation and conversion since water is a joint factor input with coal in the production of electricity and the conversion of coal to synthetic natural gas. In discussing water use in coal-fired electrical generating facilities, the rate of water withdrawal is equivalent to the rate of water depletion since there is no return flow to the water source. The no-discharge practice adopted by existing coal-fired generating units in the basin can be attributed to the Environmental Protection Agency's regulations prohibiting the discharge of heated effluent into western watercourses, the relatively high water evaporation rates, the availability of large tracts of land for wastewater retention basins, and reuse of circulating water. The use of recycled water from the production process, which in turn reduces the make-up water and hence the rate of water withdrawal, is also becoming more prevalent in the western states. Previous "water for energy" studies ignored the water recycling practice in industrial wastewater control. Site and design specificity were not considered.[25] As a consequence, many of the studies used relatively high water withdrawal estimates for coal conversion facilities. For example, much of the recent evidence supports the assertion that the actual withdrawal requirement for a coal gasification plant based on the Lurgi (with methanation) process could be one-fourth of the estimates used in the previous "water for energy" studies.[26]

[25] Site specificity refers to the characteristics of the coal mined (in particular, the heat and moisture content, which determine coal feed rates and water withdrawal requirements) and the water evaporation rate in the area of the facility, which largely determines the cooling requirement and the resulting water depletion. Design specificity refers to plant design such as type of cooling system and so forth.

[26] Two caveats should be made about water use estimates from the literature. First with regard to the nomenclature, terms like "water use" or "water requirement" make it difficult to distinguish between water withdrawals on the one hand and depletion on the other. Second, estimates of water consumption that do not stipulate plant efficiency and plant factors are virtually meaningless.

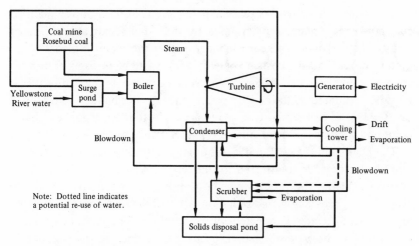

Figure 5-4. Schematic of water use in a coal-fired power plant

THE COAL-FIRED ELECTRICAL GENERATION PROCESS

In the Yellowstone River Basin where water needs for existing uses are not always met, particularly in dry years, the effects of supplying substantial quantities of water for coal-fired electrical generation must be closely assessed. In a power plant, coal is burned in a boiler to produce high-temperature, high-pressure steam. The steam passes through a turbine where a portion of the thermal energy of the steam is converted to rotating mechanical energy. The steam then passes through a condenser where the remaining thermal energy or "waste" heat is rejected to the cooling fluid. The steam is then condensed into water, which then becomes available for reuse. To ensure plant efficiency, cooling is needed in order to produce low pressure on the outlet side of the turbine. The electrical generation process is diagrammed in the flow chart of figure 5-4.

Most of the water withdrawn for coal-fired steam electric power plants is used for cooling. The remaining water is used for boiler feed,[27] ash sluicing, stack gas cleaning, and other uses. Because all but a small percentage of the water used in thermal power plants is for cooling, the amount of water used for steam electric production depends on the amount of cooling to be done and the technical efficiency with which water is used for this purpose.

[27] The amount of water used for boiler feed has little effect on the total water depletion for steam electric generation because most of it is recovered in the condensing process and reused.

The water withdrawal requirement for any coal-fired power plant or coal conversion plant is determined by the quality and availability of water, the economics of heat exchange within the plant, the cost of recycling water, and the costs associated with waste heat disposal into receiving bodies of water. The cooling demand, or the amount of heat that must be dissipated by the cooling water, on the other hand, is determined by the amount of thermal energy remaining in the steam at the exhaust point and the size and heat transfer characteristics of the condenser.[28]

The heat from the coal that is not otherwise transferred in the generation of electricity is transferred to the cooling water via the condenser. Waste heat from the process can be transferred to the atmosphere by evaporation, convection, and radiation. Most of the waste heat transferred to the cooling water is rejected by evaporation. The amount of water evaporated is the water depletion resulting from cooling. The volume of water depleted for cooling largely depends on the type of cooling system used in the power plant. It is likely that both water supply considerations and environmental constraints will determine the design of alternative cooling systems in the Yellowstone River Basin.

The basic types of cooling systems are: once-through cooling, cooling ponds, wet evaporative cooling towers, combination wet/dry (hybrid) cooling towers, and dry cooling towers. The dry cooling tower uses air to transfer the heat rather than water. However, because in dry cooling the temperature drop across the turbine is not as great as when water is used, the plant has a higher heat rate or a lower plant efficiency. This in turn means higher operating costs (and also higher capital costs) as more coal would be used in the steam electric generation and larger and more expensive condensers would be needed. The advantage, however, is that very little water is consumed in a plant with dry cooling.

Generally speaking, more water is depleted using wet evaporative cooling than cooling ponds or once-through cooling because most of the heat is rejected by evaporation, although some heat is also transferred by convection depending on the temperature and humidity conditions of the area in which the plant is located. Cooling ponds can consume either more or less water than wet evaporative cooling depending on how much of the heat is transferred by radiation and how much water is lost through seepage. Once-through cooling depletes the least volume of water but this advantage is offset by the high water withdrawal requirements. In a once-

---

[28] Paul H. Cootner and George O. Löf, *Water Demand for Steam Electric Generation: An Economic Projection Model* (Baltimore, Johns Hopkins University Press for Resources for the Future, 1965) p. 12.

through cooling system, water is withdrawn from a river, pumped through a condenser, and then discharged at an elevated temperature back into the river. Such a system requires a water source that can supply a substantial volume continuously and dependably. For example, a coal-fired 1,000-megawatt power plant operating at 100 percent capacity and using once-through cooling will withdraw about 724,000 acre-feet per year.[29] Even though this type of cooling system consumes less water than any other type, the very large water withdrawals make once-through cooling an unlikely alternative.

An alternative to once-through cooling is closed cycle cooling, which requires an offstream cooling device, such as cooling ponds or cooling towers, to transfer the waste heat to the atmosphere. With either system, make-up water is added to replace the evaporated water. Because cooling ponds receive more solar radiation by their very nature than do wet cooling towers, the amount of heat dissipated by evaporation from a cooling pond can be higher than from a wet cooling tower given the same power plant. The volume of make-up water to replace the depleted water for a 1,000-megawatt power plant (100 percent capacity factor) using a cooling pond would be approximately 14,500 to 18,000 acre-feet on an average annual basis.[30] In comparison, for the same size plant, a wet cooling tower would require an annual average make-up water rate of 10,000 to 13,000 acre-feet per year depending on the water treatment applied to the blowdown.[31] Generally speaking, less water is withdrawn for wet cooling than for either once-through cooling or a cooling pond, but more water is depleted in wet cooling at least when compared to the once-through system.

The operation of a dry cooling tower requires the least amount of water because all of the waste heat is discharged to the atmosphere by convection. Hybrid or wet/dry cooling towers have both dry and evaporative heat exchanges, and their water withdrawal and depletion rates are accordingly between those of wet and dry cooling towers. Figure 5-5 graphically illustrates the water withdrawal requirements for a 1,000-Mw-coal-fired power plant in the basin equipped with alternative cooling

[29] Bruce A. Tichenor, "Feasibility of Alternative Cooling Systems for Power Plants in the Northern Great Plains" (Pacific Northwest Environmental Research Laboratory [EPA], n.d.) p. 6.

[30] Ibid., p. 12.

[31] Ibid., p. 6. It should also be noted that the quality of water available for cooling has a large effect on the amount of water required in a wet cooling system. The higher the dissolved solids content of the water, the greater the water requirement, unless the brackish water is extensively treated.

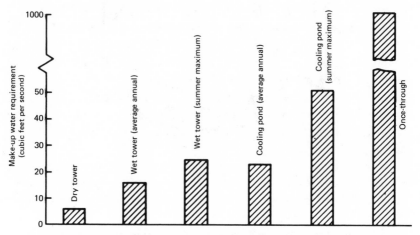

The plant size is 1,000 MW and it is assumed to be operated at a 100-percent capacity factor and equipped with flue gas desulfurization equipment.

Figure 5-5.   Water withdrawal rates for selected cooling systems for a 1,000-Mw power plant in the Northern Great Plains   *Source:* Bruce A. Tichenor, "Feasibility of Alternative Cooling Systems for Power Plants in the Northern Great Plains" (Pacific Northwest Environmental Research Laboratory [EPA] n.d.) p. 6.

systems. From a technical standpoint, the feasible cooling systems for power plants in the Yellowstone River Basin include the wet evaporative, dry, and hybrid cooling systems. From an economical standpoint new coal-fired units, Colstrip 1 and 2 at Colstrip, Montana, in the Mid-Yellow-stone subbasin are employing wet evaporative cooling systems, and such systems are proposed for units 3 and 4 as well.

WATER USE ESTIMATES

We will now estimate the water withdrawal requirements for 1,000 Mw of coal-fired operating capacity assuming a thermal efficiency of 38 per-cent and continuous operation.[32] It is also assumed that the plant is

[32] We speak of 1,000 Mw in continuous operation, realizing that this involves greater installed capacity by reason of a realistic plant factor being lower than 100 percent. 1,000 Mw at a 100 percent-capacity factor is a convenient expression for 1,000 Mw of continuously operating capacity of some amount X multiplied by the appropriate plant factor. This is equivalent to the 1,300-Mw units in the Krutilla-Fisher study operating at between 75 percent and 80 percent capacity factor. (John V. Krutilla and Anthony Fisher, with Richard E. Rice, *Economic and Fiscal Impacts of Coal Development: Northern Great Plains* [Baltimore, Johns Hopkins University Press for Resources for the Future, 1978]).

equipped with wet evaporative cooling towers and flue gas desulfurization. equipment. The water circulation rate for a plant of this type is 574,000 gallons per minute (GPM) calculated on the basis of an assumed 15° F temperature rise as it flows through the condenser.[33]

The evaporative water loss caused by cooling is the largest use of water in a power plant. The evaporated water (measured in terms of acre-feet per 1,000 Btu input to the condenser) is a function of the plant heat rate, H,[34] the condenser heat rate, kH, and the water evaporation rate, E_r (the pounds of water evaporated per 1,000 Btu input to the cooling system). The value of k is assumed to be 0.48—that is, 48 percent of the thermal heat is absorbed during condensation in accordance with general power plant operating experience. The water evaporation rate changes from about 0.65 to 0.85 lbs of water per 1,000 Btu input to the condenser depending on altitude and climatic conditions. Assuming an altitude of 4,000 feet above sea level, a relative humidity of 51 percent, and a wet bulb temperature of 38°F, the water evaporation ratio is 0.71 lbs of water evaporated hourly per 1,000-Btu input hourly to the condenser.[35] The

[33] Teknekron, Inc., *Comprehensive Standards: The Power Generation Case,* prepared for U.S. Environmental Protection Agency (Berkeley, Calif., Teknekron, Inc., March 1975) p. 135.

[34] Assuming a 38-percent-thermal efficiency for the plant and since 3,413 Btu = 1 kWh, the plant heat rate $H = \dfrac{3,413}{38}$ Btu/kWh = 9,000 Btu/kWh.

[35] See Paul Leung and Raymond Moore, *Water Consumption Determination for Steam Power Plant Cooling Towers: A Heat-and-Mass Balance Method,* ASME publication No. 69-WA/PWR-3, ASME Winter Annual Meeting, Los Angeles, November 1969. The estimated rate of water evaporation is based on an assumed altitude of 4,000 feet (p. 4, figure 3). This is in keeping with the altitude of power plants in Montana. For example, Colstrip is at an elevation of about 3,200 feet above sea level. Normal monthly data over the period of record for air temperatures and relative humidity were obtained from the U.S. Department of Commerce, National Climatic Center, *Local Climatological Data, Annual Summary with Comparative Data, 1978* for Miles City, Montana (1978). Monthly wet bulb temperatures were obtained from psychrometric charts. The heat transferred in wet cooling per unit weight of water was calculated for each month of the year, using the long-term, average ambient conditions for each month and then taking an average for all twelve months. Basing the annual water evaporation rate on the average annual ambient conditions instead could lead to considerable error in the results according to Ronald Probstein and Harris Gold, *Water in Synthetic Fuel Production, The Technology and Alternatives* (Cambridge, Mass., The MIT Press, 1978) p. 51. Therefore, calculating the long-term average for air temperature and relative humidity for each month and taking an average for all twelve months yielded an estimate of .71 lb of water evaporated/hour per 1,000 Btu heat input per hour, which is equivalent to a heat dissipation ratio of 1,408 Btu/lb of water evaporated. Note, however, that the pounds of water evaporated per 1,000 Btu heat input will increase in the summer months; that is, less heat will be dissipated per pound of water evaporated. For ex-

evaporative water loss,[36] W_E, for 1,000 Mw of capacity in continuous operation with a 38 percent thermal efficiency is estimated as

$$W_E(\text{af/yr}) = (E_r \text{ lbs}/1{,}000 \text{ Btu})(\text{gal}/8.4 \text{ lbs})(\text{af}/325{,}900 \text{ gal})$$
$$(k)(H)(\text{kWh/yr})$$

$$= (0.71 \text{ lbs}/1{,}000 \text{ Btu})(\text{gal}/8.4 \text{ lbs})(\text{af}/325{,}900 \text{ gal})$$
$$(.48)(9{,}000 \text{ Btu/kWh})(8.76 \cdot 10^9 \text{ kWh/yr})$$

$$= 9{,}815 \text{ af/yr, or in rounded form, } 9{,}800 \text{ af/yr}$$

To this estimate of evaporative water loss, we must also add the water loss caused by cooling tower blowdown and drift. Drift is airborne entrained water containing dissolved solids from an evaporative cooling tower. The amount of drift varies with local wind conditions and tower design. It is usually measured as a percentage of circulating water in the system. State-of-the-art design can obtain drift losses of 0.005 percent of the circulating flow rate for mechanical draft units and 0.002 percent for natural draft towers. However, in no case should the drift loss exceed 0.01 percent for well-designed towers.

The drift loss can be estimated by

$$D = aC$$

where

a = the percentage of the circulating flow rate in the cooling system (wet evaporative cooling tower) that is lost

C = the circulating flow rate in the system

---

ample, the average long-term calculated estimates of W_E for the months of June, July, August, and September are .78, .83, .82, and .78, respectively. The power plant would need a larger supply of water on hand in the summer months to compensate for the reduced heat dissipation rates. For example; W_E = lb of water/1,000 Btu input is equivalent to a heat dissipation rate of only 1,200 Btu/lb of water evaporated.

[36] For comparative purposes, other estimates of evaporative water loss found in the literature are the Teknekron report, which estimates 11,110 acre-feet/year based on an assumed relative humidity of 40 percent, a wet bulb temperature of 68°F, and an assumed thermal efficiency of 38 percent; and Leung and Moore, who report a theoretical average of evaporative loss of 10,946 acre-feet per year assuming the same condenser heat load. Leung and Moore's evaporative water loss estimate was scaled for 1,000 megawatts of capacity in continuous operation.

As stated previously, the circulating water between the generating plant and the wet evaporative cooling tower is 574,000 GPM. Assuming $a = .01\%$, the drift loss, D, is approximated by

$$D = (.0001)(574,000 \text{ GPM})$$

$$= 57 \text{ GPM} = 90 \text{ af/yr or in rounded form, } 100 \text{ af/yr}$$

Cooling tower blowdown is necessary in order to keep the dissolved solids from building up in the cooling water system.[37] The higher the dissolved solids content of the water, the greater the water requirement. A cycle represents the number of times that make-up water constituents are concentrated in the recirculating water. The make-up water constituents are concentrated as a result of evaporation. In the past, typical salt concentration ratios ranged from 2.5 to 5. However, the newer plants have installed brine concentrators, increasing the cycles of concentration to 10 to 15. In the existing Colstrip units 1 and 2 (330 Mw each), there are 10 to 12 cycles of concentration.[38] Based on the design of the cooling towers of the Colstrip units, we assume that the original concentration of dissolved solids in the make-up water will be increased about eleven times (that is, eleven cycles of concentration) prior to discharge in the blowdown. Blowdown serves to keep the recirculating water within acceptable solubility limits to avoid cooling system fouling. The water evaporated by blowdown B is estimated by

$$B = \frac{W_E}{C - 1}$$

where

W_E = the water evaporation rate and
C = the number of cycles of concentration in the cooling water

Therefore,

$$B = \frac{9,800 \text{ acre-feet/yr}}{11 - 1} \cong 1,000 \text{ af/yr}$$

[37] We do not explicitly account for blowdown from the boiler since we assume that boiler blowdown will be cooled and piped to the cooling tower circulating water for use in that system.

[38] Jim Rogers, Operations, Montana Power Company, Colstrip, Montana, to Constance Boris, June 7, 1978.

Since the evaporation rates are relatively high in the basin and there are large land areas, blowdown will likely go to lined settling ponds. In some power plant designs, instead of discharging the blowdown to a settling pond, it is used in the flue gas desulfurization (scrubber) system which then discharges the solids to a settling or ash pond. For example, although use of cooling tower blowdown for the scrubbers has been proposed by the Montana Power Company in its application for construction of Colstrip units 3 and 4 (700 Mw each), it is somewhat doubtful that cooling tower blowdown could be used in the scrubber system for units 3 and 4.[39]

We assume that the flue gas desulfurization system in our hypothetical 1,000 megawatts of continuously operating capacity consists of wet alkali scrubbers (single-stage venturi scrubbers) that remove fly ash as well as sulfur dioxide. In scrubbing systems, water is consumed in stack evaporative losses and in solid waste disposal. The amount of water lost through evaporation in the stack depends on the temperature in the scrubber. At 125°F, assuming the gases to be saturated, about 1,500 acre-feet per year will be carried up the stack along with the rest of the flue gases.[40]

One of the major problems inherent in scrubber systems is the production of large quantities of sludge, which itself is directly proportional to the use of coal. The solids slurry mixture from the scrubber is then discharged to an ash or settling pond. However, decanted water from the ash pond is recycled back to the scrubber system, so that make-up water is needed only for offsetting evaporative losses. If cooling tower blowdown cannot be used in the scrubber system, then an additional 600 af/yr or so would have to be withdrawn from the river for this purpose.[41]

Other water uses in the power plant include bottom ash sluicing, service water, seepage and evaporative loss from the surge pond.[42] Based on data in the environmental impact statement for Colstrip units 3 and 4, water loss attributed to bottom ash disposal (300 acre-feet per year), service water (230 acre-feet per year), and pond seepage and evaporation (1,380

[39] Montana Department of Natural Resources and Conservation, Energy Planning Division, *Draft Environmental Impact Statement on Colstrip Electrical Generating Units 3 and 4, 500 KV Transmission Lines and Associated Facilities,* Volume 3A (November 1974) p. 229.

[40] This estimate of evaporative water loss from a scrubber system using Rosebud coal is based on information obtained from the Montana Department of Natural Resources and Conservation, *Draft Environmental Impact Statement,* Volume 1, p. 93; Volume 3A, figure 8-25.

[41] Montana Department of Natural Resources and Conservation, *Draft Environmental Impact Statement.*

[42] It is very likely that surge or holding ponds will be associated with mine-mouth power plants in the basin.

Table 5-3. Water withdrawal (depletion) estimate for a 1,000-megawatt coal-fired power plant[a] in the Yellowstone Basin

Requirements for make-up water	Acre-feet/yr
Cooling tower evaporation	9,800
Cooling tower blowdown	1,000
Cooling tower drift	100
Scrubber	1,500
Other (ash disposal, service water, pond seepage and evaporation)	2,000
Total	14,400

[a] Plant is assumed to be in continuous operation.

acre-feet per year—summer rate) total about 2,000 acre-feet per year. We adopt this estimate as a working assumption for this category of plant water use.

Summarizing, make-up water requirements for our hypothetical 1,000 megawatts of continuous operating capacity assuming a 38 percent thermal efficiency are shown in table 5-3. Of course, this estimate of water withdrawal of 14,400 acre-feet per year for an annual 1,000 Mw of power production is also dependent on the other assumptions stated in this chapter such as the condenser heat rate, kH, where $k = .48$, $H = 9,000$ Btu/kWh, $E_r = .71$ lb of water evaporated per 1,000-Btu-input to the condenser, eleven cycles of concentration for blowdown, and so forth.

The amount of water withdrawn for power plant operation is also sensitive to the thermal efficiency of the process. A lower thermal efficiency implies a larger thermal waste heat dissipation and therefore an increase in water withdrawal.[43] The new Colstrip units 1 and 2 (330 Mw each), which have a design efficiency of 10,260 Btu/kWh (33.2 percent), had an average net operating heat rate of 11,381 Btu/kWh (29.7 percent) in 1976.[44] This high heat rate has been attributed to the normal start-up problems of new plants.

[43] Federal Power Commission (FPC), *Steam-Electric Plant Air and Water Quality Control Data for the Year Ended December 31, 1973, Summary Report* (March 1976). The FPC data reflect operating heat rates generally higher than nameplate heat rates. A few possible reasons for higher operating heat rates are the practice of load following, keeping a spinning reserve, and plant aging. The national average heat rate is about 10,000 Btu/kWh. The best heat rate achieved is about 9,000 Btu/kWh. It has remained at this level for the last decade.

[44] Martin A. White, Project Manager, Colstrip Complex, Western Energy Company, to Constance Boris, April 18, 1977.

The water withdrawal rate for power plant operation is also higher in the summer than in the winter. In estimating the water balance for our hypothetical power plant operation, we used representative summer water use rates.

Finally, the relatively high water evaporation rate in the basin implies that there will likely be no wastewater discharge into receiving streams. The operating practice for the newly constructed Colstrip units 1 and 2 and the proposed units 3 and 4 is to discharge the wastewater from the scrubber system and bottom ash unit to a settling pond where the water is recycled and to some extent evaporated. Because of the supply of low-cost land in the basin, a new ash pond will be constructed when the old one is filled. Therefore, physical factors such as a high water evaporation rate, the supply of land available for solids disposal, and in some cases, the lack of proximity to watercourses for wastewater discharge, and economic factors (cost of wastewater treatment) suggest that the rate of water depletion for new power plant operation will be equal to the rate of water withdrawal. Thus, the estimate of 14,400 acre-feet per year for annual water withdrawal for our 1,000-megawatt power plant in continuous operation represents the water depletion rate for such an operation in the basin.

Coal Gasification

In addition to coal being burned to produce electricity, coal can also be converted to a gaseous product. Coal gasification technology dates back to 1620.[45] There are at least five different processes for producing gas of high-Btu content from coal: Hygas, Synthane, CO_2 Acceptor, Bigas, and Lurgi. The Lurgi process, the most thoroughly proven technology, produces gas of a low-Btu content. Through an additional process called methanation, the low-Btu gas from the Lurgi process can be upgraded to a high-Btu pipeline-quality gas having about 1,000 Btu per standard cubic foot. Although there are several Lurgi coal gasification plants in operation throughout the world, the Lurgi-with-methanation process has not yet reached commercial use. While several Lurgi-with-methanation coal gasification plants have been proposed for the basin, even the firmer plans (Northern Natural Gas Company and Cities Service) have been

[45] For a brief history and description of coal gasification and technology, see Federal Energy Administration, Final Task Force Report, *Synthetic Fuels from Coal*, Project Independence Report (Washington, D.C., GPO, November 1974).

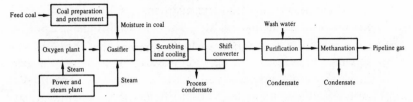

Figure 5-6. Schematic flow diagram of a Lurgi process coal gasification plant

suspended.[46] Within the study area itself, Consolidation Coal Company proposed in 1972 a complex of four 250-million-standard-cubic-foot- (MMscf)-per-day coal gasification plants on the Northern Cheyenne Reservation. (These plans seem no longer to be under consideration.)

In this study, the Lurgi-with-methanation coal gasification process was selected as the process for consideration largely because of the availability of detailed information on the method. Process and cooling water requirements will be discussed for a standard size 250-million-cubic-foot-per-day coal gasification plant following a short description of the Lurgi gasification-with-methanation process. From this point on, whenever we use the term Lurgi process, we will be referring to the process with methanation.

THE COAL GASIFICATION PROCESS

Associated with the coal gasification process is a coal mining operation and a coal preparation plant in which run-of-mine coal is crushed, sized, blended, and delivered to the coal gasification plant. The coal gasification plant includes a series of processing steps and all the auxiliary service facilities required to convert prepared coal into gas. Figure 5-6 is a schematic flow diagram of the major sections of a coal gasification plant. In the production of pipeline gas, the carbon in coal is first converted to carbon monoxide and hydrogen in an endothermic reaction. The carbon monoxide and water are then shifted to carbon dioxide (CO_2) and water to partially supply the heat for the first reaction. More hydrogen is needed to

[46] Plans for two coal gasification facilities in the Southwest, the Wesco and El Paso projects, have also been suspended. There is only one planned coal gasification plant that will likely be built in the near future if governmental loan guarantees are forthcoming. It is American Natural Resources Company's planned facilities in Mercer County, North Dakota. Unlike other plans, it will be built in two phases. Each phase will result in the production of 125 million cubic feet of gas per day assuming a 91 percent load factor.

boost the carbon monoxide (CO) and hydrogen (H_2) ratio from $1:1$ to $1:3$ in order to produce methane (CH_4). The coal itself contains a portion of the hydrogen that goes into making up the low-Btu gas. The additional hydrogen comes either from the addition of steam directly into the gasifier or through separate production of hydrogen from steam. The low-Btu gas is purified and then upgraded to high-Btu gas or pipeline-quality gas via the methanation process ($CO + 3H_2 \rightarrow CH_4 + H_2O$). For this study, we need to estimate the annual and monthly water depletion rates associated with this process.

WATER USE ESTIMATES

A necessary part of the environmental assessment of coal gasification plants is to determine the rate of water depletion. This is important in Montana where substantial coal reserves exist but water is scarce in a few subbasins during periods of low flow.

The striking feature of the published literature on estimated water withdrawal requirements for a 250-MMscf-per-day coal gasification plant is the wide range of the estimates—from 9,856 acre-feet per year to 42,560 acre-feet per year.[47] Variability in water withdrawal requirements is caused in part by the fact that the water requirements depend on the climate, the moisture content of the coal, and the supplies of raw water, as well as the type of process used, but the high end of the range now represents an outdated estimate. The high estimate can be traced to a 1973 Federal Power Commission (FPC) report of the Synthetic Gas-Coal Task Force of the National Gas Survey. The water requirements in that study ranged from 6,080 to 30,387 gallons per minute (9,810 to 49,032 acre-feet per year) for a plant producing 250 MMscf per day of synthetic pipeline-quality gas. The major variable responsible for this wide range of water requirements was the process design, specifically the use of air cooling to reduce water requirements and the amount of make-up water assumed. However, the FPC estimates were made before the commercial high-Btu coal gasification plant design data were available.[48] Water requirements for both commercially available processes and advanced-technology processes

---

[47] Estimates of water use for other coal gasification processes found in the literature are made on the assumption that there is no limitation on water availability. The summary of estimates is from G. H. Davis and L. A. Wood, *Water Demands for Expanding Energy Development*, U.S. Geological Survey Circular 703 (1974).

[48] It should be noted that later writers on the subject of water supply used the data in the Federal Power Commission study, and particularly the higher water requirements, without realizing the limitations of the initial estimates.

now appear to be at the low end of these initial estimates especially in those areas where water is limited.

The first definitive engineering data on water requirements for coal gasification plants using the Lurgi process became available when the El Paso and Wesco plants were designed for sites where water is very scarce. Consequently, the designs take maximum advantage of water reuse and conservation practices.

The major approaches to reducing make-up water requirements for coal gasification include reusing the process water effluents and substituting air cooling for wet cooling towers.[49] The tradeoff for achieving lower water requirements is the higher costs associated with dry cooling towers. Therefore, in practice, the most efficient rate of water use for a given plant is determined by the supply and demand for water resources at a given site.

For a given plant, the difference between the rate of raw water intake (water withdrawal) and the rate of effluent discharge is equal to the rate of water depletion. The designs for both the proposed Wesco and El Paso plants, which were to be sited in the arid Southwest, take maximum advantage of water reuse and conservation so that there is no wastewater effluent discharge into a receiving watercourse. The suspended Wesco plant, originally to be built in New Mexico as a joint venture of Texas Eastern Transmission Corporation and the Pacific Lighting Corporation, would have used Navajo coal as feed for the gasification process. Navajo coal has an average of 8,500 Btu/lb and 12 percent moisture by weight. This type of plant is designed to have an overall efficiency of 65.4 percent operating at a 91 percent plant factor. The coal feed rate for the production of 980 Btu per cubic feet (cf) of gas from a 250-MMscf-per-day plant is 24,820 tons of coal per day. The water balance for the Wesco plant shown in table 5-4 indicates a raw water intake rate requirement of 8,562 acre-feet per year, excluding the water produced in the methanation process (roughly 1,000 acre-feet per year) and a water depletion rate of 9,573 acre-feet per year.

The El Paso plant, on the other hand, would have used coal with a higher average heating value (8,872 Btu/lb) and a higher moisture content (16 percent by weight). Using a modified Stearns-Roger Lurgi coal

[49] The theoretical lower limit on water usage is given by the minimal requirements for the reaction with coal, which is approximately 2,000 GPM (3,226 af/yr). Water Resources Center, *Proceedings of the Workshop on Research Needs Related to Water for Energy* (Urbana, Ill., University of Illinois at Urbana-Champaign, November 1974) p. 60 (UILU-WRC-74-0093).

Table 5-4. Water balance for the proposed Wesco coal gasification plant,[a] using Navajo coal

Plant use	Gallons/minute	Percentage
Panel A. Water consumed		
Process (to supply hydrogen)	1,179	19.9
Evaporation[b]	3,900	65.7
Lime sludge and wet ash disposal	238	4.0
Plant use and selected revegetation	619	10.4
Total	5,936 (9,573 af/yr)	100.0
Panel B. Water supplied		
Raw water intake	5,309 (8,562 af/yr)	89.4
Water produced in methanation	627 (1,011 af/yr)	10.6
Total	5,936 (9,573 af/yr)	100.0

Source: The water use estimates are as of January 1976 in the U.S. Department of the Interior, Bureau of Reclamation, *Final Environmental Impact Statement, Western Gasification Company (Wesco) Coal Gasification Project and Expansion of Navajo Mine by Utah International, Inc.,* New Mexico, Volume I (January 14, 1970).

[a] This type of plant has a capacity of 250 million standard cubic feet of gas per day.

[b] This type of plant is designed to reduce water use by using cooling water only in those heat removal applications where air cooling is impractical. If water replaced air for cooling in the condensers, the evaporative water loss from the cooling tower is estimated to increase water depletion by 4,000 gpm or 6,450 af/yr. (See *Final Environmental Impact Statement, Wesco,* vol. I, p. 1–89).

gasification process design, the thermal efficiency of their Lurgi process design for converting coal to gas is 52.8 percent, and the overall plant efficiency is 67.3 percent (including by-products). To produce 972 Btu per cubic foot of gas, a coal feed rate of 26,000 tons per day is required. The water balance for the El Paso plant shown in table 5-5 indicates a raw water intake of 4,908 gallons per minute, or 7,915 acre-feet per year, and a total water depletion of 10,018 acre-feet per year. It should be noted that even for detailed designs such as these, water depletion estimates between different process designs even at the same location cannot be expected to agree to within more than 20 percent at this stage of development.[50]

We assume use of the Stearns-Roger design of the Lurgi gasification process (developed for the 250-MMscf-per-day-capacity El Paso plant) for the postulated coal gasification plant in this study.[51] Montana subbituminous coal (Rosebud and McKay coal seams) has an average of

[50] D. J. Goldstein and R. F. Probstein, "Water Requirements for an Integrated SNG Plant and Mine Operation," *Symposium Proceedings: Environmental Aspects of Fuel Conversion Technology II* (Research Triangle Park, N.C., U.S. Environmental Protection Agency, June 1976) p. 2 (Report No. EPA-600/2-76-149).

[51] We assume that the produced synthetic gas will have a heating value of 972 Btu per cubic foot.

Table 5-5. Approximate water balance for the proposed El Paso Lurgi coal gasification plant

	New Mexico coal (Navajo)		Montana coal (Rosebud)	
Item	Gallons/minute	Per-centage	Gallons/minute	Per-centage
Panel A. Water consumed				
Reaction	1,971	31.7	1,971	36.4
Evaporation	3,543	57.0	2,784[a]	51.5
Drift	260	4.2	260	4.8
Ammonia by-product	106	1.7	106	2.0
Wet ash disposal	145	2.3	145	2.7
Lime sludge	187	3.1	143	2.6
Total	6,212	100.0	5,409	100.0
Panel B. Water supplied				
River water	4,908	79.0	3,678 (5,934 af/yr)	68.0
Coal moisture	713	11.5	1,140[b](1,839 af/yr)	21.1
Water produced in methanation	591	9.5	591 (954 af/yr)	10.9
Total	6,212 (10,018 af/yr)	100.0	5,409 ≅ (8,727 af/yr)	100.0

Notes: The author was unable to balance the flows in the "Process Flow Diagram for Lurgi Dry Ash Gasification Process" in the source document on which this table is based because of lack of information in the diagram. Therefore, the adjustment for Montana coal is only approximate. The gasification plant has a capacity of 250 million standard cubic feet of gas per day and has wet evaporative cooling towers. The water consumption (depletion) estimates include the water consumption of all auxiliary facilities including a gas-fired steam plant. It is also assumed that no water is supplied from the oxygen plant condensate, use is made of air for cooling, and there is reuse of process condensate.

Source: H. Shaw and E. M. Magee, *Evaluation of Pollution Control in Fossil Fuel Conversion Processes, Section I, Lurgi Process,* prepared by Exxon Research and Engineering Company for U.S. Environmental Protection Agency, July 1974 (EPA-650/2-74-009c, also available from the National Technical Information Service PB 237-694).

[a] The evaporation rate varies with the climate. In New Mexico, the average evaporation rate is 1,100 Btu/lb of water while in Montana, it is about 1,400 Btu/lb of water (D. J. Goldstein, and R. F. Probstein, "Water Requirements for an Integrated SNG Plant and Mine Operation," *Symposium Proceedings: Environmental Aspects of Fuel Conversion Technology II* [Research Triangle Park, N.C., U.S. Environmental Protection Agency, June 1976] pp. 307–332 [Report No. EPA-600/2-76-149]). Therefore, an estimate of the water loss caused by evaporation in Montana is 11/14 of the evaporative water loss in New Mexico, or (11/14)(3,543 GPM) = 2,784 GPM.

[b] The water supply is adjusted for the coal feed rate using Montana coal in the following manner:

(27,400 tons/day)(day/24 hrs)(2,000 lbs/ton) = 2,283,333 lbs of coal/hr.

Moisture content by weight (25%):

(2,283,333 lbs/hr)(.25) = 570,833 lbs of water/hr, or 1,140 GPM.

8,500 Btu per lb of coal and a 25 percent moisture content by weight. Assuming a 52.8 percent thermal efficiency for converting Rosebud coal into 972 Btu per cubic foot of gas and an overall plant efficiency of approximately 67 percent (including by-products), the coal feed rate for the model coal gasification plant is 27,400 tons per day using a coal-fired boiler for steam production. The coal feed rate for the model plant is

Table 5-6. Approximate water depletion estimates for a 250-million-standard-cubic-foot-per-day coal gasification plant as a function of location
(million gallons per day)

Plant use	Four Corners, New Mexico (arid climate)	Campbell County, Wyoming (semiarid climate)
Process, including fuel gas generation	0.80	0.80
Cooling	3.11	1.64
Evaporation, solids disposal, and other uses	0.82	0.31
Total	4.73 (or 5,300 af/yr)	2.75 (or 4,200 af/yr)

Source: D. J. Goldstein and R. F. Probstein, "Water Requirements for an Integrated SNG Plant and Mine Operation," *Symposium Proceedings: Environmental Aspects of Fuel Conversion Technology II* (Research Triangle Park, N.C., U.S. Environmental Protection Agency, June 1976) p. 45 (Report No. EPA-600/2-76-149).

higher than in the proposed El Paso plant because Rosebud coal has a lower heating value than Navajo coal.

The approximate water balance for the Lurgi coal gasification process design (table 5-6) is adjusted for the use of Montana (Rosebud) coal in the following two ways: (1) the higher moisture content of Rosebud coal in comparison with Navajo coal (25 percent versus 16 percent), and (2) the climatic difference between Montana and New Mexico. The higher moisture content in the Rosebud coal reduces the raw water intake (or water withdrawal) requirement, and because of the difference in climate, the water evaporation rate in Montana will be different from that in New Mexico. Table 5-6 illustrates the difference in water depletion estimates depending on the location of the coal gasification plant. Plants located in the arid areas lose more water to evaporation than do plants located in semiarid areas. More specifically, the average annual rate of heat removal in New Mexico is about 1,100 Btu per lb of water evaporated and is 1,300 Btu per lb of water evaporated in the more northern locations such as Wyoming.[52] In the Yellowstone River Basin of Montana, the amount of water evaporated in Montana will be approximately $1\frac{1}{14}$ of the amount evaporated in New Mexico.

The water balance for a coal gasification plant in Montana, adjusted for both moisture and climate (table 5-6), indicates that almost two-thirds

[52] Goldstein and coauthors, *Symposium*, p. 24. The water evaporation rate for Montana is 1,400 Btu per lb of water as derived in the text and footnote 35. Note that there is also a seasonal difference in water evaporation rates as discussed in footnote 35.

of the water is lost through evaporation and drift; another one-third is lost in the gasification process itself. The total water depletion is 8,727 acre-feet per year, or in rounded form, 9,000 acre-feet per year assuming a 100 percent capacity factor. Once again, it should be noted that the raw water intake requirement is entirely consumptive; that is, no water is returned as liquid to the water supply source.[53] The raw water intake or water withdrawal requirement is 5,934 acre-feet per year, the rest of the water requirement being supplemented by moisture in the coal and water produced in the methanation process.

Based on the Stearns-Roger Lurgi coal gasification process adjusted for Montana coal, we conclude that a 250-MMscf-per-day coal gasification plant equipped with wet evaporative cooling towers would have a water withdrawal rate of about 6,000 ± 20 percent acre-feet per year. Adding the 20 percent, or 1,200 acre-feet per year, to the total to cover a margin of error, as mentioned earlier, and to be consistent with our philosophy of not underestimating water use, we find a reasonable estimate of raw water withdrawal for such a plant located in Montana to be on the order of 7,200 acre-feet per year. For convenience, we will use the rounded estimate of 8,000 acre-feet per year.

To summarize, the rates of water withdrawal for a standard-size coal gasification plant would be lower in Montana than in the more arid Southwest (roughly 1,000 acre-feet per year less water would be required) because of differences in the climate and characteristics of the coal. In addition, water withdrawal requirements for standard-size coal gasification plants employing water reuse and conservation practices will be on the low end of the wide range of estimates cited in the literature.

Coal Slurry Pipeline Transport

Replacing the traditional rail transport of coal with slurry pipelines is regarded by some as the next step in coal transport evolution. The idea, however, is not new; the basic patents were issued in 1891. The earliest recorded use of a solids pipeline was a part of a placer mining operation

---

[53] Complete water recycling within process plants is becoming a standard engineering design practice. This is caused in large part by environmental protection regulations requiring treatment of plant water discharges to about the same quality level as the raw water supply. Therefore, one caveat needs to be mentioned at this point; that is, because of continuing technological changes in the coal development processes, the above analysis of water withdrawal and depletion rates would need to be updated as new information becomes available.

in California in the late 1850s. In the past twenty years, companies built only a few slurry lines for carrying such diverse materials as copper and iron ore concentrates, coal, limestone, kaolin, and asphalt. The first long coal slurry pipeline (108 miles) operated in Ohio between 1957 and 1963 but low rail freight rates owing to introduction of the unit train concept led to its retirement after six years operation. The second coal slurry pipeline, and the only one currently operating in the nation, is the Black Mesa pipeline (273 miles) which moves coal from the Black Mesa Mine on the Navajo Indian Reservation in Arizona across the Mohave Desert to the Mohave power plant in Nevada. Both slurry pipelines operated almost continuously. A capacity factor of 98 percent was reported for the Ohio line during its period of operation and the Black Mesa line is reported to have a capacity factor of 99 percent.[54]

THE COAL SLURRY TRANSPORT PROCESS

Slurry pipelines, which appear to be suited to long distance high-volume shipments of coal from large producing mines to large consumers such as coal-fired power plants, represent an alternative to rail transport of coal. Basically, the process consists of reducing the size of the coal by crushing, adding water to the crushed coal, and then grinding it finely. The mixture is then sent to agitated storage tanks and pumped through a buried pipeline to its point of use. The economics of rail versus pipeline transport of coal is an unresolved issue because costs depend on a host of factors that vary with the circumstances in any specific case.

Proposed coal slurry pipelines in the basin include one from the coal-fields of Montana (Colstrip) and Wyoming (Gillette) to Houston, Texas, and one from Montana to Minnesota and Wisconsin. The Montana to Texas line proposed by Wytex, a joint venture between Texas Eastern Transmission Corporation and Brown and Root, Inc., is designed to be a 42-inch diameter line running 1,260 miles and to have an annual through-put of 30 to 35 million tons. The proposed Montana to Minnesota line would move 13.5 million tons per year.[55] The planned coal arteries, stretching for 1,000 miles or more, represent a quantum leap in the length

[54] T. C. Campbell and Sidney Katell, *Long Distance Coal Transport: Unit Trains or Slurry Pipelines,* U.S. Bureau of Mines, IC 8690 (1975). Once started, the slurry pipeline must continue uninterrupted or the coal will gradually settle. There is considerable technical controversy over whether the settling will clog the pipeline. To prevent settling, the Black Mesa pipeline has ponds into which the pipe discharges in the event of a break or other interruption.

[55] U.S. Congress, Office of Technology Assessment, *A Technology Assessment of Coal Slurry Pipelines* (Washington, D.C., GPO, March 1978) p. 120.

of slurry lines. Distances in excess of 1,000 miles are technically feasible, as several hundred additional miles apparently will create no special problems. Although we have not ourselves verified the economic prospects for slurry pipeline transport, markets at a distance of 1,000 to 1,500 miles are claimed to be within economic reach by the proponents of slurry pipelines.

In Montana and Wyoming, coal slurry pipeline proponents are proposing to use two sources of water—the Bighorn River and the Madison Limestone Formation, an underground aquifer. Energy Transportation Systems, Inc., has acquired a groundwater permit from the Wyoming state engineer for 15,000 acre-feet of water from the Madison Formation for their Gillette, Wyoming, to White Bluff, Arkansas, pipeline. For the Montana pipeline, the Bureau of Reclamation has suggested the use of an aqueduct to divert water from the Bighorn River. However, the use of water for coal slurry pipelines originating in Montana is improbable at this time because the 1973 Montana Water Use Act precludes the use of any water (surface or ground) for slurry to export coal. Unless the act is amended, or struck down on constitutional grounds, slurry pipelines for the out-of-state export of coal are effectively prohibited in Montana.[56] Nonetheless, for purposes of comprehensiveness in treatment and for future consideration, we discuss water withdrawal rates for coal slurry pipelines next.

We should mention that there are some technical issues related to the use of these pipelines. The fixed location of the pipeline and the need for continuous high-volume utilization in slurry systems may pose some problems in operational flexibility for the coal users. There is always the possibility of line breaks and spillage and the problem of the treatment and disposition of the wastewater when the coal is separated. Some have suggested making the coal slurry pipeline a closed loop system, which would add to operating and other costs too. That is, while one pipeline would transport coal from the mine to the power plant, another would return the water from the power plant to the mine.

WATER USE ESTIMATES

Water withdrawal requirements for a slurry pipeline range from 200 to 260 gallons per ton of coal transported. Approximately one ton of water is required to transport one ton of coal in slurry form. The high estimate

[56] Walter Kiechel, Jr., "Coal Slurry Transportation Systems and Related Water Rights and Water Quality Problems," *Natural Resources Lawyer* vol. 11, no. 3 (1979) pp. 411–417.

of water usage for coal slurry pipelines found in the literature is 260 gallons per ton of coal transported,[57] whereas operational experience of the Black Mesa line indicates the low estimate of water usage, 200 gallons per ton of coal transported, is more likely to be achieved.

The 1,036-mile coal slurry pipeline proposed by Energy Transportation Systems, Inc. (ETSI) from Wyoming to Arkansas is expected to use 15,000 acre-feet of water to move 25 million tons of coal annually, which gives us an estimate of 195 gallons of water per ton of coal moved.[58] In terms of acre-feet, one acre-foot of water will move between 1,600 and 1,700 tons of coal. It should be noted that this relationship holds true in a "steady state" sense for any distance and for any period of time because the original mix can be moved any number of miles during any period of time.[59] In this study a slurry pipeline water use rate similar to that of the ETSI and the Black Mesa pipelines of 200 gallons of water per ton of coal transported, is assumed. Therefore, a coal slurry pipeline with an annual throughput of 10 million tons of coal would have a water withdrawal rate of about 6,100 acre-feet per year, assuming no spills.

As in the case of coal gasification, water withdrawal requirements for coal slurry pipelines also depend on the moisture content in the coal as illustrated in figure 5-7. Using the average moisture content of Rosebud coal, 25 percent, then the water withdrawal rate for a coal slurry pipeline transporting the output from a mine with annual production of 10 million tons per year would be lessened by about 1,850 acre-feet per year. This is the contribution from the moisture content in the coal. Accordingly, after adjusting for the moisture content in Rosebud coal, about 4,200 acre-feet of water would be needed annually to transport the output from a 10-million-ton-per-year coal mine 1,000 miles by coal slurry pipeline

[57] U.S. Department of the Interior, Office of Coal Research, *Economic System Analysis of Coal Preconversion Technology,* R & D Report #1 (June 1974).

[58] J. V. Chambers of Energy Transportation Systems, Inc., to Constance Boris, February 12, 1976.

[59] To be precise, one would need to add the volume of a "water plug" used for normal flushing of the pipeline and for build-up and shutdown of the slurry pipeline; for example, the pipeline must be full of water to deliver the last ton of contracted-for coal. Since proposed designs of coal slurry pipelines indicate that the pipelines will run full, then a 24-inch-diameter pipeline carrying an annual coal throughput of 10 million tons over a distance of 1,000 miles would require about 380 acre-feet for the water plug. On a per-ton basis, one flushing would amount to 12 gallons per ton over 1,000 miles or 1.2 gallons per ton per 100 miles. In other words, one can consider the rate of water withdrawal for a coal slurry pipeline to have a fixed component, 200 gallons per ton, and a variable component (depending on the number of flushings), roughly 12 gallons per ton per 1,000 miles for one water plug.

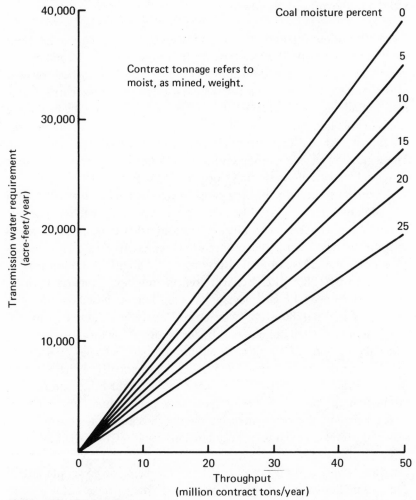

Source: Science Applications, Inc.

Figure 5-7. Transmission water requirements as a function of coal through-put and moisture content *Source:* U.S. Congress, Office of Technology Assessment, *A Technology Assessment of Coal Slurry Pipelines* (March 1978) p. 88

assuming there are no spills.[60] If the wastewater from slurry dewatering is not recycled back to the point (subbasin) of origin, the rate of water withdrawal equals the rate of water depletion.

[60] This is equivalent to 140 gallons of water per ton of Rosebud coal transported. More recent information on the proposed Montana to Minnesota/Wisconsin coal slurry pipeline indicates a water withdrawal rate of 144 gallons per ton of coal, and

Coal Development Scenarios

Since it is not our intention to predict the level and type of coal development occurring in the Yellowstone Basin during the next decade or two
but rather to play out the implications of the different options, we consider
four coal development scenarios. The first three reflect the current state
policy of mining coal for export only and represent sequentially increasing
levels of coal mining. The fourth represents a combination of mining coal
for export plus coal-fired steam electric generation and coal conversion.
These are drawn directly from Krutilla and Fisher's study of the economic
and fiscal impacts of developing Northern Great Plains coal.[61]

Scenario I represents the base case—it reflects the baseline 1975 level
of coal development of roughly 20 million tons per year with no electrical
generation or conversion facilities postulated other than those currently
operating in the Colstrip area.[62] Scenario II represents the development of
an additional increase in annual production of about 22 million tons to
be reached by 1980. This scenario "reflects the best estimates by individuals concerned with coal development in Montana based on prospects
or plans of the coal industry."[63] Scenario III considers an increase in coal
production motivated in large part by the National Energy Plan in postulating the opening of six new 10-million-ton-per-year coal mines stag-
gered over a ten-year period (1975–1985). Scenario III, which includes
the coal production postulated in scenario II, would bring annual coal
production to 102 million tons per year upon completion of the mines.

Scenario IV, the most intensive energy development strategy, consists of the level of coal mining postulated in scenario III (102 million tons
of coal) plus coal-fired steam electric generation and coal conversion
facilities—two 2,600-megawatt coal-fired steam electric power plants and
one 250-million-standard-cubic-foot-per-day coal gasification plant. Recall that in chapter 1 it was stated that RFF scenario IV, which encom-

---

the proposed Wyoming to Texas coal slurry pipeline is estimated to have a rate of
121 gallons per ton of coal transported. See U.S. Congress, Office of Technology
Assessment, *A Technology Assessment,* p. 121.

[61] The interested reader is referred to John Krutilla and Anthony Fisher, with
Richard E. Rice, *Economic and Fiscal Impacts of Coal Development: Northern
Great Plains* (Baltimore, Johns Hopkins University Press for Resources for the
Future, 1978).

[62] Two 330-Mw units, Colstrip I and II, went into operation in 1975 and 1976,
respectively, drawing water directly from the mainstem in the Mid-Yellowstone
subbasin.

[63] Ibid., p. 33.

Table 5-7. Coal development scenarios and associated water withdrawal rates, 1975–85

	For 1975			For 1985		
	Annual coal production rate (tons)	Water withdrawal rate		Annual coal production and coal conversion	Water withdrawal rate[a]	
Scenarios		(af/yr)	(af/mo)		(af/yr)	(af/mo)
RFF Scenario I	20,000,000	1,000	83			
RFF Scenario II				42,000,000 tons	2,100	175
RFF Scenario III				102,000,000 tons	5,100	425
RFF Scenario IV				102,000,000 tons, 2 (2,600-Mw) coal-fired power plants[b], 1 (250-MMscf/day) coal gasification plant	70,700	5,890

  [a] The water withdrawal rate assumes rail transport of the coal that is not converted.
  [b] The two new 330-Mw coal-fired power plants, Colstrip units I and II, are included in scenarios I–IV in the Mid-Yellowstone subbasin only, since they are currently withdrawing water from the Yellowstone mainstem.

passes the coal development activities of extraction, transport, coal-fired electrical generation, and coal gasification, is referred to as simply the "conversion" scenario. A summary of these coal development scenarios is provided in table 5-7.

Earlier, we illustrated how we estimated the water withdrawal and depletion rates for a standard-size Lurgi (with methanation) coal gasification plant adjusted for the use of Rosebud coal (8,500 Btu per lb of coal and a 25 percent moisture content by weight) and adjusted for the approximate water evaporation rate in Rosebud County, given assumptions on overall plant thermal efficiency and capacity factor. Similarly, estimates for withdrawal and depletion for a 10-million-ton-per-day coal mine and a 1,000-megawatt coal-fired power plant operating continuously (which is equivalent to a 1,300-megawatt power plant operating at a 75 percent to 80 percent capacity factor) were also discussed earlier in this chapter. Table 5-7 gives the corresponding water withdrawal rates associated with each RFF-postulated coal development scenario based on the depletion rates derived in the previous sections.

In addition to the RFF coal development levels, we include for comparative purposes, the two jointly projected coal development levels of the Department of Interior (DOI) and the Department of Energy (DOE) used in the recently issued *Draft Environmental Statement Federal Coal Management Program* and the coal development levels anticipated by

Table 5-8. Projected levels of Montana coal production from the Yellowstone River Basin

(million tons)

Year	RFF Low	RFF High	Dept. of Commerce	Depts. of Interior and Energy Low	Medium	High
1985	42.5	102.5	40.8	52.1	86.6	114.4
1990				68.6	206.8	338.7
2000			85.3			

the U.S. Department of Commerce in their report, *Preliminary Forecast of Likely U.S. Energy Consumption/Production Balances for 1985 and 2000 by States.*[64] All start at the same base level of 20 million tons of coal production in Montana. These projected coal development levels are presented in table 5-8.

As is apparent from this table, the 40.8-million-ton-1985 coal production level in the Commerce Department report is close to the low RFF level, while the year 2000 estimate is close to the DOI-DOE 1985 medium coal production level. The Department of Commerce report also includes one slurry pipeline for exporting mined coal from Montana to Texas (which is estimated to use 11,550 acre-feet of water annually).

For coal conversion, the Commerce Department report assumes two 164-million-standard-cubic-foot-per day coal gasification plants by the year 2000 in comparison to RFF's one 250-million-standard-cubic-foot-per day plant by 1985. Finally, with respect to coal-fired power generation, we have the following comparison:

Coal-Fired Steam Electric Generation
(megawatts)

	RFF	*Commerce*
1985	5,200	1,834
2000		3,271

We consider these various coal development levels for the analysis of the availability of water for energy development in chapter 9 given legal claims on water and simultaneously competing water uses.

[64] See U.S. Department of Interior, Bureau of Land Management, *Draft Environmental Statement, Federal Coal Management Program* (Washington, D.C., GPO, December 1978); and U.S. Department of Commerce, Office of Ocean, Resource and Scientific Policy Coordination, *Preliminary Forecast of Likely U.S. Energy Consumption/Production Balances for 1985 and 2000 by States* (November 1978).

Table 5-9. Comparative coal and water use requirements for coal development alternatives

Coal development alternative[a]	Capacity factor (percentage)	Coal use rate (million tons/yr)	Water withdrawal rate (acre-feet/yr)[b]	Approximate water use intensity (gallons/ton of coal input)
10-million-ton/year coal mine	—	10	500[e]	16.3
10-million-ton/year coal slurry pipeline of 1,000 mile length	100	10	4,200	136.9
250-MMscf/day coal gasification plant	100	10	8,000[d]	260.7
2,600-Mw coal-fired power plant[e]	80	10	28,800	938.6

Note: Dashes = not applicable.

[a] The quality characteristics of Rosebud coal are assumed for each alternative.

[b] Rounded estimate.

[e] It should be noted that the source of water for this alternative may be exclusively shallow groundwater rather than surface water.

[d] Recall that the water depletion rate is higher than the water withdrawal rate because additional water is supplied through the coal moisture content and the methanation process. Also, note that the coal gasification plant designs that were publicly available incorporated many water conservation and reuse features. For example, if water-cooled rather than air-cooled condensers were used, the evaporative water loss was estimated to increase by 6,400 af/yr. In that case, the total water depletion would be 14,400 af/yr, still considerably less than if the output of a 10-million-ton-per-year coal mine were used for a 2,600-megawatt coal-fired power plant.

[e] It is assumed that the plant has wet evaporative cooling towers and wet SO_2 scrubbing equipment.

Summary and Conclusions

Our analysis of the water withdrawal and depletion estimates for various coal development activities suggests a minimum usage associated with coal extraction of 500 acre-feet per year. This estimate appears to be ample for a coal mine with an annual production of 10 million tons. Exporting this annual production by rail, which is feasible in the east–west direction, is the least water-consumptive activity. Exporting the annual production from this "standard" size coal mine by slurry pipeline has the second lowest water depletion rate. Assuming that neither rights of way nor water are constraining factors (physically or legally), slurry pipeline transport could be an economical way to transport Montana coal to the Southwest where markets for this coal are in evidence. Approximately 4,200 acre-feet per year would be required to transport the output of a 10-million-ton-per-year mining operation in the basin by a slurry pipeline of 1,000 mile length.

Relaxation of the policy of "coal for export only" is represented by the conversion of coal to either electricity or synthetic gas. Using the model of a 250-million-cubic-foot-per-day coal gasification plant, an operation that would require approximately the feedstock produced by a 10-million-ton-per-year coal mining operation, we estimate that an annual withdrawal of roughly 8,000 acre-feet per year would be required. Of all of the coal-related activities with which we have been concerned, the generation of electricity is the most water-consumptive activity. Here we find that for a power generating capacity utilizing the output of a 10-million-ton-per-year mine (2,600 megawatts of installed capacity to approximate 2,000 megawatts of continuous generation), we would expect something like 28,800 acre-feet of water to be depleted annually. Table 5-9 illustrates water depletion requirements on a per-ton-of-coal-input basis.

6 Water Diversion and Depletion Estimates for Nonenergy Uses

As we learned from the review of the institutional and legal milieu governing the allocation of water rights, the amount of physically available water that will be allocated to support energy development in the Tongue, Powder, Bighorn, and Mid-Yellowstone subbasins will depend greatly on the strength of local (Montana) sentiment and the precedence of rights attaching to prior claims and future reservations to the use of water. One of the ways to understand the context in which energy-related uses will be competing for future flows, and perhaps for increased future yields from storage releases at critical periods, is to appreciate the nonenergy-related claims to the use of water in this area.

To that end, we review in this chapter the status of present uses and the reservations for future uses with which energy-related activities will have to compete. We first consider withdrawal uses such as irrigation agriculture, industrial, and municipal use. We then separate Indian reserved water right claims (estimated by both the restrictive and the expansive criteria) according to economic function. We reserve discussion of the nonwithdrawal or instream uses to chapter 7.

Irrigation Use

Irrigation has been the predominant use of water in the basin, and its dominance over other uses is assured given the approval of water reservations for the conservation and irrigation districts by the Board of Natural Resources and Conservation (BNRC). However, the use of the water reservation process (discussed in chapter 2) suggests that within the time frame of our analysis, public policy perhaps more than market forces will determine the priority of water use in the basin. Nevertheless, the question of placing additional acres under irrigation is affected by economic considerations as well.

Presently, about 650,000 acres (1976 level of irrigation) are either fully or partially irrigated in the basin, depleting approximately 1.9 million acre-feet (MMaf) of water annually.[1] Irrigable pasture (19 percent) and hay (44 percent) are the major crops in the Yellowstone Basin. Irrigated hay production accounts for 53 percent of the hay produced in the basin.[2] The importance of irrigation to produce hay for livestock was readily apparent by the late 1880s, when because of a lack of winter feed and protection from cold, 60 percent of the range cattle were estimated to have perished. A few high-cash crops such as sugar beets and dry beans are also grown on irrigated land.

It is difficult to project future irrigated acreage because the amount of acreage under irrigation in any given year, and therefore the total water depletion, are dependent on a host of factors such as the demand for crops grown under irrigation, relative price changes between various crops and livestock, governmental agricultural policies, amount of rainfall, price and type of irrigation system, and so forth. Since it is beyond the scope of this study to make independent estimates in this area, we relied on data obtained from an economic and soil reconnaissance survey recently performed by the Department of Natural Resources and Conservation (DNRC) to determine the amount of land that is economic to irrigate. Water delivery costs limit the feasibility of irrigation to areas up to 3 miles from the river and a pumping lift of 450 feet. These constraints were determined by the DNRC based on a comparison of the annualized sum of initial equipment cost (pipe, pump, and center pivot irrigation sprinklers) and operating cost using a farm budget specific to each subbasin. The results of the DNRC study indicated that the maximum additional area economically feasible to irrigate is 237,480 acres, compared with the 1976 level of 650,000 acres.

Assuming that the economic limit on delivered water will remain unchanged over the computer simulation period, we estimate water diversion and depletion for the following projected levels of expanding irrigated acreage:

1. total acreage determined by the DNRC to be economically feasible to irrigate (237,480 acres)
2. acreage projected to be irrigated in the water reservation requests

[1] Montana Department of Natural Resources and Conservation, Water Resources Division, *The Future of the Yellowstone River . . . ?* (Helena, Mont., DNRC, January 1977) p. 33.

[2] U.S. Department of Agriculture, Soil Conservation Service, *Water Conservation and Salvage Report for Montana* (Bozeman, Mont., 1976) p. 24.

Table 6-1. Projected increase in irrigated acreage in the Yellowstone River Basin (acres)

Subbasin	Economically feasible increase in irrigated acreage[a]	Increase specified in water reservation requests[b]	Increase recommended by the DNRC	Increase specified in BNRC-granted water reservations
Upper Yellowstone	38,080	65,620	24,779	46,960
Clarks Fork	2,160	21,282	5,666	10,301
Billings Area	19,410	32,186	21,647	28,186
Bighorn	13,040	52,975	8,900	10,025
Mid-Yellowstone	25,230	48,234	44,781	47,035
Tongue	21,950	8,805	0[c]	8,805
Kinsey Area	4,740	11,492	11,575	11,252
Powder	75,200	72,696	9,120	18,643
Lower Yellowstone	37,670	129,924	58,614	84,674
Total	237,480	443,214	185,082	265,881

[a] Alternatively, for the simulation analysis in chapter 9, one could assume other levels of increased acreage, for example, one-half of the projected level of economically feasible irrigable acreage.

[b] Acreage estimates by subbasin were derived by summing the acreages for which water reservations were requested in the original and amended applications submitted by the state and federal agencies.

[c] The DNRC proposed irrigating 13,000 acres in the Tongue subbasin if the DNRC's own request for multipurpose storage was granted.

      submitted to the BNRC by the irrigation and conservation districts and the state and federal agencies (443,214 acres)

3. acreage recommended by the DNRC for irrigation (185,082 acres)
4. acreage for which water has been legally reserved by the board in its December 1978 order (265,881 acres).

What is readily apparent from table 6-1 is that the increase in the irrigated acreage projected in the water *reservation applications* of conservation and irrigation districts is much higher than (nearly double) the high level of *economically feasible* irrigable acreage projected by the DNRC. Neither projection, however, represents a firm commitment to irrigate that amount of land; rather it represents a general identification of the location, extent, and quality of the irrigable areas in order to keep open the option for expanding irrigated acreage. The acreage that may eventually be practical to irrigate for one reason or another may only be half of the DNRC's projection of economically feasible irrigable land. On the other hand, the favored position of irrigation relative to energy development could continue through the water reservation process and the action by the BNRC; that is, the reservation process has the effect of granting water reservations priority over pending energy water right applications.[3] Our irrigable acre-

  [3] This was discussed in chapter 2.

age projections accordingly are useful for estimating the range of water use for irrigation purposes, thus providing some insight regarding water potentially available for other purposes.

In attempting to estimate water diversion for the projected levels of irrigable acreage, average diversion rates in the literature ranged from 3 acre-feet per acre (af/acre) by the DNRC to more than 6 af/acre by the U.S. Soil Conservation Service (SCS).[4] The DNRC assumed a diversion rate of 3 af/year based on the assumption that all new irrigation equipment would be the highly efficient variety (for example, sprinklers). This is somewhat unrealistic since it is unlikely that all new irrigators, or irrigators planning to expand, would be able to afford the capital expense of the more efficient irrigation systems.

The U.S. Soil Conservation Service, on the other hand, used a diversion rate based on the 1972 composite cropping pattern by county and the composite efficiency of conveyance and application of the diverted water. For example, the Soil Conservation Service's data for Big Horn County indicated a conveyance efficiency of 50 percent and an application efficiency of 42 percent, for a composite efficiency of 21 percent. Dividing the crop consumptive use requirements by the composite efficiency, yields an estimate of the diversion rate, which in the case of Big Horn County was 6.69 af/acre. Under the very best of conditions, a maximum conveyance efficiency of 96 percent accomplished through use of pipes rather than irrigation canals to reduce evaporation and other losses, and a sprinkler system efficiency of 70 percent would yield a composite efficiency of 67 percent. Using this "maximum composite efficiency," the diversion rate could be reduced from 6.69 af/acre to roughly 3 af/acre, but very few irrigators in the basin have such water-efficient irrigation systems.[5] On a countywide basis with the installation of more efficient water systems, the Soil Conservation Service estimated the water diversion rate to be 3.95 af/acre in the year 2000 for Big Horn County.[6]

It should be noted that the water reservation applications of the conservation districts indicated a diversion rate similar to that of the DNRC,

[4] Montana Department of Natural Resources and Conservation, Water Resources Division, *Draft Addendum Environmental Impact Statement for Water Reservation Applications in the Yellowstone River Basin, Volume II* (Helena, Mont., DNRC, 1976) p. 232; U.S. Department of Agriculture, *Water Conservation,* pp. 34–35, 62–63.

[5] Allan Dawson, Soil Conservation Service, Bozeman, Mont., to Constance Boris, December 2, 1977; John Dooley, U.S. Bureau of Reclamation, to Constance Boris, December 6, 1977.

[6] U.S. Department of Agriculture, *Water Conservation,* p. 66.

roughly 3 af/acre. Since the diversion rate is a function of the efficiency of the irrigation system, among other factors, the use of the lower diversion rate (3 af/acre) by both the DNRC and the conservation districts implies that new irrigators will install the most efficient irrigation system available. As mentioned before, this may be somewhat unrealistic because not all new irrigators will be able to afford the investment in an efficient irrigation system nor does current water law encourage efficiency in irrigation water use.[7]

Nonetheless, the choice of the irrigation diversion rate is crucial in estimating water available for other uses. Accordingly, we chose to analyze the availability of water using both the 3 af/acre diversion rate and the higher Soil Conservation Service diversion rates developed on a county basis, in order to test sensitivity of the results to the working assumptions. The use of the 3 af/acre diversion rate represents a lower bound and the Soil Conservation Service's rate provides an upper bound estimate for future irrigation diversions.

The DNRC and the Soil Conservation Service depletion rates, which consist primarily of crop consumptive and other losses, are roughly comparable, approximately 2 af/acre.

Four variants of irrigation development over the current level are presented below. Irrigation variants Ia and Ib are based on the DNRC-estimated levels of economically feasible irrigable acreage using the Soil Conservation Service's estimates of current (low) and improved (high) farm irrigation system efficiency respectively.

A brief explanation of the development of variant I using SCS data is needed. Two irrigation system efficiencies are used:

base a   present level of development (excluding water spreading) using *current* irrigation system efficiencies and crop consumptive use rates as estimated by the SCS[8]

base b   present level of development using efficiencies[9] and crop consumptive use rates as *projected* (improved efficiency) by the SCS for the year 2000.

[7] In fact, Bureau of Reclamation personnel have estimated a 50–50 split between irrigation by gravity and irrigation by the more efficient sprinkler system for new irrigation. Sprinkler irrigation systems are attractive because they are less labor intensive, but energy costs to operate the sprinkler system are increasing.

[8] All assumptions about system efficiencies, base acreages, crop consumptive depletion rates, and so forth, are based on data taken from U.S. Department of Agriculture, *Water Conservation*. Differences result from the fact that data are presented by county in the report while for our use they were worked into subbasin form.

[9] Note that conveyance and on-farm efficiencies vary by subbasin.

Specifically, the irrigation development variant I used for analysis in chapter 9 is delineated below:

variant Ia   an increase over the present level of irrigation development equivalent to all of the economically feasible acreage as determined by the DNRC using SCS-estimated current (low) irrigation system efficiencies and crop consumptive use rates

variant Ib   same acreage as variant Ia but using improved irrigation system efficiencies and crop consumptive use rates projected by the SCS for the year 2000.

Assuming typical cropping patterns for a selected subbasin, the exact method by which our irrigation diversion and depletion projections are calculated for variant I is as follows:

$$GD' = C_D A / F_E C_E$$

$$T'_L = GD' - (C_D A)$$

$$Ot'_D = (Ot_D / T_L) T'_L$$

$$T'_D = (C_D A) + Ot_D$$

$$R' = T'_L - Ot'_D$$

where

GD' = calculated gross diversion
C_D = given crop consumptive use per acre (depletion)[10]
A = projected irrigated acres
F_E = given on-farm efficiency[11]
C_E = given conveyance system efficiency[12]

[10] *Crop Consumptive Use:* the evapotranspiration of an individual crop, less the effective precipitation, over a particular period of time (usually monthly or annually). It does not include water requirements for leaching, germination, frost protection, wind erosion protection, or plant cooling. (Such requirements are accounted for in the on-farm efficiency values.)

[11] *On-Farm Efficiency:* a combined efficiency that reflects the efficiency of the on-farm distribution system and the on-farm application system. An on-farm distribution system may consist of a series of ditches or pipes, and related appurtenances, which convey the water delivered to the farm to the appropriate field. The application efficiency is the ratio of the volume of water added to the root zone of a soil during irrigation to the total volume of water applied to that soil.

[12] *Conveyance Efficiency:* the efficiency of the system that conveys the irrigation water from the diversion point to the boundary of the using farm. The loss of water from such a system includes operational losses and losses due to seepage, evaporation,

T_L = given total water losses that eventually return to the mainstem

T'_L = calculated total water losses that eventually return to the mainstem

Ot_D = given other water depletions, for example, water use by phreatophytes

Ot'_D = calculated other water depletions

T'_D = calculated total water depletion

R' = calculated return flow

This method follows, to the greatest extent possible, the method employed by the Soil Conservation Service in establishing the original data. The SCS procedure was not, however, a "synthetic" one whereby overall averages of different parameters were estimated and then cranked out mechanically for each county. Rather, the SCS study was highly disaggregated and sensitive to variations within relatively small land areas. We felt that these characteristics were desirable for our purposes. It was necessary, however, to aggregate their county data into subbasin data by estimating the proportion of each county lying within a given subbasin and weighting the SCS data accordingly as shown in the accompanying table.

Subbasin	*Estimated county composition*
Upper Yellowstone	Park, Sweetgrass, Stillwater
Clarks Fork	Carbon
Billings Area	Yellowstone
Bighorn	90 percent Big Horn
Mid-Yellowstone	70 percent Rosebud, 10 percent Custer, Treasure
Tongue	10 percent Big Horn, 30 percent Rosebud, 20 percent Custer
Kinsey Area	10 percent Custer, 10 percent Prairie
Powder	60 percent Custer, Powder River, 10 percent Prairie
Lower Yellowstone	Dawson, 80 percent Prairie, Richland, Wibaux, Fallon

Finally, brief mention of our calculation of "other depletions" (Ot'_D) resulting from irrigation should be made. The SCS calculation of other depletions involved a fairly complex procedure which we did not attempt to duplicate. Basically Ot'_D is a loss to phreatophytes and hydrophytes in

---

or transpiration by vegetation growing in or near the delivery channel. Each of these will reduce the effective conveyance efficiency. In cases where the water originated on the farm itself, such as from a well, the off-farm conveyance efficiency is assumed to be 100 percent and, consequently, the gross diversion requirement equals the farm delivery.

the irrigated area and as such is related to the total water losses (that is, all water not consumptively used by the crop under irrigation). We employed this relationship in our equation projecting other depletions.[13]

In lieu of using the U.S. Soil Conservation Service's rates of irrigation diversion and depletion, one could use the DNRC estimates (3 af/acre and 2 af/acre respectively). The use of the 3-af/acre diversion rate for new irrigation implies a lower bound for irrigation diversions because the best irrigation equipment (pipes and sprinkler systems) would have to be employed to achieve such a low diversion rate.

Variant II represents the levels of irrigable acreage and total diversion requested in the irrigation water reservation applications submitted by the irrigation and conservation districts. The increase in irrigated acreage and the associated annual rates of diversion, depletion, and return flow for variants I and II are summarized for each subbasin in tables 6-2 and 6-3.

The usefulness of any flow reservation, however, be it for a withdrawal use or an instream use, is clearly limited by the availability of unappropriated flow and, in the case of expanding irrigation, by economics including additional storage in otherwise fully allocated rivers such as the Tongue and Powder. In such cases, the competition for the unappropriated water supply may require a fairly clear showing of the need for the requested flow. The DNRC examined each of the reservation requests and made recommendations to the BNRC which were lower than the requested reservations. This is irrigation variant III (table 6-4). Generally speaking, irrigation districts with a high rate of increase in irrigable acreage over a given period (1965–75) and a high per-acre profit potential were recommended for a higher percentage of their request than their counterparts with a declining trend in increased irrigation and a lower per-acre profit potential.

In making its recommendations, the DNRC also attempted to consider the amount of water available. It is clear that an additional increase in irrigation in the Tongue and Powder subbasins is not possible without increasing storage since the flow in these subbasins at the time it would be needed is already fully allocated. The DNRC recommended that less than half of the acreage for which water reservations were requested be granted. Specifically, the DNRC recommended 474,389 acre-feet per year be granted from a total of 1.1 MMaf per year that were requested (see table 6-4). The DNRC proposed rejecting the irrigation reservations by

---

[13] This method was suggested by the Soil Conservation Service in Bozeman, Mont., as a proxy for their procedure.

federal agencies (Bureau of Land Management and Bureau of Reclamation) on the grounds of not showing a need for the reservation.

Variant IV is based on the water reservations actually granted by the board for irrigation. As mentioned in chapter 2, on December 15, 1978, the Board of Natural Resources and Conservation made its decision on the water reservation requests after months of hearings, and given the DNRC recommendations. The board signed the order granting priority among the water reservations in the following order:

1. municipal
2. instream flow—subbasins 1–3
   irrigation—subbasins 4–9
3. irrigation—subbasins 1–3
   instream flow—subbasins 4–9
4. multipurpose.

These reservations granted by the board are subject to any final determination of senior water rights in the water source including (but not limited to) any decreed rights of federal or Indian reserved rights "but not subject to any right to appropriate water which may arise from the permit applications suspended by the Yellowstone Moratorium."[14] Accordingly, a water reservation is a preferred use over any right to appropriate water that may arise from the suspended industrial permit applications for energy use that are to begin processing during 1979. The final water reservations granted to irrigation by the board are shown in table 6-5 by subbasin. The effect of these final reservations (which have a December 1978 priority date) on water available for competing uses, including energy development, is examined in chapter 9.

Associated with each irrigation diversion is a return flow. Monthly distributions for irrigation diversions and return flows unique to each subbasin were derived from the historical records of various irrigation projects. Generally speaking, irrigation diversions in the Yellowstone Basin begin approximately April 15th and end October 15th. Monthly distributions for irrigation diversions represented in the above variants by subbasin are given in table 6-6. These projected irrigation variants relate only to state holders of water rights and reservations. We must now consider the application of Indian reserved rights to irrigation.

[14] *Order of Board of Natural Resources Establishing Water Reservations* (Helena, Mont., March 1979) p. 3.

Table 6-2. Projected increase in water diversion and depletion for irrigated agriculture, based on irrigation efficiency estimates—variant I

Subbasin and variant	Irrigated acres (1,000 acres)	Base a			Base b		
		Gross diversion	Total depletion	Return flow	Gross diversion	Total depletion	Return flow
		(———————— 1,000 acre-feet ————————)			(———————— 1,000 acre-feet ————————)		
Upper Yellowstone							
Base irrigated acreage	140.4	1,092.1	226.8	865.3	556.4	234.2	322.2
Variant I	38.1	296.4	61.6	234.8	151.0	87.4	63.6
Clarks Fork							
Base irrigated acreage	96.4	843.5	175.4	668.2	395.0	162.0	233.0
Variant I	2.2	19.2	4.0	15.3	9.0	3.7	5.3
Billings Area							
Base irrigated acreage	98.8	661.5	190.4	471.2	406.8	182.7	224.1
Variant I	19.4	130.0	37.4	92.5	79.9	35.9	44.0
Bighorn							
Base irrigated acreage	56.7	378.0	99.4	278.6	223.9	98.7	125.3
Variant I	13.0	86.7	22.8	63.9	51.3	22.6	28.7

Mid-Yellowstone							
Base irrigated acreage	48.2	317.3	91.5	225.8	200.4	89.2	111.1
Variant I	25.2	165.9	47.9	118.0	104.3	46.7	58.1
Tongue							
Base irrigated acreage	24.2	152.4	44.9	107.5	96.2	44.5	51.7
Variant I	22.0	138.6	40.8	97.8	87.5	40.5	47.0
Kinsey Area							
Base irrigated acreage	4.7	26.6	8.7	17.9	18.5	9.0	9.5
Variant I	4.7	26.6	8.7	17.9	18.5	9.0	9.5
Powder							
Base irrigated acreage	28.1	127.7	49.0	78.7	113.1	55.0	58.0
Variant I	75.2	341.7	131.1	210.6	302.6	147.3	155.3
Lower Yellowstone							
Base irrigated acreage	71.6	474.8	114.5	360.2	292.2	118.5	173.7
Variant I	37.7	250.0	60.3	189.7	153.9	62.4	91.5

Note: "Base a" and "base b" represent, respectively, the SCS's estimates of the *current* and *projected* irrigation system efficiencies. The projected estimates represent higher system efficiencies than the current estimates.

Source: All data except acreages are based on U.S. Department of Agriculture, Soil Conservation Service, *Water Conservation and Salvage Report for Montana* (Bozeman, Mont., 1976).

Table 6-3. Water reservation requests for irrigation use—variant II

Subbasin	Acres	Increase in diversion (af/yr)	Increase in depletion (af/yr)	Return flow (af/yr)
Upper Yellowstone				
Park Conservation District	36,570	108,143	70,315	
Sweetgrass Conservation District	18,510	55,822	35,940	
Stillwater Conservation District	5,290	16,755	10,307	
Carbon Conservation District	630	1,890	1,260	
Department of State Lands	4,620	13,699	9,240	
Total	65,620	196,309	127,062	69,247
Clarks Fork Yellowstone				
Carbon Conservation District	20,385	45,667	37,062	
Department of State Lands	897	2,193	1,794	
Total	21,282	47,860	38,856	9,004
Billings Area				
Yellowstone Conservation District	24,835	57,963	49,262	
Huntley Irrigation District	4,000	27,372	8,000	
Department of State Lands	2,991	7,357	5,982	
U.S. Bureau of Land Management	360	720	640	
Total	32,186	93,412	63,884	29,528
Bighorn				
Big Horn Conservation District	9,175	20,190	17,030	
Department of State Lands	850	1,991	1,700	
U.S. Bureau of Reclamation	42,950	131,700	68,530	
Total	52,975	153,881	87,260	66,621
Mid-Yellowstone				
Treasure Conservation District	7,645	19,978	16,063	
Department of State Lands	3,994	10,323	7,988	
Rosebud Conservation District	34,525	87,747	73,088	
North Custer Conservation District	2,070	4,963	4,061	
Total	48,234	123,011	101,200	21,811
Tongue River				
Rosebud Conservation District	2,835	6,372	5,422	
Big Horn Conservation District	470	1,010	909	
North Custer Conservation District	4,605	10,897	9,093	
Department of State Lands	895	2,253[a]	1,790	
Department of Natural Resources and Conservation	b	b	b	
Total	8,805	20,532	17,214	3,318

Table 6-3. (continued)

Subbasin	Acres	Increase in diversion (af/yr)	Increase in depletion (af/yr)	Return flow (af/yr)
Kinsey Area				
North Custer Conservation District	5,370	13,348	10,266	
Prairie County Conservation District	5,162	15,783	9,520	
Department of State Lands	960	2,060	1,920	
Total	11,492	31,191	21,706	9,485
Powder River				
Prairie Conservation District	295	443	260	
Powder River Conservation District	34,365	89,240	59,658	
North Custer Conservation District	32,935	88,658	58,621ᶜ	
Department of State Lands	4,552	9,744	9,104	
U.S. Bureau of Land Management	549	1,098	933	
Total	72,696	189,183	128,576	60,607
Lower Yellowstone				
Prairie County Conservation District	17,079	52,241	31,503	
Dawson County Conservation District	18,127	45,855	35,575	
Richland County Conservation District	21,710	45,620	38,565	
Buffalo Rapids Irrigation District	41,306	124,435	82,612	
Little Beaver Conservation Districtᵈ	13,300	25,566	19,891ᶜ	
Department of State Lands	8,032	17,784	16,064	
U.S. Bureau of Land Management	10,370	19,681	17,711ᶜ	
Total	129,924	331,181	241,921	89,260
Basin total	443,214	1,186,561	827,680	358,881

Sources: Original water reservation request applications of the submitting state and federal agencies; Montana Department of Natural Resources and Conservation, Water Resources Division, *Draft Environmental Impact Statement for Water Reservation Applications Volume I* (Helena, Mont., DNRC, December 1976) pp. 131–173; *Volume II* December 1976, pp. 254–55; *Addendum,* June 1977, pp. 7–48; *Final Environmental Impact Statement,* February 1977, pp. 7–8.

a Of this amount, 1,821 af/yr could be supplied by the High Tongue multipurpose reservoir storage reservation request of 450,000 af proposed by the Department of Natural Resources and Conservation (DNRC).

b The DNRC application for water storage on the Tongue River could provide irrigation service for 13,000 acres on the Tongue River, 5,346 acres in Rosebud County, and 7,654 acres in Custer County. Therefore, the water reservation request for irrigating 8,805 acres of the previous four applicants (Department of State Lands, Rosebud, Big Horn, and North Custer conservation districts) could be met by the DNRC reservation request for the proposed High Tongue Dam.

c In those reservation requests specifying the acreage for water spreading, the depletion rate is estimated to be 60 percent of the diversion rate.

d The Little Beaver Conservation District requested 20,566 af/yr for the irrigation of 13,300 acres, 1,400 af/yr for recreation and wildlife ponds, and 3,600 af/yr for stock ponds.

Table 6-4. Water reservations for irrigation recommended by the Montana Department of Natural Resources and Conservation—variant III

Subbasin	Acres	Increase in diversion (af/yr)	Increase in depletion (af/yr)	Return flow (af/yr)
Upper Yellowstone				
Park Conservation District	9,548	28,262	18,376	
Sweetgrass Conservation District	7,313	22,085	14,219	
Stillwater Conservation District	3,487	11,054	6,969	
Carbon Conservation District	630	1,890	1,260	
Department of State Lands	3,801	11,636	7,757	
Total	24,779	74,927	48,581	26,346
Clarks Fork Yellowstone				
Carbon Conservation District	4,769	10,312	8,573	
Department of State Lands	897	2,193	1,462	
Total	5,666	12,505	10,035	2,470
Billings Area				
Yellowstone Conservation District	15,462	36,026	30,336	
Huntley Irrigation District	4,000	12,000	8,000	
Department of State Lands	2,185	6,147	4,098	
U.S. Bureau of Land Management	0	0	0	
Total	21,647	54,173	42,434	11,739
Bighorn				
Big Horn Conservation District	8,400	18,480	15,637	
Department of State Lands	500	1,466	977	
U.S. Bureau of Reclamation	0	0	0	
Total	8,900	19,946	16,614	3,332
Mid-Yellowstone				
Treasure Conservation District	4,122	10,758	9,134	
Department of State Lands	2,200	6,745	4,497	
Rosebud Conservation District	32,208	81,164	67,696	
North Custer Conservation District[a]	6,251	16,379	11,412	
Total	44,781	115,046	92,739	22,307
Tongue River				
Rosebud Conservation District	0	0	0	
Big Horn Conservation District	0	0	0	
North Custer Conservation District	0	0	0	
Department of State Lands	0	0	0	
Department of Natural Resources and Conservation	b	b	b	
Total	0	0	0	

Table 6-4. (continued)

Subbasin	Acres	Increase in diversion (af/yr)	Increase in depletion (af/yr)	Return flow (af/yr)
Kinsey Area				
North Custer Conservation District	6,252	16,379	11,413	
Prairie County Conservation District	5,150	15,656	9,425	
Department of State Lands	173	519	346	
U.S. Bureau of Land Management	0	0	0	
Total	11,575	32,554	21,183	11,371
Powder River				
Powder River Conservation District	9,120	13,680	9,120	
North Custer Conservation District	0	0	0	
Department of State Lands	0	0	0	
U.S. Bureau of Land Management	0	0	0	
Total	9,120	13,680	9,120	4,560
Lower Yellowstone				
Prairie County Conservation District	15,484	47,073	28,433	
Dawson County Conservation District	16,597	41,990	32,577	
Richland County Conservation District	13,517	28,386	23,996	
Buffalo Rapids Irrigation District	3,100	11,997	7,998	
Little Beaver Conservation District	6,650	12,073	8,649	
Department of State Lands	3,266	10,039	6,693	
U.S. Bureau of Land Management	0	0	0	
Total	58,614	151,556	108,346	43,210
Basin total	185,082ᶜ	474,389	349,052	125,337

Source: Montana Department of Natural Resources and Conservation, *Proposed Opinion, Findings of Fact, Conclusions of Law, and Order Submitted by the Montana Department of Natural Resources and Conservation* before the Board of Natural Resources and Conservation (1978).

ᵃ The DNRC recommended that a water diversion for 12,500 acres be reserved for the North Custer Conservation District from the mainstem. Since the diversion from the mainstem was not specified by reach, we arbitrarily assumed the diversion would be split between the Mid-Yellowstone and Kinsey Area subbasins.

ᵇ The DNRC proposed the irrigation of 13,000 acres in the Tongue subbasin if its reservation application for multipurpose storage was granted. Unless the reservoir is built, additional irrigation is not possible.

ᶜ In examining the three original Department of State Lands (DSL) applications (#9933-r) for a water reservation for irrigation, the acreage in the application totals 10,375 acres. The DNRC, in making its recommendation, used 10,875 as the total acreage. We can find no apparent reason for the use of the 10,875 acreage estimate, though the error is relatively small, only 500 acres.

Table 6-5. Water reservations for irrigation granted by the Montana Board of Natural Resources and Conservation—variant IV

Subbasin	Acres	Increase in diversion (af/yr)	Increase in depletion (af/yr)	Return flow (af/yr)
Upper Yellowstone				
Park Conservation District	21,664	64,125	41,534	
Sweetgrass Conservation District	15,313	46,245	29,890	
Stillwater Conservation District	5,290	16,755	10,307	
Carbon Conservation District	630	1,890	1,260	
Department of State Lands	4,063	12,031	8,126	
Total	46,960	141,046	91,117	49,929
Clarks Fork Yellowstone				
Carbon Conservation District	9,404	20,786	16,869	
Department of State Lands	897	2,193	1,794	
Total	10,301	22,979	18,663	4,316
Billings Area				
Yellowstone Conservation District	24,835	57,963	49,262	
Huntley Irrigation District	denied	denied	denied	
Department of State Lands	2,991	7,357	5,982	
U.S. Bureau of Land Management	360	720	640	
Total	28,186	66,040	55,884	10,156
Bighorn				
Big Horn Conservation District	9,175	20,185	17,939	
Department of State Lands	850	1,991	1,700	
U.S. Bureau of Reclamation	denied	denied	denied	
Total	10,025	22,176	19,639	2,537
Mid-Yellowstone				
Treasure Conservation District	7,035	18,361	14,870	
Department of State Lands	3,405	8,553	6,810	
Rosebud Conservation District	34,525	87,003	73,088	
North Custer Conservation District	2,070	4,953	4,061	
Total	47,035	118,870	98,829	20,041
Tongue River				
Rosebud Conservation District	2,835	7,144	5,422	
Big Horn Conservation District	470	1,034	909	
North Custer Conservation District	4,605	10,897	9,093	
Department of State Lands	895	2,253[a]	1,790	
Department of Natural Resources and Conservation[b]	[b]	[b]	[b]	
Total	8,805	21,328	17,214	4,114

Table 6-5. (continued)

Subbasin	Acres	Increase in diversion (af/yr)	Increase in depletion (af/yr)	Return flow (af/yr)
Kinsey Area				
North Custer Conservation District	5,370	13,348	10,266	
Prairie County Conservation District	5,162	15,783	9,520	
Department of State Lands	720	1,340	1,440	
Total	11,252	30,471	21,226	9,245
Powder River				
Prairie Conservation District	295	443	260	
Powder River Conservation District	9,120	13,680	8,208	
North Custer Conservation District	6,785	10,177	6,106[c]	
Department of State Lands	2,443	3,326	4,886	
U.S. Bureau of Land Management	denied	denied	denied	
Total	18,643	27,626	19,460	8,166
Lower Yellowstone				
Prairie County Conservation District	17,079	52,241	31,503	
Dawson County Conservation District	18,127	45,855	35,575	
Richland County Conservation District	21,710	45,620	38,565	
Buffalo Rapids Irrigation District	3,100	11,997	6,200	
Little Beaver Conservation District[d]	6,650	12,773	9,946[c]	
Department of State Lands	7,638	16,602	15,276	
U.S. Bureau of Land Management	10,370	19,680	17,712[c]	
Total	84,674	204,768	154,777	49,991
Basin total	265,881	655,304	496,809	158,495

Source: Order of Board of Natural Resources Establishing Water Reservations (Helena, Mont., March 1979).

a Of this amount 1,821 af/yr can be supplied from the proposed High Tongue Reservoir.

b The BNRC granted the Department of Natural Resources and Conservation a 383,000-af/yr-water reservation for the proposed High Tongue Reservoir under the conditions that the DNRC provide 7,144 af/yr to the Rosebud Conservation District, 1,034 af/yr to the Big Horn Conservation District, 10,897 af/yr to the North Custer Conservation District, and 1,821 af/yr to the Department of State Lands, for a total of 20,896 af/yr (of the requested 21,328 af/yr) to be supplied for irrigation from the proposed reservoir.

c It was assumed that the depletion rate for water spreading a given amount of acreage was 60 percent of the diversion rate.

d The BNRC granted the Little Beaver Conservation District 4,273 af/yr for irrigation, 6,000 af/yr for water spreading, 1,800 af/yr for stock watering ponds, and 700 af/yr for recreational ponds, for a total water reservation of 12,773 af/yr.

Table 6-6. Monthly distribution for irrigation diversion applications (percentage)

Subbasin	Feb.	March	April	May	June	July	Aug.	Sept.	Oct.
Upper Yellowstone	—	—	—	.03	.19	.40	.28	.09	.01
Clarks Fork	—	—	—	.03	.19	.40	.28	.09	.01
Billings Area	—	—	.02	.14	.18	.24	.22	.17	.03
Bighorn	—	—	.01	.12	.21	.32	.24	.08	.02
Mid-Yellowstone	—	—	.02	.14	.18	.24	.22	.17	.03
Tongue	—	—	.01	.10	.20	.33	.25	.10	.01
Kinsey Area	—	—	.01	.13	.17	.22	.22	.18	.03
Powder (without reservoir)	.05	.19	.62	.08	.05	.01	—	—	—
(with reservoir)	—	—	—	.13	.22	.29	.23	.13	—
Lower Yellowstone	—	—	.01	.13	.17	.22	.22	.18	.03

Note: Dashes = not applicable.

Sources: John Dooley, U.S. Bureau of Reclamation, Billings, Mont., to Constance Boris, December 9, 1977. Also see U.S. Bureau of Reclamation, Upper Missouri Regional Office, *Powder River Division Report* (Billings, Mont., December 1956) for the monthly irrigation diversion distribution for the Powder River subbasin with the proposed Moorhead storage.

Agricultural Application of Indian Reserved Water Rights

THE NORTHERN CHEYENNE TRIBE

Because Indian reserved water rights have not been quantified or adjudicated and because of the early date of their establishment, such rights inject an added layer of uncertainty in the definition of water rights and future reservations in the basin. As discussed in chapter 3, since Indian reserved water rights stem from federal law, state regulations on purpose, place, manner of use, and forfeiture of the right are not applicable to such rights. The future utilization of Indian reserved rights on the fully appropriated tributaries of the basin will divest prior users with rights established under state law subsequent to the date establishing Indian water rights. It is unclear at this time if Indian reserved water rights will be judicially determined according to a restrictive criterion (irrigable acreage) or an expansive criterion (all beneficial uses including coal development).[15] Accordingly, we will use both criteria to establish a range of the

[15] Since litigation on the reserved water rights of the Crow and Northern Cheyenne is pending, little information on these reserved rights is available. Therefore, in estimating the range of the Indian reserved water right claims, we relied on past cases dealing with reserved rights, tribal annual reports, reports by the Northern Cheyenne Research Project, and the social, economic, and cultural studies of the Crow and Northern Cheyenne funded by the Old West Regional Commission, as well as personal communication with members of the tribal staff.

Indian reserved water right claims and to estimate the effects of the application of such rights on the water available for energy development.

If Indian reserved water rights are judicially interpreted according to the restrictive criterion, then the amount of irrigable acreage on the reservation becomes the standard for estimating reserved rights. For the Northern Cheyenne Reservation, irrigation expansion is limited to the 433,434 acres within its boundaries. Presently, approximately 1,000 acres are being irrigated on the reservation using Tongue River water. Reportedly, there is a potential for expanding irrigation on the reservation to 50,000 acres.[16]

Once the potential irrigable acreage is estimated, the appropriate irrigation diversion rate must be considered. If new irrigation technology, such as irrigation sprinklers, were to be used on the reservation, the diversion rate would be roughly 3 af/acre. With present irrigation systems, the diversion rate in the Tongue subbasin is about 6 af/acre.[17] Since judicial determination will ultimately decide the appropriate diversion rate, we can only use what might be considered a plausible rate.

Some tribes have expressed a willingness to quantify their reserved water rights if the federal government would agree to help them develop their water resources in order to utilize their reserved water rights. Since the Leavitt Act[18] permits the secretary of the interior to postpone repayment of the construction costs for irrigation facilities on Indian reservations as long as the land remains in Indian possession, it is possible that the tribes together with the federal government would opt for an efficient irrigation system and, therefore, the irrigation diversion rate would be roughly 3 af/acre. However, the tribes would be responsible for operation and maintenance costs of the system. Since the more efficient sprinkler system has higher operating and maintenance costs relative to gravity systems, the tribes may opt for the gravity system and the attendant high water diversion rate of about 6 af/acre characteristic of the Tongue subbasin. Accordingly, depending on the choice of irrigation system, the reserved water rights of the Northern Cheyenne interpreted according to the restrictive criterion could range from 150,000 acre-feet (sprinkler system) assuming a diversion rate of 3 af/acre, to 300,000 acre-feet annually with the gravity system assuming a diversion rate of 6 af/acre for irrigating an additional 50,000 acres. Based on table 6-6, a diversion

[16] Eric Metcalf, Northern Cheyenne Research Project, to Constance Boris, July 1, 1977.

[17] U.S. Department of Agriculture, *Water Conservation*, p. 35.

[18] 25 U.S.C. 386a (1970).

Table 6-7. Estimates of Indian reserved water rights in Montana using the restrictive criterion

Tribe	Source of water	Increase in irrigable acreage (acres)	Month	Monthly water withdrawal rate	
				High efficiency irrigation system (af/mo)	Low efficiency irrigation system (af/mo)
Northern Cheyenne	Tongue River	50,000	January	0	0
			February	0	0
			March	0	0
			April	1,500	3,000
			May	15,000	30,000
			June	30,000	60,000
			July	49,500	99,000
			August	37,500	75,000
			September	15,000	30,000
			October	1,500	3,000
			November	0	0
			December	0	0
Crow	Bighorn River	100,000	January	0	0
			February	0	0
			March	0	0
			April	3,000	4,000
			May	36,000	48,000
			June	63,000	84,000
			July	96,000	128,000
			August	72,000	96,000
			September	24,000	32,000
			October	6,000	8,000
			November	0	0
			December	0	0

of 50,000 acre-feet in the Tongue subbasin during the irrigation season would have the monthly distribution shown in table 6-7.

The increase in agricultural development through irrigation on the Northern Cheyenne Reservation would represent a significant depletion of Tongue River water. The magnitude alone, even when interpreted according to the restrictive criterion, indicates a serious problem for downstream non-Indian appropriators with a later priority date. Assuming full utilization of the Cheyenne reserved water rights for irrigation (requiring a seasonal withdrawal of 150,000 to 300,000 acre-feet and depletion of roughly 100,000 acre-feet assuming a 2 af/acre depletion rate), the significance of Indian reserved rights for consumptive use becomes apparent when one observes that the average historical flow over the period of record on the Tongue (at Miles City) between April and October (when irrigation diversions occur) is 238,410 acre-feet.

As mentioned earlier, the Northern Cheyenne are presently irrigating about 1,000 acres on the reservation. In the entire Rosebud County area (in which the reservation is located), the Montana Department of Natural Resources and Conservation estimated that only about 1,000 additional acres could feasibly be irrigated economically using the above-stated DNRC criteria for pipe length and pump lift. However, the need for Indian tribes to utilize the limited land of their reservations may compel a less stringent standard of feasibility than is applied to non-Indian lands. It appears that an estimate of the more likely acreage to be irrigated on the Northern Cheyenne Reservation by the turn of the century may be more in the neighborhood of 10,000 acres. Accordingly, as a first approximation of the reserved right claims on the Tongue River by the Northern Cheyenne (based on the restrictive criterion), a range of 30,000 to 60,000 acre-feet during the irrigation season is used in the model simulation runs of chapter 9, depending on whether high efficiency (3 af/acre) or low efficiency (6 af/acre) irrigation practices are used.

THE CROW TRIBE

Agricultural development on the Crow Reservation can be expected to be greater than on the Northern Cheyenne Reservation because the Crow Reservation is more than three times as large and because a firm water supply is available from the Yellowtail Reservoir on the Bighorn River. The Crow are presently irrigating about 52,000 acres. Applying the restrictive criterion, roughly 400,000 acres of the 1,567,000-acre reservation are arable, but the feasibility of extending irrigation beyond 100,000 acres is reported to be in doubt.[19] As stated earlier under the provisions of the Leavitt Act, Indian tribes are not required to repay construction costs of federally built irrigation facilities. Therefore, if one assumes that the federal government will help the tribes develop and utilize their water resources by means of irrigation facilities in return for quantification of Indian reserved water rights, then more land becomes feasible for irrigation and thus more water can be requested for that use. However, the tribes must be granted the funds for irrigation facilities from Congress which in turn will be under pressure from existing state water right holders who fear a loss of water. In essence, the Indians are dependent on public funds and hence public support to exercise their reserved water rights. We

---

[19] Source confidential.

accept as a working hypothesis, then, that 100,000 acres represents the upper bound of future irrigation on the Crow Reservation.

For the purposes of this study, we assume the future expansion in irrigable acreage will occur in the Bighorn subbasin.[20] Assuming a high-efficiency irrigation system would be installed, we use a diversion rate of 3.0 af/acre planted and a depletion rate of 2.0 af/acre planted. The monthly distribution for irrigation withdrawals of 300,000 acre-feet annually from the Bighorn subbasin was shown in table 6-6.

As with the Northern Cheyenne, selecting the system for irrigating additional acreage on the Crow Reservation involves a tradeoff. The sprinkler system uses water more efficiently and more land can be irrigated, but it has higher operating costs, costs which the tribe must bear. The gravity irrigation system would mean diverting more water and constructing an adequate drainage system, but it has lower operating costs. The choice of the gravity system would mean a higher water diversion rate and therefore as a practical matter less land could be irrigated unless the volume of reserved water rights granted were also greater. If the Crow tribe are permitted the gravity irrigation system, we assume diversion of 4 af/acre, which is typical of the Bighorn subbasin under present economic conditions. In that case, irrigating an additional 100,000 acres would imply a diversion rate of 400,000 acre-feet of water annually with a return flow of 200,000 acre-feet annually. Therefore, based on the restrictive criterion, the Crow Indian reserved water rights could range from 300,000 to 400,000 acre-feet annually, assuming the irrigation of 100,000 additional acres. Table 6-7 summarizes the monthly distribution of the Crow reserved water rights based on the restrictive criterion for both the low- and high-efficiency irrigation systems. Once again, the magnitude of the Indian reserved rights indicates the seriousness of the issue of the availability of water for non-Indian uses. We defer discussion of estimating Indian reserved rights according to the expansive criterion until a later chapter.

[20] The sources of water for additional irrigation would be the Bighorn River, Little Bighorn River, and Pryor Creek. The Crows, in their petition, also claimed reserved water rights on the Tongue River and Rosebud Creek, but the Tongue abuts only a minor portion of their reservation (1,000 acres) and they would have to capture the flow and transfer it back to the reservation. We note that there is some overlapping in the projections of increased irrigation described earlier in this chapter—but it is likely to be insubstantial. For example, the DNRC projects an increase in irrigation of 1,000 acres for the entire Bighorn subbasin at a distance of 1.0 to 1.5 miles from the river. Most of the projected increase in the irrigation of 100,000 acres on the Crow Reservation will be beyond the 1.5 mile limit used by the DNRC.

We turn now to other withdrawal uses for which state water reservations have been granted by the Board of Natural Resources and Conservation—municipal use and water storage—before considering instream flow reservations in the next chapter.

Municipal Water Use

Municipal water diversions in the Montana portion of the Yellowstone Basin will be insignificant compared with the substantial water diversions for irrigated agriculture and compared with the water diversions for cooling purposes in thermal electric facilities, although it is a use that generally receives the highest priority in the water allocation schemes of many western states. It is the increase in coal development activity in the basin, and not the expansion of irrigated acreage that is responsible for increasing the municipal water diversions. As coal mining is expanded and if associated generation and conversion facilities are built, employees and families locating in the nearby communities will increase the demand for water treatment services. For example, in Rosebud County (where the coal-fired Colstrip power plant units are located), the municipal surface water diversion rose from a 1970 level of 370 af/year to 862 af/year by 1975.[21] This increase in municipal water was related to the influx of construction workers and miners into Colstrip and Forsyth. However, once construction of the power plants is completed, construction workers typically move to other areas, and municipal water demand will decrease. Eight municipalities submitted water reservation requests to the board. Seven were for reservations of water from the Yellowstone mainstem; the remaining one was for a groundwater reservation (table 6-8).

With the exception of Billings, the volume of water requested by the municipalities is quite small in comparison to the flow of the mainstem. The city of Billings submitted a water reservation request for 317,456 acre-feet per year and a peak diversion of nearly three times the requested amount. Assuming 200 gallons per capita per day (gpcd), the Billings request would serve a population of roughly twice the 1970 population of the entire state.

[21] The 1970 water withdrawal estimates are from Montana Department of Natural Resources and Conservation, *Water Use in Montana* (Helena, Mont., DNRC, 1975) p. 10 (Inventory Series Report # 13). The 1975 withdrawal figure for Rosebud County is estimated by summing the 1975 municipal water demands of Forsyth and Colstrip, which in turn were obtained from the community's water plant staff.

Table 6-8. Summary of requests and final water reservations for municipal use, by subbasin

Subbasin	Municipal use (af/yr)	Return flow[a]	
		(af/yr)	(af/mo)
Upper Yellowstone			
Request	38,978	19,489	1,624
Reservation	12,909	6,455	538
Billings Area			
Request	317,456[b]	282,536	23,545
Reservation	41,229	36,694	3,058
Mid-Yellowstone			
Request	21,720[c]	10,860	905
Reservation	2,889	1,445	120
Lower Yellowstone			
Request	12,757	6,379	531
Reservation	3,281	1,640	137
Basin Total			
Request	390,911[d]	319,264	26,605
Reservation	60,308	46,234	3,853

Note: There were no municipal requests for reserving surface water in the Clarks Fork Yellowstone, Bighorn, Tongue, Powder, and Kinsey Area subbasins.

[a] The expected rate of depletion is 50 percent of the rate of diversion.

[b] Because of Billings's new secondary treatment plant, about 89 percent of the withdrawn water is expected to be returned to the mainstem.

[c] This is the amount of water requested by Miles City, which is at the juncture of the Mid-Yellowstone and Kinsey Area subbasins.

[d] The basin total reflects surface water requests for municipal use. The town of Broadus in the Powder River subbasin requested a groundwater reservation of 605 af/yr and received a groundwater reservation of 605 af/yr.

In making its decision on the municipal water requests, the board granted only 15 percent of the total amount requested for municipal reservations in the basin, as shown in table 6-8. It should be noted that only a portion of the final water reservations will be used in the first few years. The unused portion will constitute instream flow. However, as the year 2000 is approached, most of the reservations could be utilized and little may remain as unused inchannel flow.

Water Reservations for Multiple-Use Storage

Industrial water uses are represented in the reservation application process only insofar as water is reserved for multipurpose storage. Until recently, there was only one application for industrial water use. This was the state DNRC's application for reserving the additional increment in water storage that could be obtained by raising the existing Tongue River Dam. Its application for a 450,000-acre-foot storage reservoir on the Tongue River allowed for an industrial depletion of roughly 29,000 acre-feet per year beginning with a reservoir that had first been filled. With regard to this request, the board granted a reservation of 383,000 acre-feet to protect water rights associated with the existing small Tongue River Reservoir.

Federal agencies were precluded from reserving water until state legislation was amended in mid-1977. Subsequent to the amending of state legislation allowing for the submission of reservation applications by federal agencies, the U.S. Bureau of Reclamation submitted three water reservation applications for offstream storage of mainstem water. Water would be diverted from the Yellowstone mainstem to offstream storage sites (Buffalo Creek, Cedar Ridge site on the Starved-to-Death Creek, and Sunday Creek) during periods of surplus flow for municipal, industrial, recreation, and fish and wildlife purposes. Specifically, the bureau's applications request 729,500 acre-feet per year on the Yellowstone mainstem, and the board granted these requests in full (table 6-9), but among all the water reservations granted by the board, recall that these multipurpose water reservations are last in priority.

Summary and Conclusions

It is apparent that, from an energy development standpoint, irrigation poses the most serious competition for water because of the unique opportunity for its protection afforded by state law through the water reservation process. Over a million acre-feet of water in the basin have been requested for reservation by irrigation and conservation districts. The Department of Natural Resources and Conservation recommended that less than a half million acre-feet, or 40 percent of the amount requested, be reserved for future irrigation because not all future needs of water can be fully anticipated at this time and because of equity concerns for the individual irrigators in the basin.[22] Even this lesser amount recommended for reservation for non-Indian irrigation by the DNRC would affect the

---

[22] Recall from chapter 2 that only public bodies are able to apply for water reservations; individuals are not eligible. Accordingly, an individual irrigator who undertakes to irrigate before a project using reserved water is developed would have a water right junior to the later-applied reserved water.

Table 6-9. Applications for multiple purpose storage and final reservations, by subbasin

(acre-feet/year)

Application	Amount requested	Final water reservation
Federal offstream storage[a]		
Billings Area		
U.S. Bureau of Reclamation		
(Buffalo Creek offstream storage)	68,700	68,700
Mid-Yellowstone		
U.S. Bureau of Reclamation		
(Cedar Ridge offstream storage)	121,800	121,800
Kinsey Area		
U.S. Bureau of Reclamation		
(Sunday Creek offstream storage)	539,000	539,000
Total	729,500	729,500
State onstream storage		
Tongue		
Department of Natural Resources and Conservation		
(Tongue River storage)	450,000	383,000

Sources: Montana Department of Natural Resources and Conservation, Water Resources Division, *Draft Addendum Environmental Impact Statement for Water Reservation Applications in the Yellowstone River Basin* (Helena, Mont., DNRC, June 1977); *Order of Board of Natural Resources Establishing Water Reservations* (Helena, Mont., March 1979).

[a] The purposes for water stored in offstream reservoirs as stated in the Bureau of Reclamation's applications are municipal, industrial, recreation, and fish and wildlife.

flow available for energy development in the Tongue and Powder sub-basins. The BNRC, however, granted a basin-wide reservation for irrigation equivalent to 55 percent of the amount requested.

The Crow and Northern Cheyenne reserved water right claims further complicate the issue of water potentially available for the energy development scenarios postulated in chapter 5. The increase in irrigation agriculture on the Crow and Northern Cheyenne reservations is more difficult to ascertain because of the dearth of information on irrigable acreage and also on precisely what constitutes "practicably irrigable acreage." Nonetheless, it is a most important use because of the nature of Indian reserved water rights; that is, Indian reserved rights have an early priority date and are not subject to divestiture by non-use. State holders of water rights on fully appropriated tributaries with a priority date subsequent to the treaty date establishing the reservation will be subject to a loss of a portion of their water rights upon future exercise of Indian reserved rights.

Past case law used the irrigable acreage standard for estimating Indian reserved rights. However, the quantity of water needed for irrigation is partly a function of the type of irrigation system used and its associated efficiency. As with non-Indians, the problem of choosing a representative irrigation diversion rate arises once again. The choice of the diversion rate is confounded by political considerations. Selection of an efficient irrigation system, such as the sprinkler system, would have a lower diversion rate than a gravity system, but higher operating and maintenance costs, costs the tribe would have to bear. Of course, with greater efficiency in the use of water, more land can be irrigated than is the case with the less efficient gravity irrigation systems. On the other hand, the higher the irrigation diversion rate, the greater the Indian reserved rights would be. Accordingly, depending on the irrigation system, the reserved water rights of the Northern Cheyenne could range from 30,000 to 60,000 acre-feet annually for irrigating an additional 10,000 acres, or from 150,000 to 300,000 acre-feet annually for irrigating an additional 50,000 acres. The significance of the Northern Cheyenne reserved rights, at least for the latter estimate of irrigable acreage, becomes apparent when one observes that the average historical flow over the period of record on the Tongue during the irrigation season is 238,000 acre-feet.

In a similar fashion, depending on the choice of system, irrigating an additional 100,000 acres on the Crow Reservation implies an irrigation season diversion of 300,000 to 400,000 acre-feet from the Bighorn subbasin.

Municipal and industrial uses also compete for water in the basin. However, municipal water diversions are not significant when compared with the potential diversions for irrigation agriculture and with the diversions for cooling purposes in coal conversion facilities. Although municipal water use is small, the board granted municipal use the highest priority in the basin's water allocation scheme.

Industrial water uses are represented in the water reservation application process only insofar as water is reserved for that use in multipurpose storage applications of the state DNRC and the U.S. Bureau of Reclamation, almost all of which have been granted by the board, but multipurpose reservations are last in priority.

The "water for energy" issue cannot be evaluated properly without simultaneously considering all the various uses (withdrawal and instream) with which energy must compete, taking priority and location into account. In the next chapter, instream uses are discussed and the implications of the order of priority among the reservations for nonenergy uses adopted by the board are evaluated.

7 Instream Flow Reservations

Introduction

The use of flowing water for nonconsumptive purposes has a long history involving transportation by raft and the production of power, whether mechanical or electrical. Recently, however, to these commercial services representing intermediate stages in production have been added recreational and amenity services yielding their utility in final consumption activities. The use of flowing water for instream purposes such as maintaining fisheries and water quality, and supporting other recreational activities has only recently been explicitly considered as a meaningful part of a total water management regime and as such to warrant access to water rights along with the withdrawal uses discussed in the two preceding chapters.

Historically, western state water allocation systems provided by law were concerned primarily with the use of water for extractive and consumptive purposes. In fact, development of western water law was based almost entirely on water diversions for uses such as mining and agriculture. Federal reservoirs were built for such activities as irrigation, and for vendible commercial products such as electrical power. Instream uses of water for fish and wildlife, water quality, or aesthetic purposes were not realistically valued in an era where the predominant philosophy regarding water was "use it or lose it." Consequently, most state water laws were oriented toward the regulation of rights to *private diversion* of water, which reduces inchannel flows. Recognition in state water law was not given to instream flows for fish and wildlife and aesthetic purposes until recently.

At the federal level, the first step taken to consider instream values in the use of water was the Fish and Wildlife Coordination Act of 1934, subsequently amended in 1947 and 1964. Since the 1950s, western states have shown a growing concern for the value of inchannel stream flows. The states of Montana, Oregon, Washington, and Colorado have statutes declaring that instream flows are a beneficial use.[1] Oregon and Washington, being coastal states where the economic importance of the anadromous fishery has long been recognized, were among the first to adopt policies protecting instream flows. In 1955, the Oregon State Water Resources Board adopted a policy to protect such flows. In 1971, the Washington legislature enacted the State Water Resources Act which declares that "perennial rivers and streams of the State shall be retained with base flows necessary to provide for preservation of wildlife, fish, scenic, aesthetic, and other environmental values." In other Washington state legislation (the Minimum Water Flows and Levels Act of 1969), the Department of Ecology "may establish minimum water flows or levels for streams, lakes, or other public waters for the purposes of protecting fish, game, birds, or other wildlife resources, or recreational or aesthetic values of said public waters."

By 1973, stronger legislation was passed protecting instream uses. In Montana, the 1973 Water Use Act defined fish and wildlife and recreation as beneficial uses of water and allowed for the reservation of water by state and federal agencies for such purposes. More generally, the statement of legislative policy on water needs reads:

> The legislature, noting that appropriations have been claimed, that applications have been filed for, and that there is further widespread interest in making substantial appropriations of water in the Yellowstone River Basin, finds that these appropriations threaten the depletion of Montana's water resources to the significant detriment of existing and projected agricultural, municipal, recreational and other uses, and of wildlife and aquatic habitat. The legislature further finds that these appropriations foreclose the options to the people of this state to utilize water for other future beneficial purposes, including municipal water supplies, irrigation systems, and minimum flows for the protection of existing rights and aquatic life. The legislature pursuant to its mandate and authority under Article IX of the Montana Constitution, declares that it is the policy of this state that before these proposed appropriations are acted upon existing rights to water in the Yellowstone Basin must be accurately determined for their protection, and that reservations of water within the Basin must be established as rapidly as possible for the preservation and protection of existing and future beneficial uses.[2]

[1] In some states, instream uses of water are not considered equal to a use requiring diversion.

[2] Montana Department of Natural Resources and Conservation, Water Resources Division, *Montana Water Law, Chapters 8 and 9* (Helena, Mont., July 1, 1977) section 89-8-103, p. 25.

In the same year the Colorado state legislature passed legislation declaring certain uses of water in the channel to be beneficial and allowing the state to secure water rights for such uses. The growing recognition in state laws of minimum flow as a beneficial use attests to the increasing value society is placing on *in situ* amenity services. It is difficult to provide an economic evaluation of the benefits derived from instream flow, in part because the resource services are almost invariably nonpriced. But this is no different from the valuation of navigation services or the economic services yielded from flood control systems for which the method for valuation has been developed over the past four decades. Reservoir developments, of course, have greatly reduced the length of free flowing streams and the services that they yield. As the number and length of free flowing streams diminish, the marginal value to society of remaining streams increases.

The acceptance of the concept of maintaining inchannel stream flows as a beneficial use of water and the development of institutional arrangements to protect the value of resource services provided by instream flows imply that water, at least during periods of insufficient flow, will have to be rationed between inchannel and competing uses for which water is diverted from the stream. This leads to a need for quantifying the amount of water required for instream purposes.

Initial attempts at quantifying such requirements were aimed at providing "minimum flow" releases from a dam. Typically, the minimum flow consisted of the flows required to meet downstream water rights and the flows required for maintaining aquatic habitat. The latter were usually based on the judgment of a biologist. Since then, fishery biologists have approached stream flow analysis from the viewpoint of providing habitat for fish and assuming the habitat will provide the fish.[3] Efforts have been directed toward developing analytical procedures that relate stream flow to the productivity of a fishery.[4] One such procedure is the so-called Montana Method which relates the protection of the aquatic resource to the

---

[3] An important concept in relating fish habitat to flows is that a given species of fish requires certain velocities, depth, and water temperatures depending on the state of the life cycle. Consequently, a change in water management may change the species composition by changing the competitive advantage of one species relative to another. Therefore, there is no *minimum flow* but rather a *required flow regime* for a specific productivity level of a specific mix of target fish species.

[4] For more information on this area, see U.S. Fish and Wildlife Service, Office of Biological Services, Western Water Allocation, *Methodologies for the Determination of Stream Resource Flow Requirements: An Assessment* (1976) and also publications of the Cooperative Instream Flow Service Group of the U.S. Fish and Wildlife Service.

average annual flow. For example, a minimum instantaneous flow of 10 percent of the average annual flow is said to sustain short-term survival habitat for most aquatic life forms, while 60 percent is considered to provide excellent habitat for most aquatic life forms during their primary periods of growth and for the majority of recreational uses.[5] This method provides a rule of thumb for estimating flows needed to protect the aquatic habitat. If stream flows are related directly to the fishery rather than the habitat, then the flow will be a function of the type of fishery (species composition) and the management of the fishery (put-and-take or a fishery maintained entirely by natural reproduction and growth).

Application for flow reservations for the maintenance of fish and wildlife habitat has been made for the mainstem and its tributaries in the Yellowstone Basin. In addition to fish and wildlife habitat, applications for such reservations have been made for water quality and for maintaining a water level to sustain irrigation pumping. Specifically, four instream flow reservation applications have been submitted to the Board of Natural Resources and Conservation (BNRC): (1) the Montana Fish and Game Commission for the maintenance of fish and wildlife; (2) the U.S. Bureau of Land Management for a minimum stream flow for maintenance of the riparian habitat; (3) the Montana Department of Health and Environmental Sciences (DHES) for the maintenance of water quality standards; and (4) the conservation districts to maintain the river level for existing irrigation diversions. Of these reservations, the two instream uses posing the greatest conflict with withdrawal uses are fish and wildlife habitat and water quality. We now discuss the flow regime estimated to be needed for these two instream uses.

Fish and Wildlife Resources

The Yellowstone River provides a diverse and productive natural fishery. In fact, a reach of about 100 miles on the Upper Yellowstone has been classified as a blue ribbon trout stream, having national significance in terms of productivity, degree of use, aesthetics, and availability for fishing.[6] Seventeen species of fish are found in the cold water fishery of the

[5] Donald Leroy Tennant, "Instream Flow Regimes for Fish, Wildlife, Recreation and Related Environmental Resources," *Fisheries* vol. 1, no. 4 (July–August 1976).

[6] Another reach of the Yellowstone River (from Yellowstone Lake in Yellowstone National Park to Pompey's Pillar in the Billings Area subbasin) has been proposed for inclusion in the national wild and scenic rivers system.

Upper Yellowstone. Common game fish include several species of trout and mountain whitefish. Below the mouth of the Bighorn River, the mainstem becomes a warm water fishery with about forty-five species of fish including goldeye, walleye, sauger, and northern pike.

The Montana Fish and Game Commission requested specific stream flow reservations with the following statement in their application: "The need for a reservation of water in the Yellowstone River Basin is brought about by the basic habitat requirements of all fish, wildlife and other living organisms that have through the long evolutionary process come to be totally dependent upon the natural flow of the Yellowstone River and its tributary streams."[7] Its interest is to preserve this habitat. The final requests are not, however (with the exception of the Upper Yellowstone Basin), for all of the water that has historically constituted the river habitat. Recognizing "that other uses of the water are necessary," they request only those waters which in their judgment are "absolutely necessary to sustain the organisms (dependent on the river) without significant long-term reduction in (their) quantity and quality. . ."[8] The bulk of the application details what they consider to be necessary flows, their spatial and temporal distribution, and the methods employed in their determination.

Emphasis is placed not only on the need to maintain adequate water quantity and quality but also a semblance of the seasonal variation in the flow that occurs naturally. High flows in the spring, for example, are important for the passage of some of the larger game species upriver to spawning areas.[9] High flows in the spring are also needed during the nesting period of the Canadian geese. Between May and June, the mainstem is inhabited by paddlefish on their annual spawning run from the Garrison Reservoir. Fish rearing flows, when the recently hatched fish grow to maturity, are the August through September flows. The December through February flows are generally the lowest in the mainstem. For aquatic populations, winter is the period of greatest stress and mortality. A significant depletion during this time could have severe repercussions on the fishery. In view of the importance of the natural flow regime to the continued vitality of the Yellowstone, the Fish and Game Commission's request for

[7] Montana Fish and Game Commission, *Application for Reservation of Water in the Yellowstone River Basin* (November 1, 1976) p. 4.

[8] Ibid., p. 5.

[9] All species of fish have their unique habitat requirements. Rainbow and cutthroat trout spawn in the spring while brown and brook trout and mountain whitefish spawn in the fall. Sauger spawn before the high water period in spring and the turbot spawn sometime between January and February. Therefore, analyzing the influence of flow fluctuations on the fishery in the basin is quite complex.

reservation of flows attempts to approximate the seasonal variation that occurs naturally. While such a scheme itself modifies somewhat the natural flow, it tends to preserve the seasonal variation and is thus preferable to any alternative which would fail to take into account the flow requirement for fish and wildlife.

Specifically, in the Upper Yellowstone subbasin, the commission requested the reservation of the "instantaneous streamflow subject to existing lawfully appropriated water rights in the stream reach, except during the spring high water months."[10] Justification of this request was based on the uniqueness and importance of this stretch of the river, both to Montana and the nation.[11] It was also felt that it was important to preserve the quality of the entire system. It was stated that the low flow periods between May and August were the most critical to maintain in the Upper Yellowstone and their requested flows (based on biological data and the dominant discharge concept) approached those flows that are equalled or exceeded 70 percent of the time.[12]

In cases where the flow would drop below the requested amounts, the Fish and Game Commission states:

> we fully anticipate that our requests will not be met. Under no circumstances should these figures be construed to imply that augmenting the natural flow through impoundment of flood waters for later discharge will in any way improve upon the existing natural conditions as we now find them in and along the Yellowstone River.[13]

This stance can be attributed to the fact that a reservoir would alter the natural flow and the associated fish and wildlife habitat. Therefore, even if a reservoir were constructed, the Fish and Game Commission would probably not request flow augmentation.[14]

The Fish and Game Commission's application included stream flow requests for eighty different streams and stream reaches in the basin with

[10] Montana Fish and Game Commission, *Application*, p. 161.

[11] It was classified as a blue ribbon trout stream from Gardiner to Big Timber in 1959 and again in 1965 and is the longest single reach of blue ribbon stream in Montana (452 miles).

[12] It should be noted, however, that the commission's application was not based on correlation studies between flow and biological data.

[13] Montana Fish and Game Commission, *Application for Reservation of Flows—Yellowstone River* (March 15, 1975) p. 6.

[14] This is incorporated in the operating criterion for proposed reservoirs in the hydrologic simulation model. That is, only flow surplus to that required for the irrigation and industrial use (purposes for which the reservoir would be constructed) would be passed through for fish and game. If there are no surplus flows, the commission requests that no flow augmentation be made for fish and game.

specific monthly (and many intramonthly) requests. Ideally, the streams tributary to the mainstem should not be separated from the mainstem because of inherent physical and biological relationships between the two. However, because of the spatial (subbasin) and temporal (monthly) delineation of the hydrologic simulation model, we were limited to selecting one monthly flow reservation request (twelve altogether) for each of the nine subbasins. We have attempted in our selection from among the eighty specific requests to choose those nine reaches which would most accurately represent the commission's requested flows for the nine subbasins. We chose the following stream reaches:

Subbasin	*Stream reach*
1. Upper Yellowstone	Yellowstone River from the north-south Carbon-Stillwater county lines to Clarks Fork of the Yellowstone River
2. Clarks Fork Yellowstone	Clarks Fork of the Yellowstone River from Blue Water Creek to the mouth
3. Billings Area	Yellowstone River from Clarks Fork to the Bighorn River
4. Bighorn	Bighorn River from Afterbay Dam to the mouth
5. Mid-Yellowstone	Yellowstone River from the mouth of Bighorn River to the mouth of the Powder River
6. Tongue	Tongue River from T & Y Diversion to the Yellowstone River
7. Kinsey Area	Same as Mid-Yellowstone
8. Powder	Powder River from the Little Powder River to the Yellowstone River
9. Lower Yellowstone	Yellowstone River from the mouth of the Powder River to the Montana-North Dakota state line.

The specific requests made for the above reaches by the state Fish and Game Commission are listed in table 7-1. In its application, the commission requested that when natural flows fall below these levels, diversions from future water use permits be interrupted.

Because the commission's purpose is to preserve the existing ecosystem, its reservation request represents a significant percentage of the average annual outflow from the basin. The outflow from the basin (Yellowstone River at Sidney) over the period of record averages 8.8 million acre-feet annually (unadjusted for the 1975 level of depletion) and the commission's instream flow request from the Lower Yellowstone totals 8.2 million acre-feet annually, or 93 percent of the average annual outflow from the

Table 7-1. Fish and game flow reservation requests, DNRC-recommended instream flows, and final BNRC-approved instream flow reservations, by month

	Subbasin								
	Upper Yellowstone[a]			Clarks Fork Yellowstone[b]			Billings Area[c]		
Month	Fish & game request	DNRC-recommended flow	Final BNRC flow reservation	Fish & game request	DNRC-recommended flow	Final BNRC flow reservation	Fish & game request	DNRC-recommended flow	Final BNRC flow reservation
January	98,380	58,415	81,760	15,371	15,370	278	153,719	99,770	153,058
February	88,859	52,210	73,292	13,329	13,330	287	138,843	104,400	138,186
March	110,678	61,490	82,989	14,757	14,760	298	178,314	135,500	177,648
April	136,859[d]	76,170	148,132	23,207	14,280	353	214,215	156,400	213,541
May	394,711[d]	236,115	180,454	65,792	54,110	1,000	514,710	254,040	470,664
June	896,528[d]	533,760	489,807	172,562	163,640	3,420	1,147,239	976,900	1,109,415
July	533,951[d]	257,640	232,013	86,083	35,590	1,430	577,784	358,500	529,098
August	259,834	152,490	120,220	28,899	11,680	381	295,140	163,900	251,457
September	178,512	103,550	92,508	23,802	13,090	346	220,165	138,700	203,185
October	166,016	99,695	144,463	24,595	19,370	332	221,355	166,900	220,680
November	136,859	76,770	106,488	19,636	19,640	364	208,264	163,300	207,592
December	116,826	70,715	91,596	15,987	15,990	320	172,165	121,400	171,501
Subtotal	3,118,013	1,779,020	1,843,722	504,020	392,850	8,809	4,041,913	2,994,815	3,846,025
For one 24-hr. period	58,485		36,091				68,430		68,430
Total	3,176,498		1,879,813				4,110,343		3,914,455

ᵃ See Montana Fish and Game Commission, *Application for Reservation of Flows* (March 15, 1975) p. 182. The request approximates the flow equalled or exceeded 70 percent of the time for the mainstem at Livingston. The DNRC-recommended flow is the 90th percentile monthly low flow at Livingston. The final BNRC flow reservation is approximately the 95th percentile flow at Livingston for the months of May through August and the 20th percentile flow for the remaining months.

ᵇ See *Fish and Game Application*, p. 113. Their request is 60 percent of the mean monthly discharge near Rockvale, Montana. The DNRC-recommended flow is the 95th percentile monthly low flow at Edgar. The final BNRC flow reservation is the 70th percentile flow for the months June–September and the 90th percentile for all other months.

ᶜ See *Fish and Game Application*, p. 183. The requested flows are equalled or exceeded 50 to 70 percent of the time (depending on the month) for the mainstem at Billings. The DNRC-recommended flow is the 95th percentile monthly low flow at Billings. The final BNRC flow reservation is the 50th percentile flow for January, March, and October–December. The 55th percentile flows for February and April, the 65th percentile flow for August and September, and the 85th percentile flow for May through July.

ᵈ Value equals the sum of requested intramonthly flows.

Table 7-1. (continued)

| | Subbasin | | | | | | | | |
| Month | Bighorn[e] | | | Mid-Yellowstone[f] | | | Tongue[g] | | |
	Fish & game request	DNRC-recommended flow	Final BNRC flow reservation	Fish & game request	DNRC-recommended flow	Final BNRC flow reservation	Fish & game request	DNRC-recommended flow	Final BNRC flow reservation
January	202,950	102,075	202,863	295,200	124,820	235,400	11,683	0	4,611
February	179,263	108,025	177,679	309,745	147,830	221,995	10,552	0	4,164
March	264,000	116,215	245,895	676,500	252,100	390,929	32,281	0	4,611
April	214,200	123,485	214,167	654,500	162,450	347,957	31,240	0	4,462
May	226,062[d]	103,300	233,600	773,370[d]	450,710	754,904	36,893	0	4,611
June	309,348[d]	105,735	309,352	2,272,518[d]	1,094,890	1,557,980	35,702	0	4,462
July	214,164	53,500	220,512	856,656[d]	356,020	631,856	24,963	0	4,611
August	172,200	78,090	172,127	430,500	161,100	237,415	13,835	0	4,611
September	154,700	98,790	154,676	416,500	196,370	266,682	11,306	0	4,462
October	166,050	131,590	165,979	430,500	253,330	359,578	11,683	0	4,611
November	184,450	143,120	184,421	416,500	270,750	327,730	11,306	0	4,462
December	196,800	118,675	196,716	344,400	188,150	246,466	11,683	0	4,611
Total	2,484,187	1,342,600	2,477,987	7,876,889	3,658,520	5,578,892	243,127	0	54,289

d Value equals the sum of requested intramonthly flows.

e See *Fish and Game Application*, pp. 186–189. A portion of the seasonal flows was requested based on the paddlefish migration, goose nesting season, and so forth. The DNRC-recommended flow is the 95th percentile monthly low flow at Bighorn. The final BNRC flow reservation is approximately equal to the original request.

f See *Fish and Game Application*, p. 253, and footnote e. The DNRC-recommended flow is the historic minimum flow at Miles City. The final BNRC flow reservation is the 80th percentile flow less consumptive water use reservations.

g See *Fish and Game Application*, p. 198. The requested flows are approximately 70 percent exceedance flows at the state line. The DNRC recommended a denial of the Fish and Game instream flow reservation request. The final BNRC flow reservation for the Tongue River at its mouth is 75 cubic feet per second.

Table 7-1. (continued)

	Subbasin								
	Kinsey Area[h]			Powder[i]			Lower Yellowstone[j]		
Month	Fish & game request	DNRC-recommended flow	Final BNRC flow reservation	Fish & game request	DNRC-recommended flow	Final BNRC flow reservation	Fish & game request	DNRC-recommended flow	Final BNRC flow reservation
January	295,200	124,820	235,400	4,919	310	1,961	301,350	128,510	229,831
February	309,745	147,830	221,995	4,443	185	3,986	332,271	152,430	240,281
March	676,500	252,100	390,929	30,744	4,920	17,888	676,500	319,120	416,711
April	654,500	162,450	347,957	29,752	6,490	20,643	654,500	167,800	405,031
May	773,320[d]	450,710	754,904	49,190	8,730	26,064	832,860	332,650	735,528
June	2,272,518[d]	1,094,890	1,557,980	47,603	7,320	10,946	2,427,192	1,047,290	1,495,644
July	856,656[d]	356,020	631,856	12,298	2,275	4,303	937,500	305,600	647,090
August	430,500	161,100	237,415	2,460	185	891	430,500	98,380	164,166
September	416,500	196,370	266,682	2,380	60	527	416,500	258,870	194,917
October	430,500	253,330	359,578	4,919	120	579	430,500	258,870	369,377
November	416,500	270,950	327,730	4,760	775	3,664	416,500	268,960	347,920
December	344,400	188,150	246,466	4,919	800	3,749	350,550	185,690	245,814
Total	7,876,889	3,658,520	5,578,892	198,387	32,170	95,201	8,206,723	3,429,530	5,492,310

d Value equals the sum of requested intramonthly flows.

h See *Fish and Game Application*, p. 253, and footnote e. The DNRC-recommended flow is the historic minimum monthly flow at Miles City. The BNRC flow reservation for the Yellowstone River at Miles City is the 80th percentile flow less depletions from reservations for consumptive uses.

i See *Fish and Game Application*, p. 223. The requested flows are about 70 percent of the exceedance flows at Moorhead. The DNRC-recommended flow is the historic minimum monthly flow at Locate. The final BNRC flow reservation is the 90th percentile flow at Locate (which is located near the mouth of the Powder River).

j See *Fish and Game Application*, p. 253 and footnote e. The DNRC recommended a flow equal to the historic minimum monthly flow at Sidney. The BNRC flow reservation is equal to the total of the 80th percentile flow less depletions resulting from reservations for consumptive uses.

basin. In a few of the smaller tributaries, all flows throughout the entire year (subject to existing water rights) are requested.[15]

In the spring of 1978, the Department of Natural Resources and Conservation recommended that the Fish and Game Commission instream flow reservation request be substantially reduced to between the 90th and 95th percentile monthly low flows for the upper subbasins and to the historic minimum monthly flows for the lower reaches of the mainstem and tributaries where the fishing is not as highly prized as in the upper reaches. In effect, the DNRC recommended that only 3.4 million acre-feet of the Fish and Game Commission's request of 8.2 million acre-feet be adopted for the Yellowstone River at Sidney. On the Tongue River, the DNRC recommended denial of the Fish and Game instream flow request since it would conflict with DNRC's own request for potential stored water from the proposed expansion of the Tongue River Reservoir.

In December of 1978, the Board of Natural Resources and Conservation rendered its decision on the instream flow reservations for fish and wildlife. Whereas the DNRC recommended that 3.4 million acre-feet be reserved for instream flow, the board granted a 5.5-million-acre-foot-reservation from the total amount requested of 8.2 annually (for the Yellowstone at Sidney). The specific monthly instream flow reservations for fish and wildlife that were granted by the board by subbasin are given again by subbasin in table 7-1.

Water Quality Protection

The Montana Department of Health and Environmental Sciences' instream flow request for the mainstem to maintain a given quality of water represents another sizable flow reservation (see table 7-2). Its request totals about 6.5 million acre-feet annually for the Lower Yellowstone, or about 75 percent of the average annual outflow from the basin over the period of record. The purposes of the instream flow reservation request submitted by the Department of Health and Environmental Sciences are: (1) to assure that the state water quality standards would not be violated, (2) to preserve the existing aquatic ecosystem, and (3) to prevent signifi-

---

[15] The U.S. Bureau of Land Management (BLM) also requested instream flow reservations in four subbasins for the purpose of maintaining the riparian habitat. In all subbasins except the Powder, the BLM's minimum instream flow requests were much less than those requested by the state Fish and Game Commission. However, these were denied by the board since they are effectively met by the granting of the fish and game commission's instream flow reservations.

Table 7-2. Instream flows requested for water quality by the Department of Health and Environmental Sciences for the Yellowstone River

Month	Mainstem Yellowstone, Clarks Fork River to Bighorn River			Mainstem Yellowstone, Bighorn River to Powder River			Mainstem Yellowstone, Powder River to state line		
	Flow		Percent chance exceedance	Flow		Percent chance exceedance	Flow		Percent chance exceedance
	Acre-feet	Cubic ft/ second		Acre-feet	Cubic ft/ second		Acre-feet	Cubic ft/ second	
October	237,000	3,860	50	439,000	7,150	50	600,000	9,775	15
November	232,000	3,910	30	444,000	7,470	35	602,000	10,150	3.0
December	211,000	3,440	10	457,000	7,445	5	590,000	9,610	0.7
January	400,000	6,520	<.01	512,000	8,340	7	780,000	12,700	<.01
February	217,000	3,910	5	404,000	7,280	50	627,000	11,300	12
March	210,000	3,420	25	453,000	7,380	25	673,000	11,000	52
April	197,000	3,320	70	665,000	11,200	17	983,000	16,500	8
May	65,000	1,060	>99	172,000	2,800	99	344,000	5,600	97
June	63,000	1,060	>99	167,000	2,800	99	202,000	3,400	>99
July	65,000	1,060	>99	172,000	2,800	97	209,000	3,400	95
August	160,000	2,690	90	204,000	3,430	95	319,000	5,370	61
September	227,000	3,700	50	359,000	5,850	55	536,000	8,830	15
Total	2,284,000			4,448,000			6,465,000		

Source: Montana Department of Health and Environmental Sciences, statement of testimony of Jim Thomas for the Yellowstone reservation hearings, Transcript 5, August 1977, DHES Reservation Application 10,006-4 #49.

cant degradation of state waters. The DHES developed its specific monthly instream flow requests based on meeting a recommended standard of 500 parts per million for total dissolved solids (TDS) for instream flow for August through April and requesting a seven-day ten-year low flow as a minimum instream flow for the remaining three months.

Once again, the DNRC recommended a significant reduction in the amount of such flows requested. Specifically, it recommended minimum instream flow reservations for water quality equivalent to the instream flows recommended for fish and game.

In the board's consideration of the requested reservation of instream flows for purposes of water quality maintenance, it granted an amount equivalent to that which it granted for fish and wildlife habitat preservation. Such claims on flows are not additive, since both purposes are served simultaneously.

In chapter 9, we will analyze the effect of these instream flow reservations for fish and wildlife habitat and water quality on (1) the water available for energy development and (2) on the tradeoffs between withdrawal and instream uses with respect to priority among the reservations.

However, a few preliminary observations illustrating the significance of priority among reservations are warranted at this point. The first deals with irrigation versus instream flow reservations and the second with the multipurpose storage reservations.

Priority of Instream Flow Reservations

In the first two mainstem subbasins, the board granted instream flow reservations a higher priority than irrigation. A more careful analysis of table 7-1 (especially footnotes a through c) shows that while instream use has priority over irrigation, the monthly instream flow allotments are much lower during the irrigation season (95th percentile flows, that is, those flows equalled or exceeded 95 percent of the time) than during the rest of the year (20th percentile flows) for the first mainstem subbasin (Upper Yellowstone). This probably indicates an attempt by the board to protect the highly valued fishery of the Upper Yellowstone and still provide water for future irrigation.

In the second mainstem subbasin (Billings Area) however, the board granted higher instream flow allotments to fish and game during the irrigation season—an 85th percentile instream flow for May–July and a 65th percentile instream flow for August and September. But because irrigation has a lower priority with respect to instream flows in these subbasins, this means that in order to satisfy the higher instream flow allotments in the downstream Billings Area subbasin, irrigators in the upstream subbasin (Upper Yellowstone) would have to let the water pass through unused. In effect, then, the instream flow reservation in the downstream subbasin (Billings Area) becomes a binding constraint on irrigation in the upstream (Upper Yellowstone) subbasin. Because this was likely an unanticipated outcome at the time the board made its decision, the Legislative Assembly enacted legislation that would give the board an opportunity to reallocate the instream reservations it granted.[16] Specifically, the new legislation allows the board to modify existing or future instream flow reservations by allowing for the reallocation of reserved instream flow if the board finds that "all or part of the reservation is not required for its purpose and that the need for the reallocation has been shown by the applicant to outweigh the need shown by the original reservant." The instream flow reservations may not be reallocated by the board more frequently than once every five years. It should also be noted that upon reallocation, the priority date of the new use is the date of reallocation and not the date of the original reservation. As in the case of the final order adopted by the board, municipal and domestic uses have first priority to reallocated reservations; agricultural use is second in priority.

The second observation concerns the use with the lowest priority. Flow reservations for offstream and onstream multipurpose storage reservoirs have the lowest priority among the competing uses and as such, they can only appropriate unreserved flows. This has the effect of reducing the volume of water available for capture, and thus, the economics of building offstream storage reservoirs such as those proposed by the Bureau of Reclamation under these conditions becomes doubtful.

Application of Indian Reserved Water Rights to Instream Use

Indian reserved water right claims, which could encompass instream uses under the expansive (all beneficial use) criterion, need to be examined in

---

[16] In the Forty-sixth Legislature, House Bill 0842/04, introduced by request of the Senate Water Committee, was signed by Governor Thomas Judge on May 9, 1979, by amendatory veto. In the original version sent to the governor, the bill would have eliminated the water reservations. The governor revised the bill and sent it back to the legislature. Montana law allows the governor to sign a bill if the legislature does not act on the revisions before the session ends.

order to consider all the major potential legal constraints on the amount of water available for competing uses. As discussed in chapter 3, in pending cases before the Ninth Circuit Court of Appeals (*U.S. v. Tongue River Water Users Association, The Northern Cheyenne Tribe v. Adsit,* and *U.S. v. Big Horn Low Line Canal*), the Northern Cheyenne included environmental and aesthetic purposes on their list of beneficial uses. Recall also that the Bureau of Indian Affairs, in proposed rules defining beneficial use included the use of water for aesthetic and recreational purposes and for the maintenance of adequate stream flows for fishery and environmental purposes.

It is clear that the Northern Cheyenne claim reserved rights for instream uses. It is unclear whether the court will uphold their claim for this purpose, particularly in light of *U.S. v. New Mexico* where the purposes for which the federal forest reservations were created were narrowly defined. In *U.S. v. Tongue River Water Users Association,* reserved rights claimed are to all water unappropriated as of the treaty date "which are or will become reasonably necessary for the present and future needs of the Indians."[17]

One might be able to infer needs for the near-term future from a recent survey asking members of the Northern Cheyenne Tribe what type of development they would like the tribe to undertake. The survey yielded the following options in order of declining preference: retail stores, recreation and entertainment business, timber, agriculture, a small coal mine for local use, construction, and tourism.[18] It was concluded from the survey that moves toward economic self-sufficiency would be more effective with the continued export of cattle and timber resources and efforts should be made toward establishing tribal businesses. Of these, recreation, timber, and tourism could have implications for Indian reserved right claims applied to inchannel uses. The tribe has also expressed interest in a fish hatchery.

As also discussed in chapter 3, in recent Supreme Court decisions regarding whether there is a federally reserved water right implicit in a federal land reservation, the issue is whether the government intended to reserve the unappropriated water. Intent is inferred if the unappropriated water is necessary to accomplish the purpose for which the reservation was

---

[17] Civil No. CV-75-20-BLG (D. Mont., filed August 1, 1975) at 12.

[18] Jean Nordstrom, James Boggs, Nancy Owens, Jo Ann Sooktis of the Northern Cheyenne Research Project, *The Northern Cheyenne Tribe and Energy Development in Southeastern Montana, Volume I: Social, Cultural and Economic Investigations,* prepared under a grant from the Old West Regional Commission, October 1977, p. 22.

created. The question then arises as to what the purposes of the Crow and Northern Cheyenne Indian reservations are. It is clear that agricultural development was one purpose for the establishment of Indian reservations. It can be argued that Indian reservations were intended to be places where Indians could maintain their way of life, which included hunting and fishing.[19] There does not appear to be any basis for distinguishing between agriculture and the other purposes for the establishment of Indian reservations. A few cases are pending in state and federal courts in which tribes and the United States are seeking to quantify Indian reserved rights for other purposes including hunting and fishing and the extraction and development of mineral resources.[20]

In a 1979 case, *U.S. v. Adair*,[21] the U.S. District Court for the District of Oregon ruled that members of the Klamath Indian tribe and the tribe itself have the right to sufficient water to protect their hunting and fishing rights even though the reservation had now been terminated. Protection of these rights will require the maintenance of a "natural stream flow" through both an existing marsh and forest land on the former reservation. In the decision, the court stated: "Without sufficient water to preserve fish and wildlife on the reservation lands, Indian hunting and fishing rights would be worthless." Also interesting is that the federal district court gave a priority date of "time immemorial" to these rights which are necessary to preserve their hunting and fishing rights.

The court also ruled that the Klamath Indians had reserved rights for irrigation and domestic purposes with a priority date of 1864, the year the reservation was established. In the words of the ruling:

> The principal purpose of the treaty was to provide an area for the exclusive occupation of the Indians so that they could continue to be self-sufficient. The treaty provided two ways for the Indians to be self-sufficient.

[19] In a recent but subsequently vacated case because of double jeopardy for the defendants, *U.S. v. Finch* (548 F. 2d, 822, 832 9th Cir. 1976), a court stated:

> By establishing a reservation as a "permanent home" for the Crow Indians, see Treaty with the Crows of 1868, Art. 4, 2 Kapp. 1008, 1009, the government manifestly intended to set aside lands which would provide the tribe with the food and natural resources upon which their livelihood depended. It is true that the Crow Indians were, in 1868, predominantly hunters. The aim of the United States, however, was to fix the Crows in one location and to reorient their way of life toward "agricultural and other pursuits." We find it inconceivable that the United States intended to withhold from the Indians the right to sustain themselves from any source of food which might be available on their reservation.

[20] *U.S. v. Nevada,* 412 U.S. 534 (1973), *Pyramid Lake Paiute Tribe of Indians v. Morton,* 354 F. Supp. 252 (D.D.C. 1973).

[21] No. 75-914 (D. Ore. September 29, 1979); *Environmental Law Reporter* vol. 11, no. 10 (November 1979) pp. 20733–20739.

First, by ensuring that the Indians could continue their traditional way of life which included hunting, fishing, trapping, and gathering. Article I of the treaty secured to the Indians their right to pursue their traditional way of life.

Second, by encouraging the Indians to adopt agriculture. . . .

The treaty granted the Indians an implied right to as much water on the reservation as was necessary to fulfill these purposes. The termination of the reservation did not abrogate the Indians' water rights. . . . In addition to water rights for the preservation of hunting and fishing rights, the treaty also granted the Indians an implied right to use water necessary for agriculture.[22]

In *U.S. v. Big Horn Low Line Canal,* the federal government on behalf of the Crow tribe asks for a declaration of reserved rights on the Bighorn River and other tributaries, with a priority date of 1851. In the action, the tribe states that the purposes for which the reservation was created include municipal and domestic use, irrigation, stock watering, and full utilization of the reservation and its resources. Fish and wildlife is not explicitly stated as a purpose for which the reservation was created although the latter phrase is open ended so that it is conceivable that water could be used in this way if the court determines it to be a purpose of the reservation. But since the Crow Indian Reservation occupies the uppermost reaches of the Bighorn and Little Bighorn rivers, even if reserved rights encompassed instream uses, it would not be detrimental to downstream appropriators with a later priority date. (For a map showing location of the reservations, see figure 1-3.)

The situation is more complicated with the Northern Cheyenne Reservation, however. An upper and a lower reach of the Tongue River have been designated as a class 4 fishery. If the Northern Cheyenne reserved rights were judically determined to be applicable to inchannel uses such as fisheries, recreation, and the like, then the location of the reservation becomes important. The Northern Cheyenne Reservation lies below the Tongue River Dam but still in the upper reaches of the Tongue River. A 30-mile stretch of the Tongue River forms the eastern boundary of the reservation. No information as to the volume of flow requested for instream uses is available. It is possible that the tribe may request instream flows reflecting seasonal variation as did the state Fish and Game Commission.

Absent any quantitative information regarding the Northern Cheyenne's assertion of reserved rights for "environmental and aesthetic pur-

22 Ibid., 20736-20737.

poses," we employ as a working assumption the state BNRC-granted instream flow reservation of about 4,600 acre-feet per month for the purpose of maintaining the riparian habitat. The effect of this instream flow through the reservation on competing uses is examined later in the hydrologic simulations presented in chapter 9. It is worth observing that if the Northern Cheyenne reserved rights are eventually applied to instream uses requiring a flow different from our working assumption, there would be little if any effect on downstream water right holders because of the nonconsumptive nature of such uses. However, a limited number of holders of junior rights upstream of the reservation could be affected. If additional impoundment or expansion of the existing Tongue River Dam occurs, then the additional usable supply caused by the increase in firm yield could be, under some circumstances, available for energy-related purposes. Accordingly, the Northern Cheyenne reserved rights applied to instream uses need not preclude water for energy development purposes.

Summary and Conclusions

Only recently have instream flows to maintain fisheries, water quality, and support recreational activities and amenity values been accorded explicit recognition in water law and management. In the past, only uses involving stream diversions were considered to be valid beneficial uses of water. There is now, however, a steadily growing recognition in western state laws that instream flow itself provides beneficial uses. In its 1973 Water Use Act, the state of Montana recognized fish and wildlife and recreation as beneficial uses and allowed for the reservation of water by public bodies for such purposes.

In response, the state Fish and Game Commission requested instream flow reservations for the mainstem and eighty of its tributaries. For the Yellowstone River at Sidney, their instream flow request totaled 8.2 million acre-feet annually, or 93 percent of the average annual flow over the period of record. The Board of Natural Resources and Conservation granted fish and game an instream flow of 5.49 million acre-feet, or 67 percent of the requested amount.

The state Department of Health and Environmental Sciences instream flow request represents another sizable reservation for water quality. Its request totals 6.5 million acre-feet for the Lower Yellowstone, or about 75 percent of the amount of the average annual outflow from the subbasin. The board granted simultaneously an instream flow reservation for water quality equivalent to the instream flow reservation for fish and game in the mainstem subbasins, since inchannel flow reservations are not additive. These instream flow reservations may severely limit the flow available for those uses requiring diversion from the stream if no additional impoundments are built.

Finally, not to be ignored is the issue of applying Indian reserved rights to instream uses under the expansive criterion. The Northern Cheyenne tribe claims reserved rights for "environmental and aesthetic" purposes. If the expansive criterion is assumed to prevail, we estimate the instream use portion of the Northern Cheyenne reserved rights to be equivalent, as a working hypothesis, to the state BNRC-granted instream flow reservation for maintaining the riparian habitat. The purposes for which the Crow tribe claims reserved rights do not explicitly state instream uses. Therefore, it appears that the expansive criterion applied to the Crow reserved rights claims would involve the mineral or coal resources more than inchannel uses.

At this point, we have identified and estimated the competing claims for water in the basin by economic function and by type of use (withdrawal or instream) as well as by owner. In chapter 8, we discuss the methodology by which we analyze the water available under various conditions and circumstances for these competing functions and claimants.

8 The Hydrologic Simulator for the Yellowstone River Basin

Introduction

Whether or not any given level of coal development in the Yellowstone Basin would be constrained by the amount of surface water that is available is a complex but critical question. It is complicated by the lack of quantitative information on existing state water rights[1] and by legal and institutional factors such as the new state water reservations, interstate water rights pursuant to the Yellowstone River Compact, and Indian reserved water rights. Moreover, since reserved water rights and existing state rights are not quantified for any of the rivers in the Yellowstone Basin, no existing record of valid claims and the nature of their rights to use of water in each of the subbasins is available. Estimation of relevant magnitudes is further complicated by the fact that withdrawal of water does not imply that all the withdrawn water is depleted. For example, generally speaking, about a 50 percent return flow is associated with the withdrawal of water for irrigation, but the return flow reenters the receiving water at a place downstream from which it was withdrawn and at a later time. Even the estimates of the physical volume of water available can vary depending on the period of record used, interpretation of the Yellowstone Compact,[2] the assumptions relative to other imponderables treated in the study, and the seasonal vagaries introduced by nature.

---

[1] The fact that there is unused water in the river basin does not imply that there is unappropriated water at the same time and in the place where it is needed waiting for a potential user to file for the right to use it. The availability of that water depends on the number and volume of existing rights with senior priority dates, regardless of whether or not the quantity of water attached to those rights is in use every year. The state of Montana has begun a statewide adjudication process for existing water rights. All water users must submit a statement of claim during the two and one-half year filing period.

[2] The Yellowstone River Compact, described in chapter 2, was passed by Congress in 1954, but has yet to be implemented.

To incorporate the relevant legal and institutional factors and hydrologic variables and to reflect their interaction, there is a need for a high speed calculating engine that would yield the results implicit in the simultaneous consideration of the hydrologic record, the legal rights and claims on water, the institutional and administrative processes affecting water use, the postulated coal development levels, and the competing withdrawal and instream uses of water. The calculating mechanism, the RFF/Montana Yellowstone Basin simulation model, is a hydrologic simulation model that produces quantitative results when instructed to answer questions concerning the abundance or scarcity of available water for any purpose, given different but equally probable (or plausible) outcomes of pending legal and administrative decisions.[3] The simulator can also be used to reveal the implications for the *quality* of water associated with any one of the mixes of competing water uses defined by economic function. In this chapter we describe the model which provides the apparatus that allows an integrated approach to analysis of the water issue in relation to energy (and other) developments.

The RFF/Montana Yellowstone Basin Simulation Model

DEFINING THE MODEL

The complexity of a hydrologic model is a function of the number of variables, discreteness in space and time, and the solution technique. The model used in this analysis is a hydrologic simulation model that is quasi-dynamic. That is, time is represented in discrete monthly steps over the simulation period rather than in a continuous fashion which relies on the use of transfer coefficients using differential equations. The essence of hydrologic simulation is to trace the behavior of the water system over time, given certain initial conditions and hydrologic data including inflows to the system, a set of targets, reservoir operating criteria, and legal and institutional constraints on flow.

[3] The basic hydrologic subbasin model was developed by Donald Boyd and Theodore Williams and other members of their research team at Montana State University over a five-year period. See Donald W. Boyd and Theodore T. Williams, *Development of a State Water Planning Model, Peripheral Models of Sub-Basin 43-Q of the Yellowstone Basin* (Bozeman, Mont., Montana State University, May 1976). Later, Satish Nayak, formerly with the Water Resources Division of the Montana Department of Natural Resources and Conservation, and George Cawlfield expanded the small subbasin monthly model to the nine subbasins of the Yellowstone River Basin. Further debugging, expansion, and refinement of the model was done by Constance Boris of Resources for the Future.

The RFF/Montana Yellowstone Basin simulation model can be described as a detailed hydrologic simulation model. It is an attempt to reflect the effect of alternative mixes of water use on available flow given the dynamic hydrologic characteristics of a river basin. It can do this with spatial, temporal, and hydrologic variable differentiation.

In spatial detail, the RFF/Montana model reflects the unique hydrologic characteristics of each of the nine planning subbasins of the Montana portion of the Yellowstone River Basin. This is important because the subbasins in the plains area have quite different patterns of flow compared with the subbasins in the upper mountainous reaches. The nine subbasins proceeding in a downstream fashion (illustrated in figure 4-1) are:

1. Upper Yellowstone
2. Clarks Fork
3. Billings Area
4. Bighorn
5. Mid-Yellowstone
6. Tongue
7. Kinsey Area
8. Powder
9. Lower Yellowstone

Of these nine subbasins, only the Tongue and Bighorn have existing water storage reservoirs of any significant capacity, though there are several potential storage sites in the nine subbasins.

Hydrologically, the model can be thought of generally as being divided into a surface water system and a subsurface water system. These two systems can, in turn, be further subdivided into five subsystems: (1) surface water (stream and reservoir), (2) snow, (3) runoff, (4) groundwater, and (5) soil water.

The RFF/Montana simulation model consists of five balance equations (one for each hydrologic subsystem—stream and reservoir, snow, runoff, groundwater, and soil water), eleven subsystem linking equations, and a coefficient matrix. This represents a system of simultaneous equations of the form:

$$C(I, 1)X1 + C(I, 2)X2 + \ldots + C(I, NC)XNC$$

where $1 \leq I \leq NR$ (number of rows) represents the number of endogenous variables in the system and where NC (number of columns) represents the sum of endogenous and exogenous variables.

Altogether, the simulation model consists of a set of sixteen equations which describe the hydrologic dynamics and uses encountered by water as it passes through a subbasin.[4] Formally, the system of simultaneous equations (with the endogenous variables on the left-hand side) is as follows:

$$X1 = X2 + X3 - X4 - X6 - X11 - X18$$
$$+ X19 - X27 - X28 + X31 \quad (1)$$

$$X6 = C(2, 2)X2 + C(2, 19)X19 + C(2, 28)X28$$
$$+ C(2, 31)X31 + C(2, 32)X32 \quad (2)$$

$$X10 = X7 - X8 + X9 - X11 + X12 - X26 \quad (3)$$

$$X11 = C(4, 2)X2 + C(4, 3)X3 + C(4, 4)X4$$
$$+ C(4, 19)X19 + C(4, 28)X28 + C(4, 31)X31 \quad (4)$$

$$X12 = C(5, 9)X9 + C(5, 10)X10 + C(5, 32)X32 \quad (5)$$

$$X14 = C(6, 15)X15 + C(6, 16)X16 \quad (6)$$

$$X16 = X13 - X14 + X15 - X17 + X18$$
$$+ C(7, 22)X22 + C(7, 31)X31 \quad (7)$$

$$X17 = C(8, 13)X13 + C(8, 15)X15 \quad (8)$$

$$X19 = C(9, 12)X12 + C(9, 27)X27 + C(9, 28)X28 \quad (9)$$

$$X20 = C(10, 5)X5 + C(10, 12)X12$$
$$+ C(10, 17)X17 + C(10, 28)X28 \quad (10)$$

$$X21 = C(11, 12)X12 + C(11, 27)X27 + C(11, 28)X28 \quad (11)$$

$$X22 = X5 + X12 - X13 + X17 - X19 - X20$$
$$- X21 + X27 + X28 + C(12, 31)X31 \quad (12)$$

[4] For example, a given mathematical equation can express the hydrologic dynamics of a given unit of water that falls as precipitation (rain or snow). A portion of that fallen precipitation is evaporated, a portion percolates into the ground, another portion is consumed by plants, and the remainder leaves the subbasin as stream outflow.

$$X24 = X21 + C(13, 22)X22 + X23 - X25 - X26$$

$$\text{if } FC_{\min} \leq X24 \leq FC$$

$$= FC_{\min} \qquad \text{if } X24 \; < FC_{\min}$$

$$= FC \qquad \text{if } X24 \; > FC \tag{13}$$

$$X25 = X21 + C(14, 22)X22 + X23 - X24 - X26$$

$$\text{if } X24 < FC_{\min}$$

$$= PET \qquad \text{if } X24 \geq FC_{\min} \tag{14}$$

$$X26 = C(15, 21)X21 + C(15, 22)X22$$

$$+ C(15, 23)X23 + C(15, 32)X32$$

$$\text{where } C(15, 32) = RE \qquad \text{if } X24 > FC$$

$$= 0 \qquad \text{if } X24 \leq FC \tag{15}$$

$$X29 = X28 \tag{16}$$

where the variables are defined as:

$X1$ = stream outflow
$X2$ = stream inflow
$X3$ = initial reservoir storage
$X4$ = terminal reservoir storage
$X5$ = precipitation
$X6$ = stream and reservoir evaporation loss
$X7$ = groundwater outflow
$X8$ = groundwater inflow
$X9$ = initial groundwater capacity
$X10$ = terminal groundwater capacity
$X11$ = stream and reservoir percolation
$X12$ = groundwater discharge
$X13$ = snowfall
$X14$ = sublimation loss
$X15$ = initial snow storage
$X16$ = terminal snow storage
$X17$ = snowmelt

$X18$ = ice formation
$X19$ = groundwater irrigation runoff
$X20$ = runoff evaporation loss
$X21$ = groundwater infiltration/ irrigation
$X22$ = infiltration or balance
$X23$ = initial soil water storage
$X24$ = terminal soil water storage
$X25$ = evapotranspiration loss
$X26$ = soil water percolation
$X27$ = irrigation water export
$X28$ = irrigation diversion
$X29$ = irrigation diversion deviation
$X30$ = irrigation runoff
$X31$ = precipitation runoff or balance
$X32$ = system constant

and where FC is the variable representing field capacity
FC_{min} is the minimum field capacity
RE is the groundwater recharge factor
PET is the potential evapotranspiration

The endogenous variables are $X1$ or $X4$ depending on whether or not the model is run in the with-reservoir or without-reservoir mode, $X6$, $X10$, $X11$, $X12$, $X14$, $X16$, $X17$, $X19$, $X20$, $X21$, $X24$, $X25$, $X26$, $X28$, and $X29$. The remaining variables in the set of equations are the exogenous, or independent, variables.

With regard to temporal variation, since the dimensions of hydrologic variability are better captured with smaller time units, time increments on a monthly basis are used in the model. Mean monthly data for air temperature, precipitation, potential evapotranspiration, irrigation diversions, withdrawal and return flows for withdrawal uses, flow requirements for instream uses, and in the case of reservoirs, initial reservoir storage, surface area, and PAN[5] evaporation coefficients are required data inputs.

Of the thirty-one variables in the RFF/Montana model, nine have primary values, that is, data can be obtained from historical records. Specifically, data for $X1$ (stream outflow), $X2$ (stream inflow), $X3$ (initial reservoir storage), $X4$ (terminal reservoir storage), $X5$ (precipitation), $X27$ (irrigation water export), and $X28$ (irrigation diversions) are obtained from historical records for each subbasin. Since $X7$ (groundwater outflow) and $X8$ (groundwater inflow) are functions of $X1$ and $X2$ respectively, they are calculated outside the system of equations. Secondary data (for which there is no historical record) are derived indirectly by correlating secondary variables to the primary variables through the use of regression equations. The magnitude of the regression coefficients for the secondary parameters are indirectly obtained from the theoretical literature or are specified beforehand from knowledge of the system, and others are determined by solving for nonzero coefficients. Note that the balance equations have unity coefficients which are already known by definition. Once the regression coefficients are specified, the secondary data base is generated through a calibration model. Generation of secondary data through the use of the calibration model together with the primary data yields a complete and consistent data

---

[5] Evaporation from water surfaces is commonly measured by exposing pans of water (hence the term PAN) to the atmosphere and recording evaporation losses by systematic measurements or self-registering devices.

base for the simulation model. Once the model is calibrated for each subbasin,[6] the historical subbasin outflow can be replicated for each month over the simulation period, which in this study is 360 months. Simulation of historical flow for each month over a thirty-year period constituted a first stage test of the model.[7]

Subbasin-specific monthly water withdrawal and depletion rates for alternative levels of coal development, irrigation, and municipal use as well as the monthly instream flow rates for the maintenance of fish and wildlife habitat and water quality are input to the model via a data generation program. These water use levels can be specified for either Indian or non-Indian development, or both.

The set of equations described above is the general form of the model that is applicable to any subbasin.[8] Equation (1) can be used in solving for either $X1$ (stream outflow from the subbasin) when the subbasin does not have a reservoir or $X4$ (terminal reservoir storage) and $X1$ (outflow from the dam) when the subbasin has an existing reservoir or the potential for a reservoir. Using standard matrix algebra techniques, the system of equations is solved simultaneously for the sixteen endogenous variables for each month over a thirty-year period by computer via the main source code and accompanying subroutines. The model is calibrated for each subbasin, that is, historical flow can be replicated for each month over the thirty-year period for each subbasin, providing a tool for detailed analysis of available flow and other hydrologic components of the system.

Like the data input, the model's solution set is generated on a monthly basis over a thirty-year period. The solution yielded by the model implies a standard operating procedure based on the assumption that the flow pattern of the past thirty years will be replicated. Since the historical data input to the model is based on the period 1944 to 1974, the solution set is interpreted in the following manner: if the 1944 to 1974 patterns of flow, temperature, precipitation, and the like are repeated, then the solution set reflects the effect of projected water uses on available flow over the next thirty-year period. This is admittedly not

---

[6] Calibration is the process of adjusting parameter values until agreement between simulated and observed data is obtained.

[7] The internally documented model and accompanying input data are stored on tape for further use.

[8] The specific form of the model is developed from the data for the hydrologic variables, the coefficient matrix used for solving the set of equations, the calibration process, the subroutines that internalize the hydrologic variables, and the legal and institutional variables on water use, all of which are unique to a selected subbasin.

the ideal case, but it is standard operating procedure given the resources available for topical planning purposes and policy analysis.[9]

Subbasin-dependent subroutines in the model internalize the particular set of hydrologic characteristics, existing or proposed reservoirs, and legal claims for a given subbasin under analysis. For example, the subroutine INITIA lists the initial values for precipitation, the maximum and minimum values for field capacity of a subbasin, the coefficients for calculating groundwater inflow and groundwater outflow from the subbasin, and the groundwater recharge factor.[10] The subroutine COMPUT incorporates the effects of temperature on the hydrologic system within a subbasin. Its purpose is to internalize the subbasin-specific responses (some of which are nonlinear in nature) of those variables dependent on temperature. For instance, snowfall, sublimation, ice formation, and limited evapotranspiration occur at mean monthly temperatures less than or equal to 32°F whereas rainfall, limited snowfall, snowmelt, and evapotranspiration occur at mean monthly temperatures greater than 32°F. A schematic diagram of the hydrologic model for the without-reservoir case is shown in figure 8-1.

In the with-reservoir case, the SURFAC subroutine estimates the evaporation loss from a reservoir as a function of the surface area of the reservoir and the PAN coefficients.

A serious attempt has been made to reflect the possible political constraints on available flow in the model by adding appropriate subroutines. For example, eventual implementation of the Yellowstone River Compact (which allocates flow that is surplus to the 1950 water rights on a percentage basis in the Clarks Fork, Bighorn, Tongue, and Powder subbasins between Montana and Wyoming) has implications for the flow available for Montana. The motivation for the DEPLET subroutine is to reduce the inflow to subbasins in Montana (those affected by the Yellowstone River Compact) by Wyoming's share of the compact water. Since it is not possible to calculate Wyoming's full share of the surplus flow at this time, the most likely water development and use patterns in the compact-affected subbasins are used as a basis to deplete inflow to the same subbasins in Montana on a monthly basis.

---

[9] Use of synthetic hydrologic models could be considered. These are considerably more sophisticated in concept and might be used if budgetary resources were ample enough to use them.

[10] The simulation model accounts for groundwater inflow to a subbasin and groundwater outflow. The model cannot, however, simulate the site-specific disruption of say, a coal mine, on a groundwater aquifer.

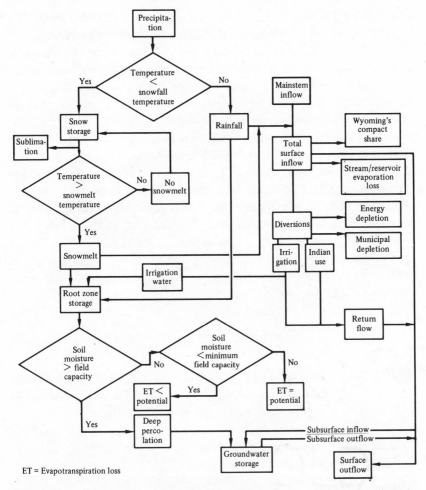

Figure 8-1. Schematic diagram of the RFF/Montana Yellowstone Basin simulation model (without-reservoir case)   *Source:* Unpublished working papers of Constance Boris; communication with Satish Nayak, April 7, 1977

Another option of the model involves the as yet judicially undetermined Indian reserved water right claims of the Wind River Indian tribes in Wyoming, and the Crow and Northern Cheyenne tribes in Montana. These subroutines and options within the model allow for much flexibility in the analysis of potential effects of plausible legal and institutional constraints on water for any use.

An additional subroutine, QUALTY, calculates the impact of projected development of competing uses on water quality, primarily on total dissolved solids (TDS) concentration. TDS is the parameter most affected by development of withdrawal uses. For example, increased irrigation diversions will produce return flows with higher TDS levels, and water depletion resulting from the operation of generation and conversion facilities will diminish the flow, which again will affect the TDS concentrations. The basic principle governing the analysis in the QUALTY subroutine is the conservation of mass–water and dissolved solids. Generally speaking, there is an inverse relationship between the flow rate or discharge[11] and the concentration of total dissolved solids except when flow regulation by a dam obscures the usual relationship. In the with-reservoir case, regression equations relating TDS to historical monthly inflow to the subbasin were used to estimate the average monthly TDS concentrations (denoted by the variable name, TDS, in the QUALTY subroutine) of the inflow to the reservoir. An average TDS concentration for the stored water (TDSR) was estimated from historical records. Complete mixing of the stored water with inflow to the reservoir is an optional assumption in the model and can be described as:

$$TDSI = \frac{(TDS)X2 + (TDSR)X3}{X2 + X3} \; .$$

where $TDSI$ = the average TDS concentration in parts per million (ppm) of the released water to be used for new irrigation or energy development below the dam

$X2$ = inflow to the dam

$X3$ = initial reservoir storage

and TDS and $TDSR$ are as defined above.

Alternatively, in the model, one can also choose the option of assuming that there is no mix of the reservoir contents with the inflow (stratification).[12]

The TDS concentration in the outflow from the subbasin will be affected by water withdrawal for energy development, new irrigation, return flows from new irrigation, and additional salt pickup in the irrigation return flow due to soil leaching. Preliminary data from the U.S. Bureau of Reclamation on irrigation return flows indicate a gross salt

---

[11] Discharge is the volume of water that passes a given point within a given period of time.

[12] This is accomplished by making a few appropriate programming changes in the QUALTY subroutine.

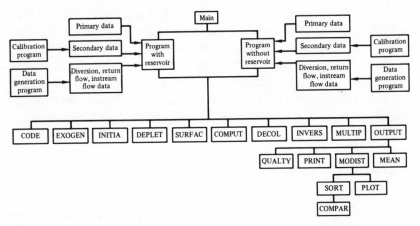

Figure 8-2. Program progression through the RFF/Montana Yellowstone Basin simulation model

pickup of one-third to one-half ton per acre per year for irrigated land in the Yellowstone drainage of Montana.[13] Ideally, return flow should remove the salt in the applied water or else salt will accumulate in the soil and reduce crop productivity. For purposes of analysis, zero salt pickup, ½ ton, and 1 ton of salt pickup per acre per year are modeled. Therefore, the outgoing salt load from the subbasin is calculated as the sum of the monthly outgoing load in the undiverted flow plus the load in the return flow from new irrigation and municipal uses and the load of additional salt pickup in the return flow from new irrigation. Dividing this sum by the monthly outflow from the subbasin and a conversion factor yields the monthly TDS concentration (in parts per million) in the outflow from the subbasin. The QUALTY subroutine is essentially the same in the without-reservoir case except that the mixing subroutine is omitted from the program logic.

Figure 8-2 illustrates the program's progression through the general subroutines and subbasin-dependent subroutines.

The remaining subroutines: CODE, EXOGEN, DECOL, INVERS, and MULTIP are used to manipulate the coefficient matrix for solving the system of simultaneous equations. The OUTPUT subroutine yields the solution of the system of equations, the simulated outflow from the subbasin, historical outflow from the subbasin, and the TDS concentrations of the simulated outflow. Within the OUTPUT subroutine, the purpose of

---

[13] U.S. Bureau of Reclamation, unpublished working documents for the ongoing water management study, Missouri River above Gavins Point.

the MODIST subroutine is to rank the outflow data on a monthly basis and calculate the 50th and 90th percentile, as well as the mean values. The MEAN subroutine calculates the time-weighted average and the volume-weighted average of the TDS concentrations by month and by year. The SORT and COMPAR subroutines are simply used for ranking the output data. The PLOT subroutine is used for plotting the 50th and 90th percentile values of subbasin inflow, outflow, and TDS concentration.

EVALUATING THE MODEL

The advantages of the model are that it can simulate the effects of any projected *individual* water use—coal development, irrigation, instream flows for water quality or fish habitat maintenance—or *combination* of uses on flow for every month over a historical period of record (which includes the lowest flow on record following conventional practice) for each subbasin. The model can be run in the with-reservoir or without-reservoir mode for a selected subbasin so that the effects of proposed reservoirs can be examined. The flexibility of the mode, accomplished through subroutines, makes it possible to examine the effects of legal and institutional constraints on available flow and water storage (existing and proposed). In addition to the quantitative assessment, the model can simulate the effects of development of competing uses on water quality. Finally, the usefulness of the model is increased by its general applicability: it can be applied to any subbasin once the values for the initial conditions and exogenous variables are supplied so that the matrix of coefficients can be derived.

The limitations of the model are similar to those of most operational hydrologic simulators; that is, an implicit assumption is made that the historic flow will be endlessly replicated except for the effects of increased drafts and reservoir regulation supplied to the model. The model uses one trace of flow obtained from an actual record of streamflows and, therefore, no information is gained on the response to other, equally likely, patterns of flow.[14] With regard to model calibration, the outflow from a subbasin can be calibrated in the without-reservoir model (that is, the historical flow trace can be replicated). However, when the model is run

[14] In Maynard M. Hufschmidt and Myron B. Fiering, *Simulation Techniques for Design of Water Resource Systems* (Cambridge, Mass., Harvard University Press, 1966), synthetic hydrology techniques are suggested to compensate for this deficiency. However, because of the limitations of time and budget, the Hufschmidt-Fiering suggestion fell outside the range of options available for this study.

in the with-reservoir mode for the case of proposed reservoirs, there are no empirical data that allow evaluating the model's performance. Historical subbasin outflows cannot be duplicated in such cases since the flows will also be determined by the operating criterion controlling releases from the proposed reservoirs.

Another limitation of the model is its inability to differentiate variations in the hydrologic characteristics *within* a given subbasin. That is, while the model is capable of reflecting the unique hydrologic characteristics among subbasins, it does not do so within a subbasin. By the same token, it cannot differentiate among the points of diversion within the subbasin. For example, a diversion would be reflected in the subbasin's outflow, but the water may not be withdrawn until near the end of the subbasin in which case the actual streamflow throughout most of the subbasin would be higher than the simulated outflow from the subbasin. Just as the points of diversion within a subbasin cannot be distinguished by the model, the same applies to tributary inflows.

While all of the deficiencies noted restrict the informational detail that the model generates, it may be fairly claimed that, from an operational viewpoint, the RFF/Montana Yellowstone Basin simulation model discriminates much more finely in the pattern of information it provides than does any other hydrologic simulator that was examined.

OPERATING THE MODEL

To provide decision makers with necessary and useful information, varying assumptions regarding the priority and extent of legal claims to water (distinguished by economic function) and alternative operating criteria for proposed reservoirs are needed. In so doing, the simulator can provide quantitative evaluations (by month and subbasin) of the amount of stored water or flow remaining for lower assigned priority uses when another use, such as irrigation, is given higher rank in a preference system. Instream uses and energy development are then ranked in descending priority. One can then examine the tradeoffs involved in adopting one water use preference system over another. For example, if energy development were given first priority for, say, national security purposes, then how much potentially irrigable acreage would have to be given up to accommodate the projected generation and coal conversion levels, and to what extent will instream uses be reduced? This can be answered by the RFF/ Montana Yellowstone Basin simulator. Analysis of simultaneously satisfying prior legal rights and claims on water before meeting the demands of water for energy development is another relevant question that can be analyzed with the aid of the model. It is integrating all the relevant hydrologic variables and legal rights and claims on water that makes this model particularly suited for assessing the physical and legal availability of water for any use.

The Mid-Yellowstone, Tongue, and Powder subbasins are of immediate interest because of the presence of the coalfields. However, as stated in chapter 4, the Powder is unregulated and cannot provide a dependable supply of water for generation and coal conversion; the same is essentially true of the Tongue since it has only a small reservoir for regulation. Both the state and private energy developers have expressed interest in constructing the proposed Moorhead Reservoir on the Powder River and in greatly expanding the existing small Tongue River Reservoir. To assess available water supplies in these subbasins, we need to examine the increase in dependable water supply that would result from the proposed new reservoirs.

In our hydrologic simulation experiments, results of which are presented in the following chapter, we consider the cases of storage (with reservoir) and no storage (without reservoir). In the case of no storage, the maximum amount of water that can be used for any given use or combination of uses is dictated by the minimum flows of the simulation period. In the case of storage, the reservoirs are operated using the following criteria:

1. withdrawal use has the highest priority and is always satisfied
2. releases from the reservoir are made to meet the water withdrawal demand for a given use (for example, irrigation) or for selected combinations of uses (irrigation, coal conversion, and the like), that is, to meet the water requirement for a selected priority use or combination of priority uses
3. if the inflow is less than the volume of water needed for the withdrawal uses, then stored water is drawn down to meet the requirement for the withdrawal uses
4. if the inflow is less than the volume of water needed for *both* the withdrawal and instream uses but is more than that needed for the withdrawal uses alone, then water is released from the reservoir equal to the inflow
5. if the inflow exceeds the volume of water needed for both the withdrawal and instream uses, the excess is stored assuming space is available.

In simultaneously satisfying a set of prior legal rights and claims delineated by water use, the monthly water requirements for the withdrawal uses (irrigation, coal development, and municipal uses) are summed. Accordingly, the model does not directly discriminate water withdrawals explicitly by use in this approach, although it can do so indirectly. For example, if the sum of monthly water requirements for irrigation, coal development, and municipal needs cannot be satisfied, then the model can be rerun without coal development if one wishes to assume irrigation and municipal needs would have preference over coal development. Or the model can be run with a reduced coal development level. Alternatively, the reservoir operating criteria can be modified in the model to grant instream use the highest priority with the shortfall in water supply experienced by the lower priority withdrawal uses.

If one assumes that the Indian reserved water rights will have precedence over new and most existing state water rights, the model is programmed with an option to show the effects of the earlier date attaching to Indian reserved water rights. Interstate water rights as allocated by the Yellowstone River Compact are also reflected in the model's logic.

Finally, the model also simulates the impact of the various uses on the quality of water; that is, the quality of the flow leaving the subbasin is a function of the remaining inchannel flow, the return flow from irrigation, and the base water quality level of the inflow to the subbasin or reservoir.

Since the development of a model that would aid in the analysis of critical and complex issues involving water for energy development in the coalfields (Powder River Basin and Fort Union Formation) in the basin was only one objective, the other being the assembling of accurate data for use of the policy analyst, the dénouement is reserved for the next chapter. There we apply the model to the carefully developed data sets, playing out the results of different possible outcomes of the pending Indian reserved rights cases, administrative actions on allocating interstate flow, and the newly enacted state water reservations that will affect the extent and mix of resource outputs in the Yellowstone River Basin of Montana.

9 An Integrated Analysis of the Availability and Quality of Water

The basic question we address in this chapter is: To what extent and under what conditions is there a dependable supply of water in the coal-bearing subbasins for the levels of coal extraction and export or conversion that were postulated in chapter 5? This question is asked within a framework which allows for the *simultaneous* consideration of both physical availability and legal availability of water with temporal and spatial differentiation of the hydrologic system.

To gain perspective we use the simulator to look first at each individual use in isolation. This will tell us if any given functional use could be met if rival uses were not a factor, or whether the reservations and projected uses are simply unrealistic given the existing legal rights and claims on flow and the basic hydrology of the region. We simultaneously evaluate water quality changes associated with different water uses as an important dimension of the problem. Next we move from the analysis of individual uses in relation to the hydrologic regime to a simultaneous consideration of various combinations of rival uses, taking into account the various institutional and legal factors that are likely to govern the level and mix of uses. This is done first for the Tongue River subbasin and then for the Powder subbasin.

The Tongue, Powder River, and Mid-Yellowstone subbasins are of special significance because federal and state owned coal deposits lie within them. The Bighorn subbasin is of importance in a somewhat different way. Since most of the coal underlying this subbasin is Indian owned, the Bighorn's significance lies principally in the large supply of water potentially available from the Yellowtail storage reservoir. While there is no storage on the Yellowstone River itself, its unregulated flow is large in relation to the tributary stream flows and could have a bearing on the water available for energy (as well as other rival uses). Later sections of the chapter deal with the evaluation of water available for energy in the

Bighorn and Mid-Yellowstone subbasins along with the water quality dimensions of the problem. In the last section of the chapter, our findings are summarized.

Analysis of the Availability and Quality of Water in the Tongue Subbasin

Recall from chapter 4 that the Tongue subbasin is characterized by agricultural and grazing lands with a low population density but a high energy development potential. Water available for any use is a function of legal as well as physical and economic variables. Since there are innumerable permutations among the priorities of existing legal claimants and prospective claimants (as reflected in the reservations requested), the action of the Board of Natural Resources and Conservation (BNRC) on these requests taken in December of 1978 has reduced somewhat the range of uncertainty involved in evaluating the amount of water available for any given purpose or combination of purposes. Since the BNRC determinations in December of 1978 may be subject to redetermination as authorized by legislation enacted during the following (Forty-sixth) Montana Legislative Assembly, it is possible that the process of political bargaining and negotiation leading to the board's 1978 determination may continue into the future. Accordingly, although we take the 1978 determination on water reservations by the BNRC as the current position, we nonetheless will want to examine other alternatives that were presented and their implications.

To review the hydrology of the Tongue subbasin, figure 4-3 reveals that August is a particularly critical month from the standpoint of stream flows. Examination of the monthly flow records adjusted for the 1975 level of depletion for the study period indicates many low flow occurrences in September and from December through February. Absence of a dependable supply of water without additional storage in the Tongue precludes expanding irrigation or converting the coal resources unless either more water-efficient irrigation systems are introduced by existing irrigators, or dry cooling is used in coal conversion. It is for this reason that building storage to increase the dependable water supply is often proposed.

One such proposal is the New High Tongue Dam which would have a total storage capacity of 320,000 acre-feet. More recently, a second stage, which would have a 450,000-acre-foot capacity (see chapter 4), has been suggested. The stage I capacity reservoir would lie totally within Montana, but the larger reservoir could increase capacity significantly at a reportedly modest increment in cost. Since the reservations granted by the Board of Natural Resources and Conservation in December 1978 determinations presuppose a storage facility of the larger capacity, we begin by reviewing the water that may be available in the Tongue River subbasin based on the assumption that a reservoir with 450,000 acre-feet of storage capacity will be built.

Table 9-1 displays a range of possible outcomes. Cases 1 through 5 are those in which only the energy development demands for water are considered. While this is not a realistic variant owing to existing rights for other purposes, it is useful to note that all of the various different levels of coal development—ranging from 100 million tons mined for export by rail only (RFF scenario III) through conversion of 30 million tons at site with the remainder (approximately 70 million tons per year) exported by either rail or slurry pipeline (RFF scenario IV)—could be accommodated with excess water in storage under the most adverse flows of record. Alternatively, the RFF scenario for high-level conversion could be accommodated with a residual corresponding to the Department of Energy (DOE) and Department of Interior (DOI) target production of approximately 339 million tons per year by 1990 (see table 5-8) exported for use outside the region.

Similarly, if we abstract from all uses other than irrigation (case 6), we see that both existing irrigation rights and irrigation reservations could be accommodated with substantial storage available for other purposes. This is true also for instream flows considered alone (case 7) or Indian (Northern Cheyenne) reserved water rights alone, estimated by the restrictive criterion, whether using water efficient systems of irrigation (case 8) or the less efficient method using 6 acre-feet of water per acre (case 15). It is only under one interpretation of the expansive criterion (suggested by the Department of the Interior—case 25) that all of the dependable yield would still be insufficient for the single claimant.[1]

---

[1] Another interpretation under the expansive criterion might be to estimate the Northern Cheyenne reserved right claims using irrigation as before but including instream use equivalent to the BNRC-granted instream reservation. If that were the case, about 258,000 acre-feet would remain in storage under hydrologic conditions corresponding to the most adverse of record if an efficient irrigation diversion rate were assumed, whereas about 185,000 acre-feet would remain if a less water-efficient rate were assumed.

It is also worth noting that viewing each of the three uses in isolation reveals the different effects on water quality of the different uses. Using the half-ton per acre salt pick-up estimate (see U.S. Department of the Interior, Bureau of Reclamation,

But since there are existing water rights allocated to irrigation and BNRC-determined instream flow reservations, along with the need to accommodate the reserved rights of the Northern Cheyenne Indian Tribe and Wyoming's interstate water claims, the more interesting cases involve what would be likely to occur if all demands were attempted to be met in some proportion simultaneously. One can see from case 9 that it would be possible to meet (1) the Northern Cheyenne reserved water rights estimated according to the restrictive criterion, (2) the existing state irrigation rights, (3) the irrigation reservations, and (4) the instream flow reservations granted by the BNRC (even assuming releases out of storage for the latter purpose) with a minimum of something over 100,000 acre-feet of month-end water in storage for conditions corresponding to the period of lowest flow of record. How much of our postulated energy development could be undertaken, then, with the residual stored water? Cases 10 through 14 provide the information for answering some aspects of this question.[2] Given all the legal claims described, it is apparent from cases 10 and 14 that a coal extraction rate of up to 339 million tons per year for export by rail only could be met with the water available as indicated by our simulator. But while up to 100 million tons of coal conceivably might be considered exportable by means of slurry (with a risk of a 19-month interruption under conditions no more severe than the most severe of record), none of the postulated coal conversion activities could be accommodated. Moreover, if the Northern Cheyenne reserved right claims corresponding to the restrictive criterion employing a less efficient irrigation system on a 10,000-acre base were considered in combination with other existing rights and water reservations granted by the BNRC (cases 17–21), only the RFF scenario III (100 million tons of coal production for export by rail only) and possibly the DOE/DOI extraction and export by rail could be accommodated. In short, reservoir shortfalls would be prevalent over so much of the period for any additional (conversion) energy activity that conversion activities would be infeasible. Indeed, in pending litigation if it were determined that the reserved right claims of the Northern Cheyenne Indian Tribe were to be adjudicated on a 50,000-acre base, even the other nonenergy claims could not simultaneously be accommodated (cases 23–24).

---

unpublished working documents for the ongoing Water Management Study, Missouri River Above Gavins Point [1976]), we can observe the increase in total dissolved solids associated with each of the independent irrigation simulations.

[2] One can also observe the effects of energy development options on the TDS values.

Table 9-1. Stored water available assuming prior legal claims and the BNRC-granted water reservations in the Tongue River subbasin with the High Tongue Reservoir (stage II) 450,000 acre-feet

| | Potentially realizable Northern Cheyenne Indian Tribe claims on Tongue River water (acre-feet/yr) | | | Existing state irrigation rights (acre-feet/yr) | BNRC-granted state reservations | | Residual stored water available for other claims (acre-feet) |
| | Restrictive criterion (irrigation only) | | Expansive criterion (DOI) | | | | |
Case	at the rate of 3 af/acre	at the rate of 6 af/acre	Expansive criterion (DOI)	Existing state irrigation rights (acre-feet/yr)	Irrigation (——— acre-feet/yr ———)	Instream flow	Residual stored water available for other claims (acre-feet)
1	—	—	—	—	—	—	—
2	—	—	—	—	—	—	—
3	—	—	—	—	—	—	—
4	—	—	—	—	—	—	—
5	—	—	–	—	—	—	—
6	—	—	—	42,000	20,896 (for 8,805 acres)	—	271,327
7	—	—	—	—	—	54,289	315,605 (9/61)
8	30,000 (for 10,000 acres)	—	—	—	—	—	331,738 (9/61)
9	30,000 (for 10,000 acres)	—	—	42,000	20,896 (for 8,805 acres)	54,289	106,026 (9/61)
10	30,000 (for 10,000 acres)	—	—	42,000	20,896 (for 8,805 acres)	54,289	106,026 (9/61)
11	30,000 (for 10,000 acres)	—	—	42,000	20,896 (for 8,805 acres)	54,289	106,026 (9/61)
12	30,000 (for 10,000 acres)	—	—	42,000	20,896 (for 8,805 acres)	54,289	106,026 (9/61)

Lowest month-end acre-feet of water in storage after meeting potential demands of energy developments on Tongue River water required for:					Water quality TDS concentration ≥1,000 ppm (90th percentile value)[f]
RFF scenario III (coal for export)		RFF scenario IV conversion with export of residual		DOE/DOI 1990 level for export by rail[e]	
By rail[a]	By slurry[b]	By rail[c]	By slurry[d]		
380,866 (9/61)	—	—	—	—	None
—	324,045 (9/61)	—	—	—	None
—	—	294,435 (9/61)	—	—	None
—	—	—	234,720 (1/62)	—	None
—	—	—	—	365,043 (9/61)	None
—	—	—	—	—	1,634 (Aug.–Sept.)
—	—	—	—	—	None
—	—	—	—	—	1,563 (August)
—	—	—	—	—	None
96,075 (9/61)	—	—	—	—	None
—	Reservoir shortfall for 19 months (7/61–5/62, 8/62–3/63)	—	—	—	None
—	—	Reservoir shortfall for 34 months (8/60–5/63)	—	—	None

(continued)

Table 9-1 (continued)

| | Potentially realizable Northern Cheyenne Indian Tribe claims on Tongue River water (acre-feet/yr) | | | Existing state irrigation rights (acre-feet/yr) | BNRC-granted state reservations | | Residual stored water available for other claims (acre-feet) |
| | Restrictive criterion (irrigation only) | | Expansive criterion (DOI) | | | | |
Case	at the rate of 3 af/acre	at the rate of 6 af/acre			Irrigation (———	Instream flow acre-feet/yr ———)	
13	30,000 (for 10,000 acres)	—	—	42,000	20,896 (for 8,805 acres)	54,289	106,026 (9/61)
14	30,000 (for 10,000 acres)	—	—	42,000	20,896 (for 8,805 acres)	54,289	106,026 (9/61)
15	—	60,000 (for 10,000 acres)	—	—	—	—	276,647 (9/61)
16	—	60,000 (for 10,000 acres)	—	42,000	20,896 (for 8,805 acres)	54,289	Reservoir shortfall of 4,768 (9/61 only)
17	—	60,000 (for 10,000 acres)	—	42,000	20,896 (for 8,805 acres)	54,289	Reservoir shortfall of 4,768 (9/61 only)
18	—	60,000 (for 10,000 acres)	—	42,000	20,896 (for 8,805 acres)	54,289	Reservoir shortfall of 4,768 (9/61 only)
19	—	60,000 (for 10,000 acres)	—	42,000	20,896 (for 8,805 acres)	54,289	Reservoir shortfall of 4,768 (9/61 only)
20	—	60,000 (for 10,000 acres)	—	42,000	20,896 (for 8,805 acres)	54,289	Reservoir shortfall of 4,768 (9/61 only)
21	—	60,000 (for 10,000 acres)	—	42,000	20,896 (for 8,805 acres)	54,289	Reservoir shortfall of 4,768 (9/61 only)

Lowest month-end acre-feet of water in storage after meeting potential demands of energy developments on Tongue River water required for:					Water quality TDS concentration $\geq 1,000$ ppm (90th percentile value)[f]
RFF scenario III (coal for export)		RFF scenario IV conversion with export of residual		DOE/DOI 1990 level for export by rail[e]	
By rail[a]	By slurry[b]	By rail[c]	By slurry[d]		
—	—	—	Reservoir short-fall for much of the simulation period	—	—
—	—	—	—	73,001 (9/61)	None
—	—	—	—	—	None
—	—	—	—	—	None
Reservoir short-fall for 8 months (8/61–3/62)	—	—	—	—	None
—	Reservoir short-fall for 45 months (7/60–5/63, 8/63–5/64)	—	—	—	—
—	—	Reservoir short-fall for much of the simulation period	—	—	—
—	—	—	Reservoir short-fall for almost the entire simulation period	—	—
—	—	—	—	Reservoir short-fall for 17 months (7/61–5/62, 8/62–1/63)	None

(continued)

Table 9-1 (continued)

	Potentially realizable Northern Cheyenne Indian Tribe claims on Tongue River water (acre-feet/yr)			Existing state irrigation rights (acre-feet/yr)	BNRC-granted state reservations		Residual stored water available for other claims (acre-feet)
	Restrictive criterion (irrigation only)		Expansive criterion (DOI)			Instream flow	
Case	at the rate of 3 af/acre	at the rate of 6 af/acre			Irrigation (	acre-feet/yr)	
22	150,000 (for 50,000 acres)	—	—	—	—	—	77,937 (9/61)
23	150,000 (for 50,000 acres)	—	—	42,000	20,896 (for 8,805 acres)	54,289	Reservoir shortfall for 175 months (7/54–3/69)
24	—	300,000 (for 50,000 acres)	—	—	—	—	Reservoir shortfall for 240 months (8/53 to end of study period)
25	—	—	109,200 (irrigation) 196,920 (other incl. energy)	—	—	—	Reservoir shortfall for 239 months (9/53 to end of study period)

Notes: All data on stored water available are net of the water due Wyoming under the interstate Yellowstone River Compact. Dashes = not applicable. DOE = U.S. Department of Energy. DOI = U.S. Department of the Interior. TDS = total dissolved solids. ppm = parts per million. It is assumed that appropriate releases from storage are made to maintain the instream flow.

a Requires 5,100 acre-feet per year for 100 million tons per year.

b Requires 47,940 acre-feet per year for 100 millon tons per year.

To help readers view the results given in table 9-1 and the other tables in this chapter from an appropriate perspective, the principal working assumptions underlying the simulation results are specified below.

a. The 1985 coal development levels (RFF scenarios II–IV) postulated in chapter 5 are assumed to be attained by the beginning of the simulation period

b. The proposed reservoirs are assumed to be full at the beginning of the simulation period

c. One thirty-year trace of monthly inflows containing the most ad-

Lowest month-end acre-feet of water in storage after meeting potential demands of energy developments on Tongue River water required for:					Water quality TDS concentration $\geq 1,000$ ppm (90th percentile value)[f]
RFF scenario III (coal for export)		RFF scenario IV conversion with export of residual		DOE/DOI 1990 level for export by rail[e]	
By rail[a]	By slurry[b]	By rail[e]	By slurry[d]		
—	—	—	—	—	1,286 (July) 1,346 (Aug.–Nov.)
—	—	—	—	—	—
—	—	—	—	—	—
—	—	—	—	—	—

e Requires a combination of process water, along with water for mining, of 70,704 acre-feet per year assuming export of the difference (approximately 70 million tons) by rail.

d Requires a combination of process water, along with water for mining, of 100,944 acre-feet per year assuming export of the difference (approximately 70 million tons) by slurry.

e 16,935 acre-feet per year required for mining of 339 million tons and export by rail only.

f The TDS calculations cannot be meaningful estimates for reservoir shortfalls of long duration and therefore are excluded under such circumstances.

verse annual flow of record corresponding to each of the nine subbasins gives results good to a first approximation

d. Inflows to the state reflect Wyoming's share of Yellowstone compact water likely to be depleted during the simulation period[3]

[3] In chapter 4, Wyoming's share of the surplus flow likely to be used was estimated to be 7,500 af per month, and this withdrawal rate is assumed to be associated with a 3,000-af-per-month depletion. If the monthly flow to Montana is greater than 7,500 af per month, then the inflow is depleted by 3,000 af per month. If not, then the flow is depleted by 40 percent of the inflow reflecting Wyoming's percentage allocation under the terms of the Yellowstone River Compact.

e. The reservoir operating criteria release stored water first to meet all legal obligations, that is, Indian reserved water rights, existing basin rights (in those cases where they are not arbitrarily displaced for alternative assessment purposes), and then the municipal, irrigation, and instream flow reservations[4]

f. The complexion of the state, interstate, and Indian legal claims on flows remains invariant throughout the simulation period

g. In simulating water quality changes, irrigation withdrawals and associated total dissolved solids (TDS) loads are made according to the monthly distributions for irrigation diversions specified by subbasin (table 6-6). The diverted load is assumed to return to the stream with an additional ½ ton salt pickup per irrigated acre before the beginning of the next irrigation season. No return flows are associated with energy withdrawals of water.

While these assumptions are reflected in our simulation runs, the model, as can be observed, is flexible enough to accommodate alternative reservoir operating criteria: (1) changes in the disposition of legal claims, (2) different storage capacities and alternative reservoir operating criteria, and (3) related modifications appropriate to various times and circumstances.

For example, in table 9-1 it is assumed that water will be released from storage in order to maintain the instream reservations. Since instream flow reservations are accorded a lower priority than Indian reserved water rights, existing irrigation rights, and even irrigation reservations in some subbasins such as the Tongue, it is not likely water would always be released from storage to support minimum instream flows.[5] Were that

[4] Priority of rights in Montana involves the Indian reserved water rights, existing state water rights, and state water reservations for irrigation and inchannel uses (excluding municipal allocations in the Tongue). Among the state water reservations, irrigation reservations have priority over instream reservations, and municipal reservations take precedence over both in subbasins 4 through 9. In the upstream subbasins, instream reservations have priority over irrigation reservations.

[5] The reservoir operating criterion can be altered to reflect changing circumstances. In the original fish and game reservation application, the commission requested that there be no flow augmentation for any shortfalls that may occur. If it is assumed that irrigation has priority over instream use, the operating criterion would reflect this scheme for a given monthly inflow, for example, 1,500 af, in the following way:

a. if the sum of the state water reservations is greater than the monthly inflow of 1,500 af, for example,

irrigation reservation	800 af/mo
fish and game reservation	900 af/mo
	1,700 af/mo

to be the case, the residual stored water available for other claims would be greater than that shown for case 9 (table 9-1) and cases 10 through 14 (where the instream flow reservations granted by the BNRC are reflected). The shortfall of a modest 4,768 acre-feet in one month (case 16) would not occur at all. This is shown in table 9-2 (in case 6) where there is a stored water residual of about 96,000 acre-feet under conditions corresponding to the most adverse of record after accommodating a liberal irrigation diversion rate based on the restrictive criterion for estimating Indian reserved right claims, along with existing state irrigation rights, the irrigation reservations, and the instream flow reservation (which is not augmented by releases from storage except during surplus flow months). Indeed, the above claims could be served along with coal extraction corresponding to RFF's scenario III postulating 100 million tons of coal mined for export only by rail (case 7) or even the larger DOE/DOI high projections of coal extraction for the year 1990 if mined for export only using rail transportation (case 9). Note, however, that this is an illustrative example only since the instream flow reservation is, in essence, a water right with a December 1978 priority and would precede any later applications for coal development.

It is interesting to check whether all of the state reservation *requests* could have been accommodated with storage of 450,000-acre-foot capacity. Table 9-3 shows that the reservations, even without regard to the Indian reserved water rights cannot be attempted without reservoir shortfalls (case 1). This is true even when it is assumed no water is released from storage to maintain instream flows. If releases are made from storage to maintain the instream flow reservation, there would be a reservoir shortfall for the bulk of the entire simulation period. If, on the other hand, the Indian reserved water rights (estimated by the restrictive criterion with an

---

then, because the 1,500-af/mo inflow is less than the total required 1,700 af/mo, the irrigation reservation is met first because it has a higher priority, and the remaining flow is passed through but there is no augmentation for the 200-af/mo shortfall in the fish and game instream flow reservation

b. if the sum of the state water reservations is less than the monthly inflow of 1,500 af,

irrigation reservation	800 af/mo
fish and game reservation	500 af/mo
	1,300 af/mo

then, since the inflow is greater than the sum of the reservations, the excess, 200 af/mo, is stored in the reservoir assuming storage space is available.

Since the BNRC issued its final order on the water reservations, the instream reservation is treated as a minimum flow that must be met, and therefore the reservoir operation reflects flow augmentation for instream uses when needed.

Table 9-2. Stored water available assuming prior legal claims and BNRC-granted water reservations without instream flow augmentation in the Tongue River subbasin with the High Tongue Reservoir (stage II) 450,000 acre-feet

| | Potentially realizable Northern Cheyenne Indian Tribe claims on Tongue River water (acre-feet/yr) | | | Existing state irrigation rights (acre-feet/yr) | BNRC-granted state reservations | | Residual stored water available for other claims (acre-feet) |
| | Restrictive criterion (irrigation only) | | Expansive criterion (DOI) | | | | |
Case	at the rate of 3 af/acre	at the rate of 6 af/acre			Irrigation (———acre-feet/yr———)	Instream flow	
1	30,000 (for 10,000 acres)	—	—	42,000	20,896	54,289	165,785 (9/61)
2	30,000 (for 10,000 acres)	—	—	42,000	20,896	54,289	165,785 (9/61)
3	30,000 (for 10,000 acres)	—	—	42,000	20,896	54,289	165,785 (9/61)
4	30,000 (for 10,000 acres)	—	—	42,000	20,896	54,289	165,785 (9/61)
5	30,000 (for 10,000 acres)	—	—	42,000	20,896	54,289	165,785 (9/61)
6	—	60,000 (for 10,000 acres)	—	42,000	20,896	54,289	96,055 (9/61)
7	—	60,000 (for 10,000 acres)	—	42,000	20,896	54,289	96,055 (9/61)
8	—	60,000 (for 10,000 acres)	—	42,000	20,896	54,289	96,055 (9/61)
9	—	60,000 (for 10,000 acres)	—	42,000	20,896	54,289	96,055 (9/61)
10	—	—	109,200 (irrigation), 196,920 (other)	42,000 42,000	20,896 20,896	54,289 54,289	Reservoir shortfall over most of the simulation period

Notes: All data on stored water available are net of the water due Wyoming under the interstate Yellowstone River Basin Compact. Dashes = not applicable. DOE = U.S. Department of Energy. DOI = U.S. Department of the Interior. TDS = total dissolved solids. ppm = parts per million. It is assumed that appropriate releases from storage are made to maintain the instream flow reservation.

ᵃ Requires 5,100 acre-feet per year for 100 million tons per year.

ᵇ Requires 47,940 acre-feet per year for 100 million tons per year.

Lowest month-end acre-feet of water in storage after meeting potential demands of energy developments on Tongue River water required for:					Water quality TDS concentration $\geq 1,000$ ppm (90th percentile value)[f]
RFF scenario III (coal for export)		RFF scenario IV conversion with export of residual		DOE/DOI 1990 level for export by rail[e]	
By rail[a]	By slurry[b]	By rail[e]	By slurry[d]		
—	—	—	—	—	1,493 (August)
156,545 (9/61)	—	—	—	—	1,491 (August)
—	44,593 (9/61)	—	—	—	1,477 (August)
—	—	Reservoir short-fall for 11 months (7/61–5/62)	—	—	1,465 (August)
—	—	—	—	136,783 (9/61)	1,492 (August)
—	—	—	—	—	1,072 (August)
81,970 (9/61)	—	—	—	—	1,070 (August)
—	Reservoir short-fall for 20 months (6/61–5/62, 8/62–3/63)	—	—	—	1,057 (August)
—	—	—	—	22,773 (9/61)	1,066 (August)
—	—	—	—	—	—

[e] Requires a combination of process water, along with water for mining, of 70,704 acre-feet per year assuming export of the difference (approximately 70 million tons) by rail.

[d] Requires a combination of process water, along with water for mining, of 100,944 acre-feet per year assuming export of the difference (approximately 70 million tons) by slurry.

[e] Requires 16,935 acre-feet per year for mining of 339 million tons and export by rail only.

[f] The TDS calculations cannot be meaningful estimates for reservoir shortfalls of long duration and therefore are excluded under such circumstances.

efficient irrigation system) were considered along with existing water rights and the state reservation requests for irrigation and instream flows (excluding industrial reservations), the reservoir shortfall would occur in forty-six months distributed over three different periods as shown in case 2 in table 9-3.

Another plausible variation of the reservations might have involved the Department of Natural Resources and Conservation's (DNRC's) recommended levels of reservations following study of the state reservation requests. This is not presented to imply that there is some special merit to the DNRC recommendations which escaped the BNRC's attention, but only to identify another plausible set of allocations, taking into account the department's considered views.

In table 9-4 we review the tradeoffs assuming we need not repeat the exercise of considering any single use independently, having done so previously in connection with our discussion of table 9-1. Inspection of the tradeoffs is left to the interested reader, but a few cases merit observation. Cases 6 through 10 may be compared with cases 11 through 14. Here the effective difference is the postulated efficiency of the irrigation system on the 10,000 acres of irrigation agriculture taken as a plausible working assumption in connection with adjudication of the Northern Cheyenne reserved water right claims employing the restrictive criterion. After meeting (1) the allotment for irrigating 10,000 acres on the Northern Cheyenne Indian Reservation, (2) honoring existing state irrigation rights (3) reserving 28,750 acre-feet for industrial purposes, and (4) reserving 29,250 acre-feet for expansion of future irrigation agriculture (the DNRC did not recommend instream flow reservations), the difference in residual stored water (case 6 compared with case 11) is roughly cut in half by use of a technically efficient as compared with a "current practices" irrigation system. If we wish to postulate various energy development scenarios for the nondescript "industrial reservation" specified in the DNRC recommendations, we can do so. Thus, comparing cases 7 and 8 with cases 12 and 13, we can see what tradeoff in terms of potential energy development would be precluded by adoption of a technically less efficient irrigation system on the Northern Cheyenne Indian Reservation.

Another significant implication of the difference between the DNRC recommendations and the BNRC rulings shows up in a comparison of the water quality columns of tables 9-1 and 9-4. Absence of instream flow in the DNRC recommendations would provide less flow for dilution purposes, hence increasing the concentration of dissolved solids. Indeed,

Table 9-3. Stored water available assuming prior legal claims and state requests for water reservations in the Tongue River subbasin with the High Tongue Reservoir (stage II) 450,000 acre-feet

Case	Potentially realizable Northern Cheyenne Indian Tribe claims on the Tongue River water (acre-feet/yr)			State water reservation requests[a]				
	Restrictive criterion (irrigation only)		Expansive criterion (DOI)	Existing state irrigation rights (acre-feet/yr)	Industrial	Irrigation	Instream flow (without augmentation)	Residual stored water available for other claims
	at the rate of 3 af/acre	at the rate of 6 af/acre			(——————————— acre-feet/yr ———————————)			
1	—	—	—	42,000	28,750	29,250	243,127	Reservoir shortfall for 19 months
2	30,000 (for 10,000 acres)	—	—	42,000	—	29,250	243,127	Reservoir shortfall for 46 months (10/58–2/59, 10/59–2/60, 5/60–5/63)

Notes: The simulations are net of the flow likely to be depleted in Wyoming under the Yellowstone River Compact. Dashes = not applicable. DOI = U.S. Department of the Interior.
[a] In the "with augmentation" simulation of instream flows (that is, when the instream flows are considered as minimum flows that must be met each month), there is a reservoir shortfall for most of the simulation period even without including the minimally estimated Northern Cheyenne reserved water right claims (30,000 af/yr).

207

Table 9-4. Stored water available assuming prior legal claims and the DNRC reservation recommendations in the Tongue River subbasin with the High Tongue Reservoir (stage II) 450,000 acre-feet

	Potentially realizable Northern Cheyenne Indian Tribe claims on Tongue River water (acre-feet/yr)			Existing state irrigation rights (acre-feet/yr)	DNRC recommendations for state reservations		
	Restrictive criterion (irrigation only)		Expansive criterion (DOI)				
Case	at the rate of 3 af/acre	at the rate of 6 af/acre			Industrial (⸻	Irrigation ⸻acre-feet/yr⸻	Instream flow ⸻)
1	—	—	—	42,000	28,750	29,250	0.0
2	—	—	—	42,000	—	29,250	0.0
3	—	—	—	42,000	—	29,250	0.0
4	—	—	—	42,000	—	29,250	0.0
5	—	—	—	42,000	—	29,250	0.0
6	30,000 (for 10,000 acres)	—	—	42,000	28,750	29,250	0.0
7	30,000 (for 10,000 acres)	—	—	42,000	—	29,250	0.0
8	30,000 (for 10,000 acres)	—	—	42,000	—	29,250	0.0
9	30,000 (for 10,000 acres)	—	—	42,000	—	29,250	0.0

Residual stored water available for other claims (acre-feet)	Lowest month-end acre-feet of water in storage after meeting potential demands of energy developments on Tongue River water required for:					Water quality TDS concentration ≥1,000 ppm (90th percentile value)[f]
	RFF scenario III (coal for export)		RFF scenario IV conversion with export of residual		DOE/DOI 1990 level for export by rail[e]	
	By rail[a]	By slurry[b]	By rail[c]	By slurry[d]		
209,400 (9/61)	—	—	—	—	—	1,831 (August), 1,814 (Sept.–Oct.)
209,400 (9/61)	—	170,638 (9/61)	—	—	—	1,803 (August), 1,795 (Sept.–Oct.)
209,400 (9/61)	—	—	125,231 (9/61)	—	—	1,781 (Aug.–Sept.), 1,775 (Oct.–Nov.)
209,400 (9/61)	—	—	—	41,473 (9/61)	—	1,777 (Aug.–Sept.), 1,754 (Nov.–Dec.)
209,400 (9/61)	—	—	—	—	233,247 (9/61)	1,827 (Aug.–Oct.)
136,921 (9/61)	—	—	—	—	—	1,619 (Aug.–Oct.), 1,591 (November)
136,921 (9/61)	—	98,954 (9/61)	—	—	—	1,614 (Aug.–Oct.), 1,572 (Nov.–Dec.)
136,912 (9/61)	—	—	32,005 (9/61)	—	—	1,613 (Aug.–Nov.), 1,551 (Dec.–Jan.)
136,921 (9/61)	—	—	—	Reservoir shortfall for 23 months (4/61–5/62, 7/62–4/63)	—	1,599 (Aug.–Jan.)

(*continued*)

Table 9-4 (continued)

Case	Potentially realizable Northern Cheyenne Indian Tribe claims on Tongue River water (acre-feet/yr)			Existing state irrigation rights (acre-feet/yr)	DNRC recommendations for state reservations		
	Restrictive criterion (irrigation only)		Expansive criterion (DOI)		Industrial	Irrigation	Instream flow
	at the rate of 3 af/acre	at the rate of 6 af/acre			(	acre-feet/yr	)
10	30,000 (for 10,000 acres)	—	—	42,000	—	29,250	0.0
11	—	60,000 (for 10,000 acres)	—	42,000	28,750	29,250	0.0
12	—	60,000 (for 10,000 acres)	—	42,000	—	29,250	0.0
13	—	60,000 (for 10,000 acres)	—	42,000	—	29,250	0.0
14	—	60,000 (for 10,000 acres)	—	42,000	—	29,250	0.0
15	—	—	109,200 (irrigation), 194,200 (industrial)	42,000	—	29,250	0.0

Notes: All data on stored water available are net of the water due Wyoming under the interstate Yellowstone River Basin Compact. Dashes = not applicable. DOE = U.S. Department of Energy. DOI = U.S. Department of the Interior. TDS = total dissolved solids. ppm = parts per million.

a Requires 5,100 acre-feet per year for 100 million tons per year.

b Requires 47,940 acre-feet per year for 100 million tons per year.

c Requires a combination of process water, along with water for mining, of 70,704 acre-feet per year assuming export of the difference (approximately 70 million tons) by rail.

Residual stored water available for other claims (acre-feet)	Lowest month-end acre-feet of water in storage after meeting potential demands of energy developments on Tongue River water required for:					Water quality TDS concentration $\geq 1,000$ ppm (90th percentile value)[f]
	RFF scenario III (coal for export)		RFF scenario IV conversion with export of residual		DOE/DOI 1990 level for export by rail[e]	
	By rail[a]	By slurry[b]	By rail[c]	By slurry[d]		
136,921 (9/61)	—	—	—	—	160,680 (9/61)	1,628 (Aug.–Oct.), 1,603 (November)
65,829 (9/61)	—	—	—	—	—	1,117 (Aug.–Nov.), 1,094 (December)
65,829 (9/61)	—	Reservoir shortfall for 6 months (8/61–1/62)	—	—	—	1,069 (July), 1,111 (Aug.–Nov.), 1,108 (Dec.–Jan.)
65,829 (9/61)	—	—	Reservoir shortfall for 19 months (1/61–5/62), 8/62–3/63)	—	—	1,104 (Aug.–Jan.)
65,829 (9/61)	—	—	—	—	89,022 (9/61)	1,121 (Aug.–Oct.), 1,084 (Nov.–Dec.)
Reservoir shortfall over much of the simulation period	—	—	—	—	—	—

d Requires a combination of process water, along with water for mining, of 100,944 acre-feet per year assuming export of the difference (approximately 70 million tons) by slurry.

e Requires 16,935 acre-feet per year for mining of 339 million tons and export by rail only.

f The TDS calculations cannot be meaningful estimates for reservoir shortfalls of long duration and therefore are excluded under such circumstances.

there is a question of whether the increase in salinity associated with simulating the DNRC-recommended water allocations would prevent the productive application of allotted water.

We have presumed that the incremental construction costs of storage, comparing the proposed stage I (320,000 acre-feet) and stage II (450,000 acre-feet) reservoirs, would merit the larger capacity reservoir (for which the BNRC granted the DNRC a water reservation). There could be some questions concerning the larger project since it would inundate land across the state line in Wyoming, with the associated transactions cost this factor may impose, or, conceivably, there could be differentially larger environmental costs not reckoned in construction costs. Since we do not know whether or not this would turn out to be the case, it is useful to consider the performance characteristics of the smaller stage I reservoir in the event that it should. There are two aspects that might be considered: one, the performance characteristics of stage I as an independent alternative; and two, the comparative performance of the two differently scaled facilities, to the extent permitted by our model. The actual evaluation of transactions costs and the conceivable difference in environmental costs (or various other third party costs not reckoned in the construction cost estimates) fall outside the scope of our analysis. However, the data generated by us in the process are not elsewhere available. Such data should be useful to anyone responsible for making a decision that may require more complete environmental and economic analyses. Accordingly, we present in table 9-5 the results of the simulation study involving the 320,000-acre-foot reservoir net of Wyoming's share of compact water likely to be depleted over the simulation period.

The smaller stage I reservoir would provide for existing state irrigation rights and for the BNRC's 1978 determination of water reservations for irrigation and instream use (excluding consideration of Indian reserved water rights), with some 66,000 acre-feet of residual storage available for other purposes (case 1). Alternatively, it could accommodate all of the existing state irrigation and state reservations for irrigation and instream flows and, in addition, the irrigation of 10,000 acres of Northern Cheyenne tribal lands (assumed for the restrictive criterion in determining Indian reserved water rights along with use of the technically water-efficient irrigation system hereafter referred to as the restrictive/efficient case) leaving a modest residual in storage under the hydrologic conditions comparable to the most adverse of record (case 6). Indeed it would be possible to do the above with the irrigation of 10,000 acres of Northern

Cheyenne Reservation lands with the less water-efficient irrigation practices except for one nine-month period under the most adverse hydrologic conditions experienced during the thirty-year historical record (case 11). It would not be possible, however, to meet the Indian reserved water rights under the expansive criterion (case 12). Looking beyond the Indian reserved water rights, the existing irrigation rights, and the irrigation and instream flow reservations, it seems possible to accommodate only the RFF scenario III (100 million tons of coal mined for export by rail only) with the smaller reservoir (case 7). Even this case would involve a brief shortfall during one month under conditions similar to those experienced under the most adverse hydrologic conditions of record.

If we consider, for illustrative purposes, the alternative of not augmenting instream flows except when there is water surplus to higher priority uses, we get a somewhat different pattern of results as illustrated in table 9-6. By operating the reservoir to reflect this assumed adjustment in instream flows, some additional "beneficial consumptive" uses would be possible, but the extent would be limited. Basically, the RFF scenario III with coal extraction for export only and use of a slurry pipeline would be possible, but it is difficult to imagine that such an option would be exercised under the scarce water conditions. The RFF scenario IV, involving the conversion of 30 million tons of coal annually with the remainder to be exported by rail, in addition to all of the other uses, might be considered. That is, there would be seventeen months of shortfall over a thirty-year hydrologic trace experienced in two periods, one of a twelve-month and the other of a five-month duration assuming a repeating hydrologic pattern (case 10). Not all of the purposes could be served simultaneously, however, throughout. Indeed there is no case in which all of the prior non-energy claims could be met along with the conversion of coal postulated in RFF scenario IV. However, all could be met (assuming the Indian restrictive/efficient case) with the high projection of coal extraction postulated by DOE/DOI for 1990 if the coal were exported from the basin by rail (case 11). But again, this is assuming that releases would not be made to augment the instream flow reservation except during times of surplus flow. Recall that the instream flow reservation has a 1978 priority date and would likely precede any application for surface water withdrawal for coal extraction.

How does the stage I, 320,000-acre-foot-capacity, reservoir perform in comparison with the larger stage II reservoir? Tables 9-1 and 9-5 indicate the reduced storage capacity would result in the elimination of all energy

Table 9-5. Stored water available assuming prior legal claims and the BNRC-granted water reservations in the Tongue River subbasin with the High Tongue Reservoir (stage I) 320,000 acre-feet

| | Potentially realizable Northern Cheyenne Indian Tribe claims on Tongue River water (acre-feet/yr) | | | Existing state irrigation rights (acre-feet/yr) | BNRC-granted state reservations | | Residual stored water available for other claims (acre-feet) |
| | Restrictive criterion (irrigation only) | | | | | | |
Case	at the rate of 3 af/acre	at the rate of 6 af/acre	Expansive criterion (DOI)		Irrigation	Instream flow	
1	—	—	—	42,000	20,896 (for 8,805 acres)	54,289	66,183 (9/61)
2	—	—	—	42,000	20,896 (for 8,805 acres)	54,289	66,183 (9/61)
3	—	—	—	42,000	20,896 (for 8,805 acres)	54,289	66,183 (9/61)
4	—	—	—	42,000	20,896 (for 8,805 acres)	54,289	66,183 (9/61)
5	—	—	—	42,000	20,896 (for 8,805 acres)	54,289	66,183 (9/61)
6	30,000 (for 10,000 acres)	—	—	42,000	20,896 (for 8,805 acres)	54,289	6,402
7	30,000 (for 10,000 acres)	—	—	42,000	20,896 (for 8,805 acres)	54,289	6,402
8	30,000 (for 10,000 acres)	—	—	42,000	20,896 (for 8,805 acres)	54,289	6,402
9	30,000 (for 10,000 acres)	—	—	42,000	20,896 (for 8,805 acres)	54,289	6,402
10	30,000 (for 10,000 acres)	—	—	42,000	20,896 (for 8,805 acres)	54,289	6,402

Lowest month-end acre-feet of water in storage after meeting potential demands of energy developments on Tongue River water required for:					Water quality TDS concentration ≥ 1,000 ppm (90th percentile value)[f]
RFF scenario III (coal for export)		RFF scenario IV conversion with export of residual		DOE/DOI 1990 level for export by rail[e]	
By rail[a]	By slurry[b]	By rail[c]	By slurry[d]		
—	—	—	—	—	None
56,176 (9/61)	—	—	. —	—	None
—	Reservoir shortfall for 8 months (10/61–8/62)	—	—	—	None
—	—	Reservoir shortfall for 22 months (2/61–5/62, 9/62–2/63)	—	—	None
—	—	—	—	33,124 (9/61)	None
—	—	—	—	—	None
Reservoir shortfall for 1 month (9/61)	—	—	—	—	None
—	Reservoir shortfall for 15 months (11/61–5/62, 8/62–4/63)	—	—	—	None
—	—	Reservoir shortfall for 43 months (7/60–5/63, 9/63–5/64)	—	—	None
—	—	—	—	Reservoir shortfall for 7 months (8/61–2/62)	None

(continued)

Table 9-5 (continued)

	Potentially realizable Northern Cheyenne Indian Tribe claims on Tongue River water (acre-feet/yr)			Existing state irrigation rights (acre-feet/yr)	BNRC-granted state reservations		Residual stored water available for other claims (acre-feet)
	Restrictive criterion (irrigation only)						
Case	at the rate of 3 af/acre	at the rate of 6 af/acre	Expansive criterion (DOI)		Irrigation (———acre-feet/yr———)	Instream flow	
11	—	60,000 (for 10,000 acres)	—	42,000	20,896 (for 8,805 acres)	54,289	Reservoir shortfall for 9 months (7/61–3/62)
12	—	—	109,200 (irrigation), 196,920 (other)	42,000	20,896 (for 8,805 acres)	54,289	Reservoir shortfall over most of simulation period

Notes: All data on stored water available are net of the water due Wyoming under the interstate Yellowstone River Basin Compact. Dashes = not applicable. DOE = U.S. Department of Energy. DOI = U.S. Department of the Interior. TDS = total dissolved solids. ppm = parts per million. It is assumed that appropriate releases from storage are made to maintain the instream flow reservation.

ª Requires 5,100 acre-feet per year for 100 million tons per year.

ᵇ Requires 47,940 acre-feet per year for 100 million tons per year.

development scenarios if Indian reserved water rights, the existing irrigation rights, and the irrigation and instream flow reservations were honored, except possibly for coal extraction for export by rail only (cases 7 and 10, table 9-5). Moreover, the capacity of the reservoir would scarcely permit the irrigation of 10,000 acres of Northern Cheyenne land if the technically less water-efficient irrigation system were employed. That is, meeting the Indian reserved water rights assuming 10,000 acres irrigated at a rate of 6 acre-feet per acre, along with the other irrigation and instream flow reservations, would result in a shortfall of 9 months within the thirty-year trace during the irrigation season (case 11, table 9-5). Moreover, it would not augur well for any coal development in the basin, but in this respect it does not differ so greatly from the situation for the larger reservoir (see cases 16 through 21, table 9-1) when the less technically efficient irrigation system is considered for the postulated 10,000 acres of Indian irrigation agriculture under the restrictive criterion. The situation in this respect would be exacerbated were the Indian reserved water right claims to be based on the expansive criterion.

Lowest month-end acre-feet of water in storage after meeting potential demands of energy developments on Tongue River water required for:					Water quality TDS concentration $\geq 1,000$ ppm (90th percentile value)[f]
RFF scenario III (coal for export)		RFF scenario IV conversion with export of residual		DOE/DOI 1990 level for export by rail[e]	
By rail[a]	By slurry[b]	By rail[c]	By slurry[d]		
—	—	—	—	—	None
—	—	—	—	—	—

[c] Requires a combination of process water, along with water for mining, of 70,704 acre-feet per year assuming export of the difference (approximately 70 million tons) by rail.

[d] Requires a combination of process water, along with water for mining, of 100,944 acre-feet per year assuming export of the difference (approximately 70 million tons) by slurry.

[e] Requires 16,935 acre-feet per year for mining of 339 million tons and export by rail only.

[f] The TDS calculations cannot be meaningful estimates for reservoir shortfalls of long duration and therefore are excluded under such circumstances.

Analysis of the Availability and Quality of Water in the Powder River Subbasin

The Tongue subbasin displays a richness of options to consider with its diverse economic development possibilities including both withdrawal and instream uses, alternative water storage volumes, and the array of potential federal and state legal constraints on the use of water. The Powder, on the other hand, is a somewhat simpler case because it does not involve any Indian claims for reserved water rights. There are, however, state water reservations granted for various uses. Moreover, the Yellowstone River Compact, which allocates interstate water rights on the Powder, affects the water available in Montana.[6] There are also two proposed reservoirs, the Moorhead and the Intake, similar to the situation in the Tongue subbasin.

[6] For the Powder subbasin, Wyoming's share under the Yellowstone Compact assumed likely to be depleted over the simulation period is estimated to be 42 percent of the inflow up to a maximum of 5,000 acre-feet per month.

Table 9-6. Stored water available assuming prior legal claims and the BNRC-granted water reservations without instream flow augmentation in the Tongue River subbasin with the High Tongue Reservoir (stage I) 320,000 acre-feet

| | Potentially realizable Northern Cheyenne Indian Tribe claims on Tongue River water (acre-feet/yr) | | | Existing state irrigation rights (acre-feet/yr) | BNRC-granted state reservations | | Residual stored water available for other claims (acre-feet) |
| | Restrictive criterion (irrigation only) | | Expansive criterion (DOI) | | | | |
Case	at the rate of 3 af/acre	at the rate of 6 af/acre			Irrigation (———acre-feet/yr	Instream flow ———)	
1	—	—	—	42,000	20,896 (for 8,805 acres)	54,289	124,003 (9/61)
2	—	—	—	42,000	20,896 (for 8,805 acres)	54,289	124,003 (9/61)
3	—	—	—	42,000	20,896 (for 8,805 acres)	54,289	124,003 (9/61)
4	—	—	—	42,000	20,896 (for 8,805 acres)	54,289	124,003 (9/61)
5	—	—	—	42,000	20,896 (for 8,805 acres)	54,289	124,003 (9/61)
6	—	—	—	42,000	20,896 (for 8,805 acres)	54,289	124,003 (9/61)
7	30,000 (for 10,000 acres)	—	—	42,000	20,896 (for 8,805 acres)	54,289	65,097 (9/61)
8	30,000 (for 10,000 acres)	—	—	42,000	20,896 (for 8,805 acres)	54,289	65,097 (9/61)
9	30,000 (for 10,000 acres)	—	—	42,000	20,896 (for 8,805 acres)	54,289	65,097 (9/61)
10	30,000 (for 10,000 acres)	—	—	42,000	20,896 (for 8,805 acres)	54,289	65,097 (9/61)

Lowest month-end acre-feet of water in storage after meeting potential demands of energy developments on Tongue River water required for:					Water quality TDS concentration $\geq 1,000$ ppm (90th percentile value)[f]
RFF scenario III (coal for export)		RFF scenario IV conversion with export of residual		DOE/DOI 1990 level for export by rail[e]	
By rail[a]	By slurry[b]	By rail[c]	By slurry[d]		
—	—	—	—	—	1,621 (August)
114,539 (9/61)	—	—	—	—	1,765 (July), 1,615 (August)
—	48,869 (9/61)	—	—	—	1,574 (August)
—	—	12,294 (9/61)	—	—	1,568 (August)
—	—	—	Reservoir short-fall for 24 months (11/61–5/62, 9/62–11/63)	—	1,539 (August)
—	—	—	—	94,393 (9/61)	1,602 (August)
—	—	—	—	—	1,492 (August)
56,248 (9/61)	—	—	—	—	1,488 (August)
—	Reservoir short-fall for 3 months (9/61–1/62)	—	—	—	1,471 (August)
—	—	Reservoir short-fall for 17 months (6/61–5/62, 9/62–1/63)	—	—	1,435 (August)

(continued)

Table 9-6 (continued)

	Potentially realizable Northern Cheyenne Indian Tribe claims on Tongue River water (acre-feet/yr)						
	Restrictive criterion (irrigation only)			Existing state irrigation	BNRC-granted state reservations		Residual stored water avail-
Case	at the rate of 3 af/acre	at the rate of 6 af/acre	Expansive criterion (DOI)	rights (acre-feet/yr)	Irrigation (———acre-feet/yr———)	Instream flow	able for other claims (acre-feet)
11	30,000 (for 10,000 acres)	—	—	42,000	20,896 (for 8,805 acres)	54,289	65,097 (9/61)
12	—	60,000 (for 10,000 acres)	—	42,000	20,896 (for 8,805 acres)	54,289	Reservoir short-fall for 1 month (9/61)
13	—	60,000 (for 10,000 acres)	—	42,000	20,896 (for 8,805 acres)	54,289	Reservoir short-fall for 1 month (9/61)
14	—	60,000 (for 10,000 acres)	—	42,000	20,896 (for 8,805 acres)	54,289	Reservoir short-fall for 1 month (9/61)
15	—	—	109,200 (irrigation), 196,950 (other)	42,000	20,896 (for 8,805 acres)	54,289	Reservoir short-fall over much of the simula-tion period

Notes: All data on stored water available are net of the water due Wyoming under the interstate Yellowstone River Basin Compact. Dashes = not applicable. DOE = U.S. Department of Energy. DOI = U.S. Department of the Interior. TDS = total dissolved solids. ppm = parts per million.

    [a] Requires 5,100 acre-feet per year for 100 million tons per year.

    [b] Requires 47,940 acre-feet per year for 100 million tons per year.

    [c] Requires a combination of process water, along with water for mining, of 70,704 acre-feet per year assuming export of the difference (approximately 70 million tons) by rail.

The predominant irrigation method used in the Powder subbasin is the spreading of water on the land during periods of high flows to bring up the soil moisture. Expanding irrigation agriculture appears to be limited by the lack of a dependable supply of water and by the heavy silt loads in July and August as well as the high naturally occurring total dissolved solids (TDS) concentrations.

In 1944, the Bureau of Reclamation first proposed the Moorhead Reservoir which has a total storage capacity of 1,150,000 acre-feet. Enthusiasm for it by the states of Montana and Wyoming, which would share the stored water in the Moorhead, has been high during periods of ex-

Lowest month-end acre-feet of water in storage after meeting potential demands of energy developments on Tongue River water required for:					Water quality TDS concentration $\geq 1,000$ ppm (90th percentile value)[f]
RFF scenario III (coal for export)		RFF scenario IV conversion with export of residual		DOE/DOI 1990 level for export by rail[e]	
By rail[a]	By slurry[b]	By rail[e]	By slurry[d]		
—	—	—	—	36,875 (9/61)	1,479 (August)
—	—	—	—	—	1,065 (August)
Reservoir shortfall for 4 months (9/61–1/62)	—	—	—	—	1,065 (August)
—	—	—	—	Reservoir shortfall for 7 months (8/61–2/62)	1,062 (August)
—	—	—	—	—	—

[d] Requires a combination of process water, along with water for mining, of 100,944 acre-feet per year assuming export of the difference (approximately 70 million tons) by slurry.

[e] Requires 16,935 acre-feet per year for mining of 339 million tons and export by rail only.

[f] The TDS calculations cannot be meaningful estimates for reservoir shortfalls of long durations and therefore are excluded under such circumstances.

treme high or low flows but low during periods of normal runoff. Farmers and ranchers have appeared to be interested in additional water for irrigation, but have been reluctant to support a federal reclamation project because of associated acreage limitations and long-term contractual commitments.

The Moorhead Reservoir is not considered to be an economic undertaking for the original purposes of irrigation, flood control, power, fish and wildlife, and recreation, but would be considered economically justified if a large part of the active storage could be marketed for industrial use rather than substantial downstream irrigation.

Operation of the reservoir would reduce the variability in flows but the heavy sediment load would accumulate in the reservoir.[7] In fact, the requirement for sediment deposition—estimated to be 625,000 acre-feet in seventy-seven years—means that a disproportionate share of the 1,150,000-acre-foot storage capacity must be reserved for that purpose. An additional 250,000 acre-feet are reserved for flood control, leaving only 275,000 acre-feet of active storage.[8] Besides the Bureau of Reclamation, Intake Water Company (a subsidiary of Tenneco Corporation) also filed an application to build a 564,000-acre-foot reservoir at the Moorhead site. Utah International has a more modest application for storage on the Powder River for 40,000 acre-feet.

Having noted the possible options for improved dependable water flows, the federally proposed Moorhead Reservoir and the privately proposed Intake Reservoir are singled out for analysis. Before discussing the performance of the reservoirs, we emphasize that the active storage used in all of the simulations presupposes use of some storage capacity that would not be available beyond a thirty-year period owing to the accumulation of sediment. But since at least the energy conversion facilities would not have an economic life exceeding thirty years, there is warrant for considering use of the storage for this purpose, recognizing that only a lesser amount of active storage capacity would be available over the longer life cycle of the reservoir.

In table 9-7 we show the outcomes involving water used for different purposes both singly and in different combinations for the proposed Moorhead Reservoir. Again we note that if we look at each use separately (cases 1 through 5 for energy, case 6 for irrigation, case 7 for instream flow maintenance using stored water for augmentation), any individual use can be accommodated with residual stored water available for other uses. Indeed if one looks at any one of the different combinations of uses, one observes that any combination we have postulated can be accom-

---

[7] The Powder River carries the highest average concentration of sediment of any of the major streams in the Yellowstone and Missouri river basins. The annual sediment load of the Powder River at the Moorhead Dam site is estimated at 8,500 acre-feet compared with average annual flows of about 322,000 acre-feet with 8,100 acre-feet of sediment being retained in the reservoir. See U.S. Department of the Interior, Bureau of Reclamation, *Reconnaissance Report on Moorhead Unit Montana-Wyoming* (October 1969) p. 8.

[8] Since some activities can be undertaken with facilities having a life cycle of less than thirty years, which would utilize the additional storage representing the difference between thirty and seventy-seven years of sedimentation, the active storage for the Moorhead Reservoir will be taken as 657,000 acre-feet in our simulation runs. See table 4-4.

modated simultaneously with any other, with month-end water remaining in storage under hydrologic conditions corresponding to the most adverse of record. Case 17 is the most demanding; the BNRC-granted irrigation and instream flow reservations are satisfied along with the RFF scenario IV (which postulates conversion of 30 million tons of coal per year) and the export of the remainder by *slurry pipeline.* There appears to be no case without going into higher levels of energy conversion where the reservoir would be emptied assuming hydrologic conditions no more severe than the most adverse of record. These results warrant a number of observations.

First, there are neither Indian reserved water right claims in the subbasin nor a record of existing irrigation rights. The former represent a straightforward situation, but the latter has some ambiguities. Currently, irrigation is by water spreading, which entails diverting water out of the stream in periods of spring freshets or heavy rainfalls to maximize the soil moisture for carrying over into the drier growing season. Because of this practice, it is expected that, of the estimated 11,000 water rights in this subbasin, about three-fourths are use rights (rights acquired by direct use for which there is no record). Related to this observation is the high dissolved solids concentration of the water, shown in the last column of table 9-7. The natural salinity of the Powder River is very high except during periods of high flows at which time dilution of the dissolved solids takes place. However, once impounded, and particularly if used for irrigation purposes where additional salts are leached from the soils and conveyed back to the stream in return flows, the total dissolved solids reach concentrations that are problematic. We defer discussion of the matter until later. Secondly, without storage, not even the state BNRC-granted reservations for irrigation and instream flows can be met. This is likely one reason the board granted a reservation only for water spreading and not full-service irrigation. Also, instream use which has a lower priority than irrigation, would be protected more by a practice of water spreading than by full-service irrigation since the latter method would contribute to diverting water in the critically low flow summer months.

Would our assessment of the availability of water for different purposes be greatly altered if the DNRC recommendations had been adopted by the BNRC in its ruling? Since the DNRC (see table 9-8) recommended both a lesser amount for irrigation and for instream flows for fish and wildlife habitat maintenance, a larger amount is available for other uses, but in either event the level of coal conversion already postulated is sufficiently high for any single subbasin to raise questions regarding the ability

Table 9-7. Stored water available assuming the BNRC-granted water reservations in the Powder River subbasin with the Moorhead Reservoir—657,000 acre-feet

	BNRC-granted state reservations			Residual stored water available for other claims (acre-feet)
Case	Irrigation (——————————————	Instream flow[a] ——acre-feet/yr——	Instream flow[b] ——————————)	
1	—	—	—	—
2	—	—	—	—
3	—	—	—	—
4	—	—	—	—
5	—	—	—	—
6	27,626 (for 18,643 acres)	—	—	568,739 (1/62)
7	—	—	95,201	483,063 (1/62)
8	27,626 (for 18,643 acres)	—	—	568,739 (1/62)
9	27,626 (for 18,643 acres)	—	—	568,739 (1/62)
10	27,626 (for 18,643 acres)	—	—	568,739 (1/62)
11	27,626 (for 18,643 acres)	—	—	568,739 (1/62)

Lowest month-end acre-feet of water in storage after meeting potential demands of energy developments on Powder River water required for:					Water quality TDS concentration $\geq 1,000$ ppm (90th percentile value)
RFF scenario III (coal for export)		RFF scenario IV conversion with export of residual		DOE/DOI 1990 level for export by rail[g]	
By rail[c]	By slurry[d]	By rail[e]	By slurry[f]		
611,306 (1/62)	—	—	—	—	1,200 (September)
—	541,310 (1/62)	—	—	—	1,500 (August)
—	—	503,937 (1/62)	—	—	1,500 (August)
—	—	—	453,710 (1/62)	—	1,500 (August)
—	—	—	—	592,461 (1/62)	1,500 (August)
—	—	—	—	—	2,000 (August), 1,300–1,500 (Sept.–Nov.)
—	—	—	—	—	1,600 (August), 1,200 (Sept.–Nov.)
560,302 (1/62)	—	—	—	—	2,000 (Aug., Dec.), 1,300–1,500 (Sept.–Nov.)
—	489,778 (1/62)	—	—	—	2,400 (Aug., Dec.), 2,300 (September), 1,400–1,600 (Oct., Nov.)
—	—	452,123 (1/62)	—	—	4,000 (Sept., Dec.), 3,100 (August), 2,000 (October), 1,400 (November)
—	—	—	402,533 (1/62)	—	4,000–4,200 (Aug.–Jan.)

(continued)

Table 9-7 (continued)

Case	BNRC-granted state reservations			Residual stored water available for other claims (acre-feet)
	Irrigation	Instream flow[a]	Instream flow[b]	
	(——————————————— acre-feet/yr ———————————————)			
12	27,626 (for 18,643 acres)	—	—	568,739 (1/62)
13	27,626 (for 18,643 acres)	—	95,201	432,325 (1/62)
14	27,626 (for 18,643 acres)	—	95,201	432,325 (1/62)
15	27,626 (for 18,643 acres)	—	95,201	432,325 (1/62)
16	27,626 (for 18,643 acres)	—	95,201	432,325 (1/62)
17	27,626 (for 18,643 acres)	—	95,201	432,325 (1/62)
18	27,626 (for 18,643 acres)	—	95,201	432,325 (1/62)
19	27,626 (for 18,643 acres)	95,201	—	517,821 (1/62)
20	27,626 (for 18,643 acres)	95,201	—	517,821 (1/62)

| Lowest month-end acre-feet of water in storage after meeting potential demands of energy developments on Powder River water required for: | | | | | Water quality TDS concentration ≥1,000 ppm (90th percentile value) |
| RFF scenario III (coal for export) | | RFF scenario IV conversion with export of residual | | DOE/DOI 1990 level for export by rail[g] | |
By rail[e]	By slurry[d]	By rail[e]	By slurry[f]		
—	—	—	—	540,860 (1/62)	2,100 (August), 1,300–1,600 (Sept.–Nov.)
—	—	—	—	—	2,000 (August), 1,300–1,800 (Sept.–Nov.)
424,021 (1/62)	—	—	—	—	2,000 (Aug., Dec.), 1,300–1,800 (Sept.–Nov.)
—	350,578 (1/62)	—	—	—	2,900 (September), 2,400 (August), 1,400–1,900 (Oct.–Nov.)
—	—	307,748 (1/62)	—	—	3,000–3,100 (Aug., Sept.), 1,700–2,000 (Oct.–Jan.)
—	—	—	102,252[h] (1/62)	—	3,000–3,200 (Aug., Sept.), 2,900 (October), 1,600–1,800 (Nov.–Jan.)
—	—	—	—	404,178 (1/62)	2,100 (Aug., Dec.), 1,400–1,900 (Sept.–Nov.)
—	—	—	—	—	2,000 (Aug., Dec.), 1,300–1,800 (Sept.–Nov.)
513,892 (1/62)	—	—	—	—	2,100 (Aug., Dec.), 1,300–1,800 (Sept.–Nov.)

(continued)

Table 9-7 (continued)

Case	BNRC-granted state reservations Irrigation (	Instream flow[a] —acre-feet/yr	Instream flow[b])	Residual stored water available for other claims (acre-feet)
21	27,626 (for 18,643 acres)	95,201	—	517,821 (1/62)
22	27,626 (for 18,643 acres)	95,201	—	517,821 (1/62)
23	27,626 (for 18,643 acres)	95,201	—	517,821 (1/62)
24	27,626 (for 18,643 acres)	95,201	—	517,821 (1/62)

Notes: All data on stored water available are net of the water due Wyoming under the interstate Yellowstone River Basin Compact. Dashes = not applicable. DOE = U.S. Department of Energy. DOI = U.S. Department of the Interior. TDS = total dissolved solids. ppm = parts per million.

[a] This does not accommodate releases from storage to maintain minimum instream flows unless water is available for prior accommodation of all other reservations.

[b] This assumes appropriate releases from storage to maintain minimum instream flows.

[c] Requires 5,100 acre-feet per year for 100 million tons per year.

[d] Requires 47,940 acre-feet per year for 100 million tons per year.

to increase industrial or energy uses without confronting environmental difficulties.

Next we consider the effects of the reduction in storage capacity that would attend the construction of the smaller reservoir proposed by the Intake Water Company on the Moorhead site.[9] These effects are shown

[9] Just as in the case of the Moorhead Reservoir, we have taken the usable additional storage over the first thirty-year life of the Intake Reservoir as available for active storage in our simulation runs to provide information for comparative purposes with the Moorhead facility.

Lowest month-end acre-feet of water in storage after meeting potential demands of energy developments on Powder River water required for:					Water quality TDS concentration ≥1,000 ppm (90th percentile value)
RFF scenario III (coal for export)		RFF scenario IV conversion with export of residual		DOE/DOI 1990 level for export by rail[g]	
By rail[e]	By slurry[d]	By rail[e]	By slurry[f]		
—	469,710 (1/62)	—	—	—	3,000 (September), 2,400 (August), 1,400–1,900 (Oct.–Dec.)
—	—	439,888 (1/62)	—	—	3,100 (Aug., Sept.), 2,000 (October), 1,700–1,900 (Nov., Dec.)
—	—	—	353,238 (1/62)	—	3,600 (August), 3,000 (September), 2,800 (October), 1,600–2,000 (Nov., Dec.)
—	—	—	—	503,545 (1/62)	2,100 (Aug., Dec.), 1,400–1,900 (Sept.–Nov.)

[e] Requires a combination of process water, along with water for mining, of 70,704 acre-feet per year assuming export of the difference (approximately 70 million tons) by rail.

[f] Requires a combination of process water, along with water for mining, of 100,944 acre-feet per year assuming export of the difference (approximately 70 million tons) by slurry.

[g] 16,935 acre-feet per year required for mining of 339 million tons and export by rail only.

[h] Sediment storage after 30 years is estimated to have a volume of 243,000 acre-feet. Therefore any simulated monthly terminal reservoir storage below that level indicates a dipping into the sediment storage portion of the reservoir capacity.

in table 9-9. The interested reader may inspect various aspects of the comparison with the larger Moorhead Reservoir. Suffice it here to say only that the reduction of close to 100,000 acre-feet of storage capacity would result in a reservoir shortfall of a six-month period for the most demanding case (case 17 in both table 9-7 and 9-9) and a more frequent use of the "interim" storage reserved for sedimentation beyond the first thirty years. But while the volume of water is available for all purposes except the unlikely case of the RFF scenario IV conversion level (with the

Table 9-8. Stored water available assuming the DNRC reservation recommendations in the Powder River subbasin with the Moorhead Reservoir—657,000 acre-feet

	DNRC recommendations for state reservations			Residual stored water available for other claims (acre-feet)
Case (	Irrigation	Instream flow[a]	Instream flow[b]	
		———acre-feet/yr———		)
1	13,680 (for 9,120 acres)	—	32,170	546,119 (1/62)
2	13,680 (for 9,120 acres)	—	32,170	546,119 (1/62)
3	13,680 (for 9,120 acres)	—	32,170	546,119 (1/62)
4	13,680 (for 9,120 acres)	—	32,170	546,119 (1/62)
5	13,680 (for 9,120 acres)	—	32,170	546,119 (1/62)
6	13,680 (for 9,120 acres)	—	32,170	546,119 (1/62)

Lowest month-end acre-feet of water in storage after meeting potential demands of energy developments on Powder River water required for:					Water quality TDS concentration $\geq 1,000$ ppm (90th percentile value)
RFF scenario III (coal for export)		RFF scenario IV conversion with export of residual		DOE/DOI 1990 level for export by rail[g]	
By rail[e]	By slurry[d]	By rail[e]	By slurry[f]		
—	—	—	—	—	1,800 (August), 1,300 (Sept.–Nov.), 2,000 (December)
537,751 (1/62)	—	—	—	—	1,800 (August), 1,300 (Sept.–Nov.), 2,000 (December)
—	466,884 (1/62)	—	—	—	1,900 (August), 1,300–1,700 (Sept.–Nov.), 2,200 (December)
—	—	429,542 (1/62)	—	—	2,400 (September), 1,400–2,000 (Aug., Oct., Nov.), 2,200 (December)
—	—	—	380,150 (1/62)	—	3,100–3,500 (Sept.–Oct.), 1,800–2,300 (Aug., Nov.– Dec.)
—	—	—	—	518,244 (1/62)	1,800 (August), 1,300 (Sept.–Nov.), 2,000 (December)

(*continued*)

Table 9-8 (continued)

Case	DNRC recommendations for state reservations			Residual stored water available for other claims (acre-feet)
	Irrigation (—————————	Instream flow[a] —————acre-feet/yr———	Instream flow[b] —————)	
7	13,680 (for 9,120 acres)	32,170	—	560,202 (1/62)
8	13,680 (for 9,120 acres)	32,170	—	560,202 (1/62)
9	13,680 (for 9,120 acres)	32,170	—	560,202 (1/62)
10	13,680 (for 9,120 acres)	32,170	—	560,202 (1/62)
11	13,680 (for 9,120 acres)	32,170	—	560,202 (1/62)
12	13,680 (for 9,120 acres)	32,170	—	560,202 (1/62)

Notes: All data on stored water available are net of the water due Wyoming under the interstate Yellowstone River Basin Compact. Dashes = not applicable. DOE = U.S. Department of Energy. DOI = U.S. Department of the Interior. TDS = total dissolved solids. ppm = parts per million.

[a] This does not accommodate releases from storage to maintain minimum instream flows unless water is available for prior accommodation of all other reservations.

[b] This assumes appropriate releases from storage to maintain minimum instream flows.

[c] Requires 5,100 acre-feet per year for 100 million tons per year.

Lowest month-end acre-feet of water in storage after meeting potential demands of energy developments on Powder River water required for:					Water quality TDS
RFF scenario III (coal for export)		RFF scenario IV conversion with export of residual		DOE/DOI 1990 level for export	concentration $\geq 1,000$ ppm (90th percentile
By rail[e]	By slurry[d]	By rail[e]	By slurry[f]	by rail[g]	value)
—	—	—	—	—	1,800 (August), 1,300 (Sept.–Nov.), 2,000 (December)
553,510 (1/62)	—	—	—	—	1,800 (August), 1,300 (Sept.–Nov.), 2,000 (December)
—	497,818 (1/62)	—	—	—	1,900 (August), 1,300–1,700 (Sept.–Nov.), 2,200 (December)
—	—	467,929 (1/62)	—	—	2,400 (September), 1,400–2,200 (Aug., Oct.–Dec.)
—	—	—	423,715 (1/62)	—	3,200–3,700 (Sept.–Oct.), 1,800–2,300 (Aug., Nov.–Jan.)
—	—	—	—	538,045 (1/62)	1,800 (August), 1,300 (Sept.–Nov.), 2,000 (December)

d Requires 47,940 acre-feet per year for 100 million tons per year.

e Requires a combination of process water, along with water for mining, of 70,704 acre-feet per year assuming export of the difference (approximately 70 million tons) by rail.

f Requires a combination of process water, along with water for mining, of 100,944 acre-feet per year assuming export of the difference (approximately 70 million tons) by slurry.

g Requires 16,935 acre-feet per year for mining of 339 million tons and export by rail only.

Table 9-9. Stored water available assuming the BNRC-granted water reservations in the Powder River subbasin with the Intake Reservoir—564,400 acre-feet

	BNRC-granted state reservations			Residual stored water available for other claims (acre-feet)
Case	Irrigation (———————	Instream flow[a] ——————acre-feet/yr——	Instream flow[b] ————————)	
1	—	—	—	—
2	—	—	—	—
3	—	—	—	—
4	—	—	—	—
5	—	—	—	—
6	27,626 (for 18,643 acres)	—	—	463,980 (1/62)
7	—	—	95,201	377,179 (1/62)
8	27,626 (for 18,643 acres)	—	—	463,980 (1/62)
9	27,626 (for 18,643 acres)	—	—	463,980 (1/62)
10	27,626 (for 18,643 acres)	—	—	463,980 (1/62)
11	27,626 (for 18,643 acres)	—	—	463,980 (1/62)
12	27,626 (for 18,643 acres)	—	—	463,980 (1/62)
13	27,626 (for 18,643 acres)	—	95,201	324,985 (1/62)

Lowest month-end acre-feet of water in storage after meeting potential demands of energy developments on Powder River water required for:					Water quality TDS concentration $\geq 1,000$ ppm (90th percentile value)
RFF scenario III (coal for export)		RFF scenario IV conversion with export of residual		DOE/DOI 1990 level for export by rail[g]	
By rail[e]	By slurry[d]	By rail[e]	By slurry[f]		
507,419 (1/62)	—	—	—	—	1,600 (August)
—	436,156 (1/62)	—	—	—	1,600 (August)
—	—	398,296 (1/62)	—	—	1,600 (August)
—	—	—	347,623 (1/62)	—	1,600 (August)
—	—	—	—	487,958 (1/62)	1,600 (August)
—	—	—	—	—	4,191 (August), 1,300–1,800 (Sept.–Jan.)
—	—	—	—	—	1,600 (August), 1,200 (Sept.–Nov.)
455,486 (1/62)	—	—	—	—	2,221 (August), 1,300–1,600 (Sept.–Jan.)
—	384,048 (1/62)	—	—	—	4,086 (September), 1,400–2,880 (Aug., Oct.–Jan.)
—	—	345,880 (1/62)	—	—	4,100 (Aug.–Sept.), 1,800–2,200 (Oct.–Nov.)
—	—	—	295,454 (1/62)	—	4,200 (Aug.–Jan.)
—	—	—	—	435,693 (1/62)	2,330 (August), 1,300–1,700 (Sept.–Nov.)
—	—	—	—	—	2,191 (August), 1,400–1,900 (Sept.–Nov.)

(continued)

Table 9-9 (continued)

| Case | BNRC-granted state reservations | | | Residual stored water available for other claims (acre-feet) |
| | Irrigation | Instream flow[a] | Instream flow[b] | |
	(—————————— acre-feet/yr ——————————)			
14	27,626 (for 18,643 acres)	—	95,201	324,985 (1/62)
15	27,626 (for 18,643 acres)	—	95,201	324,985 (1/62)
16	27,626 (for 18,643 acres)	—	95,201	324,985 (1/62)
17	27,626 (for 18,643 acres)	—	95,201	324,985 (1/62)
18	27,626 (for 18,643 acres)	—	95,201	324,985 (1/62)
19	27,626 (for 18,643 acres)	95,201	—	412,234 (1/62)
20	27,626 (for 18,643 acres)	95,201	—	412,234 (1/62)
21	27,626 (for 18,643 acres)	95,201	—	412,234 (1/62)

Lowest month-end acre-feet of water in storage after meeting potential demands of energy developments on Powder River water required for:					Water quality TDS concentration $\geq 1,000$ ppm (90th percentile value)
RFF scenario III (coal for export)		RFF scenario IV conversion with export of residual		DOE/DOI 1990 level for export by rail[g]	
By rail[e]	By slurry[d]	By rail[e]	By slurry[f]		
316,493 (1/62)	—	—	—	—	2,227 (August), 1,400–1,900 (Sept.–Nov.)
—	241,856[h] (1/62)	—	—	—	3,066 (September), 2,939 (August), 1,700–1,900 (Oct.–Dec.)
—	—	157,285 (1/62) (8 months into sediment storage)	—	—	3,200 (August), 3,000 (September), 1,800–2,200 (Oct.–Dec.)
—	—	—	Reservoir short-fall for 6 months (8/61–1/62) (23 months into sediment storage)	—	3,200 (August), 3,000 (September), 1,700–2,900 (Oct.–Dec.)
—	—	—	—	295,924 (1/62)	2,800 (September), 1,400–2,100 (Oct.–Dec.)
—	—	—	—	—	2,100 (August), 1,400–2,100 (Sept.–Dec.)
408,274 (1/62)	—	—	—	—	2,200 (August), 1,400–2,100 (Sept.–Dec.)
—	363,645 (1/62)	—	—	—	3,200 (September), 2,900 (August), 1,500–1,900 (Oct.–Dec.)

(continued)

Table 9-9 (continued)

Case	BNRC-granted state reservations			Residual stored water available for other claims (acre-feet)
	Irrigation	Instream flow[a]	Instream flow[b]	
	(————————————————————acre-feet/yr————————————————————)			
22	27,626 (for 18,643 acres)	95,201	—	412,234 (1/62)
23	27,626 (for 18,643 acres)	95,201	—	412,234 (1/62)
24	27,626 (for 18,643 acres)	95,201	—	412,234 (1/62)

Notes: All data on stored water available are net of the water due Wyoming under the interstate Yellowstone River Basin Compact. Dashes = not applicable. DOE = U.S. Department of Energy. DOI = U.S. Department of the Interior. TDS = total dissolved solids. ppm = parts per million.

[a] This does not accommodate releases from storage to maintain minimum instream flows unless water is available for prior accommodation of all other reservations.

[b] This assumes appropriate releases from storage to maintain minimum instream flows.

[c] Requires 5,100 acre-feet per year for 100 million tons per year.

[d] Requires 47,940 acre-feet per year for 100 million tons per year.

remaining 70 million tons annually shipped out of the basin by slurry pipeline), the effects of including different uses on the water quality is more pronounced. The concentration of total dissolved solids in table 9-9 reflects the reduction in dilution effects occasioned by the lesser storage capacity.

The Water Quality Dimension

We have noted in the discussion of the various outcomes presented in the tables in this chapter that the total dissolved solids concentration under some options would prove to be problematic.[10] In particular, soil

[10] The 90th percentile values for TDS concentrations (that value equaled or exceeded 90 percent of the time) are displayed in the tables.

Lowest month-end acre-feet of water in storage after meeting potential demands of energy developments on Powder River water required for:					Water quality TDS
RFF scenario III (coal for export)		RFF scenario IV conversion with export of residual		DOE/DOI 1990 level for export by rail[g]	concentration $\geq 1,000$ ppm (90th percentile value)
By rail[e]	By slurry[d]	By rail[e]	By slurry[f]		
—	—	333,435 (1/62)	—	—	3,600 (August), 3,000 (September), 1,800–2,200 (Oct.–Dec.)
—	—	—	202,418 (1/62) (5 months into sediment storage)	—	3,800 (August), 3,100–3,200 (Sept.–Oct.), 1,600–2,100 (Nov.–Dec.)
—	—	—	—	397,869 (1/62)	2,300 (August), 1,600–2,100 (Sept.–Dec.)

[e] Requires a combination of process water, along with water for mining, of 70,704 acre-feet per year assuming export of the difference (approximately 70 million tons) by rail.

[f] Requires a combination of process water, along with water for mining, of 100,944 acre-feet per year assuming export of the difference (approximately 70 million tons) by slurry.

[g] 16,935 acre-feet per year required for mining of 339 million tons and export by rail only.

[h] Sediment storage after 30 years is estimated to have a volume of 243,000 acre-feet. Therefore, any simulated monthly terminal reservoir storage below that level indicates a dipping into the sediment storage portion of the reservoir capacity.

and water salinity are problems for agriculture in the Tongue and Powder subbasins. The difference in the amount of water used for one or another purpose, particularly where irrigation is involved, will have a substantial effect on the water quality that results. Before discussing these results, we would like to acknowledge that our results are indicative rather than definitive. The reasons for this relate in part to the rather limited research that has been done on the salt pickup in irrigation return flows under varying conditions in the Yellowstone Basin, although it is known that the phenomenon is a function of a complex set of factors.[11] In addition, our model for each subbasin does not disaggregate the watercourse into segments for computing the salinity at various points along the entire stream-

[11] R. S. Ayres and D. W. Wescot, *Water Quality for Agriculture,* Irrigation and Drainage Paper #29 (Rome, U.N. Food and Agriculture Organization, 1976).

course. The informational requirements for calibrating such a model are excessive for a planning and policy level analysis such as we are conducting, and thus we are restricted to a model that takes the TDS concentration at the point of entry into the Montana portion of the basin to give the naturally occurring TDS and then takes into account the withdrawals, depletions (evapotranspiration and other nonreturn phenomena), return flows, and the additional salt pickup (about one-half ton per irrigated acre) in return flows, the effects of which are all accounted for at the exit point of the subbasin. Accordingly, the TDS concentration estimates shown in the last columns of all the tables represent the cumulative effect of all of the processes at the end point of the accounting process. Nevertheless, while it would be desirable to have a more finely calibrated model, the necessary information does not exist. Moreover, we feel the additional complexity is not warranted for this level of analysis. Accordingly, with these caveats cautioning against overinterpreting the results, we draw attention to some of the findings which are *indicated*.

Comparing the differences in the TDS levels between the BNRC rulings and the DNRC's recommendations (which excluded instream flows for the Tongue subbasin), we find that absence of instream flow provisions in the DNRC recommendations makes for a very substantial difference. Once irrigation is admitted as a use without instream flows being augmented by releases of stored water, we find the TDS concentrations to be at levels which translate into severe problems.[12]

Indeed, if we consult cases 6 or 8 in table 9-1 (two sets of irrigation cases with different amounts of land under irrigation and no instream flow), both show TDS concentrations unsuitable for irrigation of crops. Although the results are displayed for the months with the highest concentrations during the year, concentrations during most of the growing season appear to be too high to be conducive to proper germination and growth.[13] (Simulating the subbasin exit concentrations only does not flaw our argument.) Since Northern Cheyenne Indian reserved right claims applied to irrigation (case 8, table 9-1) would take place just below the storage reservoir, the highly saline return flow would affect downstream users from the point of return to the exit point in the subbasin. However, compare these results with those shown in case 9, where both the Northern Cheyenne Indian irrigation of 10,000 acres, the existing irrigation with established

---

[12] Ayres and Wescot, *Water Quality;* L. A. Richards, ed., *Diagnosis and Improvement of Saline and Alkali Soils,* Agricultural Handbook No. 60, U.S. Department of Agriculture (February 1954).

[13] Richards, *Diagnosis and Improvement.*

rights to 42,000 acre-feet annually, and the additional irrigation reservations are considered together with instream flows of 54,289 acre-feet annually supported as necessary with appropriate releases from storage. With instream flows serving also to dilute the total dissolved solids concentrations, the problem we encountered in the absence of the instream flow reservation does not occur. It would appear, then, that only if provision is made for instream flows—consistent with the BNRC's December 1978 determinations—could any irrigation take place in the Tongue subbasin additional to what would correspond to the Northern Cheyenne irrigation consistent with our postulated restrictive/efficient case.

Proceeding to the Powder subbasin, there appears to be a quantity of water sufficient for every combination of cases we have postulated, including the RFF and DOE/DOI high level coal development scenarios respectively, provided the Moorhead Reservoir is built and operated to employ storage over the first thirty years. This storage will be needed for sediment accumulation beyond that time. As previously mentioned, however, water spreading is practiced in the Powder subbasin, and some beneficial use associated with this practice is served on some 28,000 acres. In fact, the irrigation water reservations granted by the BNRC were for water spreading. All full-service irrigation requests were denied by the board because there currently is no storage on the Powder River. Simulating the case for proposed storage we find the salinity problem intrudes again. Water spreading during spring freshets employs water with dissolved solids concentrations substantially more dilute than the regulated outflows from the reservoir. The TDS concentration of released water from the reservoir exceeds values conducive to proper germination and growth of crops. Accordingly, if impounded to provide more dependable flows, the Powder River seems to provide little by way of quality water for irrigation because of the TDS concentration occurring naturally, regardless of whether the BNRC or the DNRC outcomes would be considered.[14]

We summarize then, as follows: since (1) there are no Indian reserved right claims at issue in the Powder subbasin, (2) the majority of existing irrigation water rights are use rights associated with water spreading, and (3) there appears to be adequate water for all combinations of uses to the levels postulated (albeit irrigation uses may not be compatible with the naturally occurring dissolved solids in concentrations found in storage

---

[14] We point out here that the state water quality standards specify an instream TDS concentration of 500 ppm. The TDS standard for these two rivers is currently undergoing revision with 1,500 ppm being suggested as the TDS standard for the Powder River.

releases), the Powder subbasin—were storage to be developed—would be quite favorably situated for the provision of water in quantities required by our postulated energy scenarios. Whether the Powder could accommodate the concentration of energy developments implied in our higher level scenarios if various environmental factors not addressed here were considered is not known. However, it appears that energy development would have a lesser impact on water quality than even the limited amount of irrigation recommended by the DNRC.

Analysis of the Availability and Quality of Water in the Bighorn Subbasin

The Bighorn subbasin is the last of the tributary subbasins selected for analysis. It lies somewhat removed from the coal resources, and like the other subbasins, has numerous actual and potential claimants to its flows. Unlike the previous two, however, where the reservoirs are in the proposal stage, the Bighorn subbasin has a large-capacity federal reservoir near the Montana-Wyoming state line located on the Crow Reservation—the 1,375,000-acre-foot Bureau of Reclamation Yellowtail Dam and Reservoir.

Recall from chapter 4 that it was stored water from the Yellowtail Reservoir for which energy companies competed in the late 1960s and early 1970s through option contracts. Several major energy companies took out such contracts totaling 258,000 acre-feet annually with applications for an additional 502,000 acre-feet (see table 4-1). By the spring of 1978, however, the water option contracts for energy had dwindled to 70,000 acre-feet per year, held by Gulf Oil and Shell Oil.[15]

The Yellowtail project is currently operated primarily for hydroelectric (peaking) power, flood control, recreation, and fish and wildlife enhancement. If industrial use materializes, the reservoir might be used to provide service to the industrial water user.[16] In other words, because the Yellowtail Reservoir is a federal reservoir, the Bureau of Reclamation appears to

[15] The bureau regards the water option contracts as preliminary allocations. The option contracts do not require the bureau to retain the quantity of water under contract in storage.

[16] As mentioned in chapter 4, the bureau's industrial water marketing program was challenged by the *Environmental Defense Fund v. Kleppe* (renamed *Andrus*) suit. As a result of the suit, a moratorium on entering into such contracts was imposed.

retain jurisdiction over the use and distribution of stored Yellowtail water after releases are made to satisfy existing water rights.[17]

Under the Yellowstone Compact, the surplus flow allocation terms provide Montana with 20 percent of the firm annual yield and Wyoming with 80 percent. It appears unlikely, at this time, that Wyoming could use its full share of the allocation,[18] and our simulations reflect this assumption. Other legal claimants to the flow of the Bighorn include the Wind River Indian tribes in Wyoming where adjudication of their reserved rights on the upstream reaches of the Bighorn River has recently been initiated. The importance of these Indian reserved right claims is that consumptive utilization of these rights may diminish inflow to the Yellowtail Reservoir and consequently the inflow and stored water available to the users in Montana.

Within Montana, the Crow tribe (upon whose reservation the Yellowtail is located) claims in its adjudication suit that it has reserved rights on the Bighorn River. In addition, federal and state agencies (and other public entities of the state) have filed water reservation requests for irrigation, municipal, and instream uses of water for preservation of water quality and fish and game habitat.

To give a perspective on the levels of development for which water reservation requests have been submitted, the Bureau of Reclamation requested a reservation for irrigating 42,950 new acres out of the total of 52,975 acres for which reservations were submitted (see table 6-3). The DNRC, on the other hand, recommended that water for irrigating only 8,900 acres be reserved, while the BNRC granted an irrigation reservation for 10,025 acres. In addition, the state fish and game commission requested an instream flow reservation of almost 3,000,000 acre-feet annually. The DNRC recommended an instream flow reservation of slightly less than one-half that amount, while the BNRC granted an instream flow reservation of 2,477,987 acre-feet. It is not clear to what extent the state water reservations, especially the instream flow reservation, will be hon-

---

[17] The Supreme Court's majority opinion in the *California v. U.S.* case stated that a state could impose conditions on the distribution of water from federal impoundments provided they were consistent with Congressional authorization for the dam.

[18] An array of twelve monthly values was developed from the Wyoming Framework Plan (Wyoming State Engineer's Office, *Wyoming Framework Water Plan* [Cheyenne, Wyoming, May 1973] p. 140) to reflect Wyoming's use of compact water over the simulation period. If Wyoming's 80-percent share of the monthly inflow exceeded the corresponding value in array C for that month, then the inflow was depleted by only the C array value; at all other times it was depleted by 80 percent.

ored by the bureau's operation of the Yellowtail Reservoir since it is an unsettled legal question as to who has title to the stored water and what conditions the state can impose on the use and distribution of stored water after existing rights are honored. In any event, it may be useful to consider various alternative outcomes to see their quantitative implications.

Given the large volume of storage involved, it goes without saying that there would be an adequate supply of water for any single use in Montana considered individually. However, it must be recognized that the Indian claims to reserved water rights in amounts representing the expansive criterion (Department of Interior estimates) for the Wind River Indian tribes in Wyoming and the Crow in Montana would basically exhaust the water available for any other claimants. This can be observed in table 9-10, case 3. On the other hand, irrigation of up to 200,000 acres of land on the Wind River Reservation along with 100,000 acres on the Crow would be possible with residual stored water available for other claims ranging from two-thirds of a million (restrictive/efficient case) down to a half million (restrictive/nonefficient case) as seen respectively in cases 1 and 2.[19] The use of such a large amount of water could be problematic, however, owing to the salinity issue discussed in the previous section. But given the amount of residual stored water after accommodating the Indian reserved water rights (restrictive/efficient case), we would antici-pate that some water would be available for other purposes as well. Ex-amining cases 4 through 8, we observe that the BNRC-granted irrigation reservation could be accommodated along with the Indian reserved water rights and leave remaining substantial amounts of water in storage for energy development purposes. But, this would not accommodate the BNRC instream reservation of 2,477,987 acre-feet annually (case 14), which in any event could not be met except in favorable water years, if Indian reserved rights and the BNRC-granted irrigation reservation were to be simultaneously honored. Indeed, excluding the instream flow reser-vation, not only could all the energy scenarios we have considered be ac-commodated under those circumstances without reservoir shortfalls, but Indian reserved water rights with less water-efficient practices could be accommodated along with the irrigation reservation (cases 9 through 13).[20]

---

[19] The estimated reserved right claims of the Wind River Indian tribes, based on 200,000 acres, may be an exaggerated estimate. It is also somewhat doubtful when this level of irrigation could be achieved, if at all.

[20] It is conceivable that, were the expansive criterion used to adjudicate the Crow Indian reserved right claims, water for energy development on the Indian reservation would take precedence over the state reservations including the large BNRC-granted instream flow reservation.

Consider the possibility that we may have been unrealistically high in our estimates of what the courts might provide the various Indian tribes under the restrictive criterion. Were we to reduce the implied allocation of close to 900,000 acre-feet per year in the aggregate to only 500,000 acre-feet per year among all of the tribes, then we would be able to satisfy the irrigation reservations, the instream flow reservation to a limited extent (by releases from storage when there is surplus water after accommodating prior reservations), and any combination of energy developments represented by our standard option scenarios. These observations are results of simulation runs that, however, are not displayed in table 9-10.

The options on the Bighorn are intriguing because of the numerous possible tradeoffs we have witnessed and the issue of how the waters stored as a result of federal project construction are ultimately to be allocated. The Bureau of Reclamation obviously intended to use the increased dependable yields of the Bighorn resulting from the federal Yellowtail Dam and Reservoir for industrial purposes. The action taken by the Environmental Defense Fund (*EDF v. Kleppe,* now *EDF v. Andrus*) challenged the statutory authority of the Bureau of Reclamation to do so. The litigation had a long, drawn out history, being resolved on appeal only in June of 1979. Although the U.S. District Court in Montana ruled against the position advanced by the Environmental Defense Fund, on appeal, the Ninth Circuit Court of Appeals has placed constraints on the Bureau of Reclamation's latitude in making industrial water sales. It is also unclear whether sales of water could be made to the state of Montana for instream flow purposes, and if not, whether the instream flow reservation would be honored. It should also be recognized that without instream flows to provide dilution during the months of July and August when the major part of the irrigation water is applied, severe salinity problems would be encountered.

Finally, assuming water for industrial purposes could be made available from the Yellowtail Reservoir, it would need to be transported out of the subbasin to the vicinity of the coalfields. This would entail a delay, given the conditions that the Ninth Circuit Court of Appeals imposed on the Bureau of Reclamation (*EDF v. Andrus*) in relation to the environmental impact studies including the potential effect on agriculture. Moreover, the delay might be compounded in obtaining rights of way and construction of the conveyance system. It is not clear under the circumstances that the existence of a reservoir in the Bighorn subbasin would necessarily make water available in the Powder any more rapidly than the construction of the Intake or Moorhead storages in the Powder itself.

Table 9-10. Stored water available assuming prior legal claims and the BNRC-granted water reservations in the Bighorn subbasin with the Yellowtail Reservoir—1,375,000 acre-feet

| Case | Potentially realizable Crow Indian Tribe claims on the Bighorn River water (acre-feet/yr) | | | Potentially realizable Wind River Indian Tribe reserved right claims upstream in Wyoming (acre-feet/yr) | | BNRC-granted state reservations | |
| | Restrictive criterion (irrigation only) | | Expansive criterion (DOI) | | | Irrigation | Instream flow[a] |
	at the rate of 3 af/acre	at the rate of 4 af/acre		RFF	DOI	(————— acre-feet/yr —————)	
1	300,000 (for 100,000 acres)	—	—	480,000 (irrigation) (for 200,000 acres)	—	—	—
2	—	400,000 (for 100,000 acres)	—	480,000 (irrigation) (for 200,000 acres)	—	—	—
3	—	—	1,080,000 (irrigation), 198,550 (other)	—	1,920,000 (irrigation), 965,080 (other)	—	—
4	300,000 (for 100,000 acres)	—	—	480,000 (irrigation)	—	22,176 (for 10,025 acres)	—
5	300,000 (for 100,000 acres)	—	—	480,000 (irrigation)	—	22,176 (for 10,025 acres)	—
6	300,000 (for 100,000 acres)	—	—	480,000 (irrigation)	—	22,176 (for 10,025 acres)	—
7	300,000 (for 100,000 acres)	—	—	480,000 (irrigation)	—	22,176 (for 10,025 acres)	—
8	300,000 (for 100,000 acres)	—	—	480,000 (irrigation)	—	22,176 (for 10,025 acres)	—
9	—	400,000 (for 100,000 acres)	—	480,000 (irrigation)	—	22,176 (for 10,025 acres)	—
10	—	400,000 (for 100,000 acres)	—	480,000 (irrigation)	—	22,176 (for 10,025 acres)	—

| Residual stored water available for other claims[b] (acre-feet) | Lowest month-end acre-feet of water in storage after meeting potential demands of energy developments on Bighorn River water required for: | | | | | Water quality TDS concentration ≥1,000 ppm (90th percentile value)[h] |
| | RFF scenario III (coal for export) | | RFF scenario IV conversion with export of residual | | DOE/DOI 1990 level for export by rail[g] | |
	By rail[e]	By slurry[d]	By rail[e]	By slurry[f]		
666,035 (8/61)	—	—	—	—	—	2,025 (August)
578,544 (8/61)	—	—	—	—	—	1,472 (August)
Reservoir shortfall over most of simulation period	—	—	—	—	—	—
646,659 (8/61)	645,021 (8/61)	—	—	—	—	2,100 (August)
646,659 (8/61)	—	631,145 (8/61)	—	—	—	2,100 (August)
646,659 (8/61)	—	—	623,734 (8/61)	—	—	2,100 (August)
646,659 (8/61)	—	—	—	613,917 (8/61)	—	2,100 (August)
646,659 (8/61)	—	—	—	—	641,192 (8/61)	2,100 (August)
559,120 (8/61)	557,461 (8/61)	—	—	—	—	1,500 (August)
559,120 (8/61)	—	543,566 (8/61)	—	—	—	1,500 (August)

(continued)

Table 9-10 (continued)

	Potentially realizable Crow Indian Tribe claims on the Bighorn River water (acre-feet/yr)			Potentially realizable Wind River Indian Tribe reserved right claims upstream in Wyoming (acre-feet/yr)		BNRC-granted state reservations	
	Restrictive criterion (irrigation only)		Expansive criterion (DOI)			Irrigation	Instream flow[a]
Case	at the rate of 3 af/acre	at the rate of 4 af/acre		RFF	DOI	(———— acre-feet/yr ————)	
11	—	400,000 (for 100,000 acres)	—	480,000 (irrigation)	—	22,176 (for 10,025 acres)	—
12	—	400,000 (for 100,000 acres)	—	480,000 (irrigation)	—	22,176 (for 10,025 acres)	—
13	—	400,000 (for 100,000 acres)	—	480,000 (irrigation)	—	22,176 (for 10,025 acres)	—
14	300,000 (for 100,000 acres)	—	—	480,000 (irrigation)	—	22,176 (for 10,025 acres)	2,477,987

Notes: The maximum capacity of the Yellowtail Reservoir is 1,375,000 af. Of this total, 259,000 af are reserved for flood control. In addition, 3,662 af/yr was assumed to be the annual rate of sediment accumulation, so that over a 30-year period, 109,883 af would be reserved for sediment storage. Finally, 168,361 af are reserved for inactive storage and 18,967 af for dead storage. Therefore, if the simulated reservoir capacity goes below 297,211 af, it is dipping into the inactive and sediment storage. Dashes = not applicable. DOE = U.S. Department of Energy. DOI = U.S. Department of the Interior. TDS = total dissolved solids. ppm = parts per million.

a If the BNRC-granted instream flow reservations are considered to be minimum flows that must be met every month, then there would be a reservoir shortfall much of the time.

b All data on stored water available are net of the water due Wyoming under the interstate Yellowstone River Basin Compact.

Analysis of the Availability and Quality of Water in the Mid and Lower Yellowstone Subbasins

Unlike the other subbasins discussed, which are tributaries, the Mid-Yellowstone subbasin encompasses the middle reach of the unimpeded mainstem Yellowstone River. This subbasin presently best illustrates the potential conflict between the instream and the withdrawal uses of water. A portion of the mainstem in this subbasin has been proposed for inclusion in the wild and scenic rivers system while elsewhere water is being withdrawn from the mainstem for operating the Colstrip coal-fired units 1 and 2. During the water reservation hearings, many individuals spoke of

Residual stored water available for other claims[b] (acre-feet)	Lowest month-end acre-feet of water in storage after meeting potential demands of energy developments on Bighorn River water required for:					Water quality TDS concentration ≥1,000 ppm (90th percentile value)[h]
	RFF scenario III (coal for export)		RFF scenario IV conversion with export of residual		DOE/DOI 1990 level for export by rail[g]	
	By rail[e]	By slurry[d]	By rail[e]	By slurry[f]		
559,120 (8/61)	—	—	532,072 (8/61)	—	—	1,500 (August)
559,120 (8/61)	—	—	—	493,932 (8/61)	—	1,500 (August)
559,120 (8/61)	—	—	—	—	553,627 (8/61)	1,500 (August)
Reservoir shortfall over much of simulation period	—	—	—	—	—	—

e Requires 5,100 acre-feet per year for 100 million tons per year.

d Requires 47,940 acre-feet per year for 100 million tons per year.

e Requires a combination of process water, along with water for mining, of 70,704 acre-feet per year assuming export of the difference (approximately 70 million tons) by rail.

f Requires a combination of process water, along with water for mining, of 100,944 acre-feet per year assuming export of the difference (approximately 70 million tons) by slurry.

g Requires 16,935 acre-feet per year for mining of 339 million tons and export by rail only.

h The TDS calculations cannot be meaningful estimates for reservoir shortfalls of long durations and therefore are excluded under such circumstances.

the need to preserve this unique long stretch of free flowing water in the mainstem and to preserve the fish and wildlife resources which the river supports.

The legal claims on water are not as complex in this subbasin as in the tributary subbasins discussed earlier. The mainstem is not subject to the claims of Indian reserved water rights nor to provisions of the Yellowstone River Compact. There are, however, state water reservations for irrigation, municipal use, and instream flow.

Because the Mid-Yellowstone lies in the middle of the basin, it was necessary to postulate economic development levels for those subbasins feeding into the Mid-Yellowstone. A sequential approach was used; for

Table 9-11. Assumed development levels in subbasins upstream of the Mid-Yellowstone subbasin

(acre-feet per year)

Subbasin	Crow Indian reserved rights	Wind River Indian reserved rights	State BNRC-granted irrigation reservation	State BNRC-granted municipal reservation
Upper	—	—	141,046 (for 46,960 acres)	12,909
Clarks Fork	—	—	22,979 (for 10,301 acres)	—
Billings Area	—	—	66,040 (for 28,186 acres)	41,229
Bighorn	400,000 (for 100,000 acres)	480,000 (for 200,000 acres)	22,176 (for 10,025 acres)	—

Note: Dashes = not applicable.

example, the sum of the simulated outflows from the Upper and Clarks Fork subbasins becomes the inflow for the Billings Area subbasin. In turn, the sum of the simulated outflows from the Billings Area subbasin and the Bighorn subbasin becomes the inflow for the Mid-Yellowstone subbasin.

Instream flow reservations in the upper subbasins do not diminish flow available in the downstream subbasin. Thus we used development levels for withdrawal uses only. In the upper subbasins these are irrigation and to a much less extent, municipal use. The development levels assumed for irrigation and municipal use are the reservations for these uses granted by the BNRC.

There are no Indian reserved right claims in the subbasins upstream of the Mid-Yellowstone except for the Bighorn subbasin in which we assumed Wind River and Crow reserved right claims to be 880,000 acre-feet annually, nor are there interstate water right claims except for the Clarks Fork and Bighorn subbasins.[21] In table 9-11, the assumed development levels in the subbasins upstream of the Mid-Yellowstone are shown.

The outflows resulting from these development levels in the upstream subbasins become the inflow to the Mid-Yellowstone subbasin. What,

[21] According to the *Wyoming Framework Water Plan*, little development is projected for the Clarks Fork subbasin in Wyoming. The Bighorn subbasin is net of Wyoming's share of compact water likely to be depleted.

then, are the results of the simulations which assume the developments as described above for the upstream subbasins and the BNRC-granted reservations for municipal use, irrigation, and instream flow in the Mid-Yellowstone?

First, if the municipal, irrigation, and instream flow reservations granted by the BNRC for the Mid-Yellowstone are implemented, there would not be flows available for any other use in that reach of the stream for about a third of the time, not necessarily over consecutive months (see case 12, table 9-12). If only the municipal and irrigation reservations were implemented, there would be a minimum flow of 68,065 acre-feet in the month corresponding to the most adverse hydrologic conditions of record (case 6), and 94,216 acre-feet per month under like hydrologic conditions, were only the municipal reservations implemented (case 1). On the other hand, if only the municipal and instream flows of 5.6 million acre-feet per year (omitting the irrigation) were implemented, dropping the irrigation would still leave flows unavailable for industrial or energy uses for from a quarter to a third of the time, again not necessarily during a consecutive month period (case 11).

Would the results be effectively altered were we to assume again that we have made unrealistic assumptions regarding the court's generosity in adjudicating Indian reserved right claims? Although not reflected in table 9-12, if the upstream Indian reserved water right claims were again assumed to be reduced from the near 900,000 acre-feet per year in the Bighorn subbasin to 500,000 acre-feet, the difference in the flow available for other uses would be only marginally affected. That is, given the BNRC-granted reservations in the Mid-Yellowstone along with each of the several energy development scenarios, there would still be inadequate flows for roughly 20 percent of the time, not necessarily over consecutive months.

Recall that in each of the subbasins, we have imposed iteratively the *total* of the energy developments postulated onto that subbasin. That is, the BNRC-granted reservations for the Mid-Yellowstone subbasin, which effectively precluded the appropriation of flow for significant energy development in that subbasin, do not imply that energy development of the intensities we have postulated would be precluded for the entire group of subbasins. Indeed, coal extraction for export in the Tongue could be as large as projected by the DOE/DOI high scenarios, and, in addition, an equivalent amount along with the RFF energy conversion variant could be undertaken in the Powder while honoring all of the BNRC reservations.

Table 9-12. Instream water available assuming the BNRC-granted water reservations in the Mid-Yellowstone subbasin

| | BNRC-granted state reservations | | | Residual flow available for appropriation for other claims (acre-feet) | Lowest monthly instream flow (in acre-feet) after meeting potential demands of energy developments on Mid-Yellowstone River water[a] required for: | | | | | Water quality TDS concentration ≥1,000 ppm (90th percentile value) |
| | Municipal[b] | Irrigation | Instream flow[c] | | RFF scenario III (coal for export) | | RFF scenario IV conversion with export of residual | | DOE/DOI 1990 level for export by rail[h] | |
Case	(—— acre-feet/yr ——)				By rail[d]	By slurry[e]	By rail[f]	By slurry[g]		
1	2,889	—	—	94,216 (8/61)	92,721 (8/61)	—	—	—	—	None
2	2,889	—	—	94,216 (8/61)	—	89,160 (8/61)	—	—	—	None
3	2,889	—	—	94,216 (8/61)	—	—	86,603 (8/61)	—	—	None
4	2,889	—	—	94,216 (8/61)	—	—	—	84,754 (8/61)	—	None
5	2,889	—	—	94,216 (8/61)	—	—	—	—	91,738 (8/61)	None
6	2,889	118,870 (for 47,035 acres)	—	68,065 (8/61)	66,570 (8/61)	—	—	—	—	None
7	2,889	118,870 (for 47,035 acres)	—	68,065 (8/61)	—	63,009 (8/61)	—	—	—	None

8	2,889	118,870 (for 47,035 acres)	—	68,065 (8/61)	—	60,452 (8/61)	—	—	None
9	2,889	118,870 (for 47,035 acres)	—	68,065 (8/61)	—	—	58,603 (8/61)	—	None
10	2,889	118,870 (for 47,035 acres)	—	68,065 (8/61)	—	—	—	65,587 (8/61)	None
11	2,889	—	5,578,892	100 months flow unavailable	—	—	—	—	None
12	2,889	118,870 (for 47,035 acres)	5,578,892	104 months flow unavailable	—	—	—	—	None

Notes: In order to simulate the flows for the Mid-Yellowstone subbasin, which is the fifth in order proceeding downstream, depletions occurring in the four upstream subbasins must be accounted for. In these simulations we have assumed depletions corresponding to the BNRC-granted reservations. In addition, we have assumed the restrictive criterion (4 acre-feet per year) for estimates of the reserved water rights of the Crow Indian Tribe and depletions corresponding to 480,000 acre-feet of reserved water rights for the Wind River Indian tribes' irrigation along with the Wyoming share depletions, all in connection with the Bighorn subbasin. Dashes = not applicable. DOE = U.S. Department of Energy. DOI = U.S. Department of the Interior. TDS = total dissolved solids. ppm = parts per million.

a All of the energy scenarios, including the "non-conversion" scenarios, do include the water currently withdrawn for the Colstrip 1 and 2 steam electric plants.

b This is the amount of water granted by the BNRC to Miles City, which is at the junction of the Mid-Yellowstone and Kinsey Area subbasins.

c There is no onstream reservoir to augment flow for instream or any other use.

d Requires 5,100 acre-feet/year for 100 million tons per year.

e Requires 47,940 acre-feet/year for 100 million tons per year.

f Requires a combination of process water, along with water for mining, of 70,704 acre-feet/year assuming export of the difference (approximately 70 million tons) by rail.

g Requires a combination of process water, along with water for mining, of 100,944 acre-feet/year assuming export of the difference (approximately 70 million tons) by slurry.

h Requires 16,935 acre-feet/year for mining of 339 million tons and export by rail only.

253

Table 9-13. Assumed development levels in subbasins downstream of the Bighorn subbasin

(acre-feet per year)

Subbasin	Northern Cheyenne reserved rights	State BNRC-granted municipal reservation	State BNRC-granted irrigation reservation	Energy development
Mid-Yellowstone	—	2,889	118,870 (for 47,035 acres)	29,820[a]
Tongue[b]	60,000 (for 10,000 acres)	—	21,328 (for 8,805 acres)	—
Kinsey Area	—	—	30,471 (for 11,252 acres)	—
Powder[c]	—	—	27,626 (for 18,643 acres)	70,704[d]

Note: Dashes = not applicable.

[a] This level reflects the sum of the water withdrawal rates for the existing Colstrip units 1 and 2 and for DOE/DOI's coal production target of 339 million tons exported by rail. Note that alternative coal development levels can be specified.

[b] The proposed stage II (450,000-af capacity) of the Tongue River Reservoir is assumed to be in place and Wyoming's share of the Yellowstone Compact water likely to be depleted is reflected in the simulation.

[c] Wyoming's share of compact water likely to be depleted is reflected in the simulation.

[d] The proposed Intake Reservoir (564,400-af capacity) is assumed in this subbasin along with the RFF scenario IV coal conversion level with the remainder exported by rail.

Finally we address the Lower Yellowstone as the last downstream subbasin, the outflow from which provides a summary account of the cumulative interactions of the hydrologic variables and the consumptive use demands associated with the legal claims on flow taking place upstream of the North Dakota boundary. To undertake this, we must first specify a plausible level of consumptive use development for the eight upstream subbasins, the first four of which we prepared for table 9-11, in order to do simulations for the Mid-Yellowstone subbasin. The additional information for the remaining subbasins is given in table 9-13. There a plausible set of activities incorporating BNRC-granted reservations for withdrawal uses only and the Northern Cheyenne reserved right claims based on the restrictive/low efficiency irrigation diversion rate are assumed. In the Lower Yellowstone subbasin itself, the BNRC-granted reservations for municipal use and irrigation are assumed. Given the above, would there be any flow available for appropriation at the exit point of the Yellowstone in Montana at the North Dakota border? The simulation results (not shown) indicate that there would be substantial flows into North Dakota except for one month corresponding to the most severe flow conditions of record when the flow would be close to nonexistent. In our simulated runs, the proposed stage II High Tongue Reservoir and the proposed Intake Reservoir are operated to meet consumptive uses only with the latter being operated to meet the additional demand of coal conversion (RFF scenario IV) in the Powder subbasin. If, on the other hand, the two proposed reservoirs are operated also to satisfy the BNRC-granted instream flow reservations for the Tongue and Powder subbasins respectively, then even in the critical low flow month of record, there is shown to be a flow into North Dakota in excess of 3,000 acre-feet for that critical month. Accordingly, the runs for the Lower Yellowstone subbasin indicate that the Montana water reservations are not detrimental to North Dakota. In addition, the runs illustrate the capability of the model to account for different development levels occurring in the upstream subbasins and provide a summary account for the entire Yellowstone Basin.

Conclusions

We set out to examine whether the availability of water or water quality might be constraints on development of energy from the Fort Union Formation. Various opinions were expressed regarding the availability or absence of water for energy activities in the Yellowstone River Basin. A review of the flow conditions in the Tongue and Powder subbasins clearly indicates that without storage in the Powder subbasin or expansion of existing storage in the Tongue, there is not a dependable supply of water in these coal-bearing subbasins even for expanding existing uses, let alone coal conversion. It was clear from our analysis that assuming proposed storage facilities in either subbasin are in place, then any use considered singly and independently of other simultaneous competing projected uses could easily be accommodated insofar as the availability of water is concerned. It is not clear, however, that the level of irrigation reflected in the reservation requests or even the BNRC-granted irrigation reservations (and where applicable, the additional Indian communities' postulated irrigation under the reserved rights doctrine) would be feasible from the water quality rather than the availability standpoint. This would very likely be the case in each of the tributary subbasins, although not a problem in the Mid-Yellowstone. Moreover, so far as the Tongue, Powder, and Bighorn subbasins are concerned, it is clear that the level of irrigation we have mentioned would not be consistent with maintenance of current state water quality standards, quite apart from the issue of the suitability of the TDS concentrations for irrigating crops.

When we considered various competing claims simultaneously, it appears that there will be, under certain circumstances, water available for energy development while meeting all of the state BNRC-granted reservations in some of the subbasins. It does not follow that all of the reservations and the total of the most intensive energy developments could occur in every one of the subbasins, although it does seem possible in the Powder, assuming proposed storage is built to provide for more dependable supplies of water. But even in subbasins where all of the reservations and the most intensive energy development scenario cannot be wholly accommodated within the particular subbasin, varying degrees of energy development can take place in individual subbasins short of the total we have postulated for the entire Yellowstone Basin. This is true of the Tongue as well, again provided storage is built on the Tongue and assuming the Northern Cheyenne reserved right claims are based on the restrictive/efficient criterion. While water from the Yellowtail Reservoir may not be available for energy development purposes, depending on a number of still unresolved issues, it appears that it would need to be transported outside the basin in any event if it were to be used for any coal conversion other than that on the Crow Reservation and could be displaced by Powder River water, provided storage is built at the Moorhead site.

To conclude, it appears that the amount of water hydrologically available, if impounded in proposed storage reservoirs, would provide sufficient water so as not to constrain coal conversion in the Powder River subbasin or coal extraction in the Tongue subbasin, or more generally, the Yellowstone River Basin. This could be done while simultaneously satisfying all of the BNRC-granted reservations, the interstate water right claims likely to be depleted over the simulation period, and the Indian reserved water right claims estimated by the restrictive criterion.

Under the current situation, however, without the proposed storage, surface water would be legally unavailable for appropriation for the postulated coal extraction and conversion levels in the Tongue and Powder subbasins just as it is in the free-flowing Mid-Yellowstone subbasin. In the Bighorn subbasin, which has the existing Yellowtail Reservoir, the court imposed restrictions on the Bureau of Reclamation that, until they are met, do not allow the bureau to market the stored water. Therefore, while water is physically available in the Bighorn and Mid-Yellowstone subbasins, it may not be legally available for our postulated coal development levels.

10 Summary and Conclusions

Summary

With reemergence of the prospect that coal will play a major role in meeting the nation's energy needs, the Northern Great Plains, and particularly the Fort Union Formation in the Colstrip-Gillette Oval, are being looked to as the source of a major expansion of coal production that would make a significant contribution to the nation's energy goals. But many problems beset a quick and large-scale expansion of coal extraction and conversion in this area. The nature and scale of economic and fiscal impacts have been examined in a companion study.[1] The problem of finding cooperating factors, such as water, which is essential both as process water (in coal mining and in conversion processes or other economic activities) on the one hand, and as an aesthetic attribute of the environment on the other, is another major issue. There are others as well, but in this study we have limited ourselves to developing an integrated approach to the assessment of the amount of water which might become available in the Yellowstone River Basin, the major surface source of water for the Montana portion of the Fort Union Formation.

Just as we know there is enough fixed carbon in the nation's coal deposits to supply all U.S. needs for a very long time barring other important constraints on its unlimited use, we also know that the Yellowstone River Basin will provide an ample supply of water for any foreseeable energy development in eastern Montana, provided there are no other significant factors inhibiting its use for such development. In fact, however, there are vigorous claims being made on the use of Yellowstone River Basin water that are incompatible with making it available solely for energy development.

[1] John V. Krutilla and Anthony C. Fisher, with Richard E. Rice, *Economic and Fiscal Impacts of Coal Development: Northern Great Plains* (Baltimore, The Johns Hopkins University Press for Resources for the Future, 1978).

There are two aspects to the problem. One is: How will, or should, the water supplies of the Yellowstone River Basin be allocated functionally among different economic and social purposes? The other is a step more proximate: namely, What are the relative legal rights and obligations among competing corporate, communal, and other private or public entities to these waters, and what latitude do these entities have in the matter of transferring their rights? The more proximate aspect of the problem, of course, is the key to answering the ultimate question. For this reason we began with a careful review and evaluation of both the relative rights among contending parties, and the legal and administrative actions that are being used to clarify or perhaps redefine the relative rights. These actions consist of the administrative processes under Montana water legislation, and the court proceedings in which state and federal reserved water rights legislation may be in conflict. We did this to learn what we could, from case law and other sources, about the probable range of outcomes. We are also aware that rights are not absolute and decisions affecting the outcome of these processes may themselves be influenced by the objective implications of one or another criterion or course in reaching decisions. By exploring the quantitative implications of alternative courses of action, administrative decisions, and court opinions, this study is intended to be of assistance in providing information relevant to the decisions themselves.

In chapter 2 we learned that Montana water law tends strongly to favor allocation of natural (unregulated) flows to support an agrarian oriented society. This means that transfer of water rights in sizable quantity among owners is prohibited if it results in a change from agricultural to industrial uses. We have learned, however, that increased dependable yields from storage regulation provided by federally built projects can be transferred to the state for a consideration equal to the costs to the federal government, and in turn, subject to allocation by auction. If an unfettered market develops for new supplies (that is, increases in dependable yield), then we could see a two-tiered allocative mechanism with industry legally able to compete for water on the same terms as agriculture; namely, for a price up to the value of the marginal product of water in the more productive application. This would provide a source of supply to the industrial sector, provided that new projects are built, although such construction is not a forgone conclusion.

A review of the legal issues arising out of the federal reserved rights doctrine, however, suggests a challenge to the primacy of the western states in their traditional right to allocate water within their boundaries.

The problem here has two aspects. In several recent cases, the federal government has asserted under the federal reservation doctrine a right to the waters necessary to carry out the purposes for which the various federal land withdrawals such as national forests, national wild and scenic rivers, national parks, and the like were set aside. (In some areas there have been federal withdrawals for coal extraction purposes, but this does not appear to have been a problem of any real importance in Montana.) What appears to be of much greater significance are the Indian reserved water rights that have their legal basis in the same doctrine and refer to Indian rights of access to water for economic activities on their reservations. Because these rights have existed since the establishment of the reservations, they are senior to the rights of most individuals in the non-Indian community.

There are different courses which the courts may adopt in adjudicating Indian water rights. One, which we refer to as the "restrictive criterion," would limit the right to water that is used only for irrigating arable land. The other, the "expansive criterion," would place no limitation on the economic purposes for which water could be applied. As there is generally a wider range of options where energy commodities and their conversion are concerned (for example, in the case of the Crow and Northern Cheyenne Indian tribes), the expansive criterion would presumably result in a much larger reservation of water for the Indian community, and consequently, a much smaller volume that would fall within the jurisdiction of the state to allocate. Unless the aspirations and objectives of the Indian tribes happen to coincide with the dominant interests in the state that would influence the character of the priority and extent of water reservations filed under state law and administrative proceedings, the resulting water allocation would likely differ markedly under a ruling using the expansive compared with the restrictive criterion.

Lay analysts of the problem, of course, cannot predict the outcome under the circumstances. Indeed, there are differences of opinion within the legal fraternity about the rights under the laws, for its members can be found on opposite sides of each case bearing on the issue. Nor can we find unambiguous evidence that the courts lean heavily in one direction since our review of the cases suggests different emphases in different courts. Our review also shows that on occasion judicial opinions are overturned on appeal. Faced with the imponderables, then, we have simply attempted to identify the critical factors and assessed the probable range of values the variables may take to provide the parameters with which to carry out the analysis.

While the law and the courts may confound the lay members of society, the professional literature dealing with normalized inputs of water per unit of output in the various agricultural and industrial activities has at times been equally ambiguous. Fortunately, application of careful methods of analysis that make assumptions explicit and include the chemical analysis of the coal as well as local ambient conditions for careful and critical analysis of industrial water coefficients, has permitted the development of a methodology and data file that we trust will serve other analysts equally well (see chapter 5).

Our estimates for *nonindustrial* water uses are based on the experience in the region and the expertise provided by federal agency personnel and academic researchers who have dealt with agronomy, soil mechanics, agricultural uses of water, and instream uses for maintenance of fish and wildlife habitat and water quality. While there doubtless is room for improvement in any data used in the study, it is beyond our competence to do so in our survey of the materials relevant to these technical factors and related water management issues. Our efforts have been directed, however, toward obtaining the most accurate information about the technical factors of, and the potential outcomes from, pending administrative and legal decisions currently in process, preparatory to the systematic evaluation of water supplies for coal extraction and energy development. A major part of our effort, reflected in chapters 5, 6, and 7, relates to the assembling of the most trustworthy information currently possible to obtain for the purpose of estimating the amounts of water that are being claimed or reserved by state or federal policy by each of the several public and private entities who are making claims to the use of the Yellowstone River Basin water. Through an analysis of the interests and objectives of each of the different entities, we worked toward an identification of the functional (economic) distribution of claims for this water to the extent it is possible.

The basic mechanism for the simultaneous analysis of interdependent factors is the RFF/Montana Yellowstone Basin simulation model. This is a hydrologic model that will simulate the quantitative implications of information fed into it concerning the whole array of data; for example, hydrologic, chemical, and technical relations between water required and unit (or total) output of any relevant economic activity (and under different assumptions about technical efficiencies or assumptions about the outcomes of administrative or litigative processes). The attractive feature of this planning tool is that it is disaggregated by subbasins, thus allowing different conditions with respect to the occurrence of coal, hydrologic variability, and the aspirations of the particular entities involved (plus other conditions where it is desirable for policy purposes to be able to discriminate finely) to be addressed by this planning tool. Aside from its "spatial fine tuning," it is designed to address either the implications of the water reservations for a single purpose independently or any level or mix of several activities simultaneously in terms of their joint feasibility given dependable supplies of water. In the latter case, the feasibility may be constrained by a probability that water supplies will need to be interrupted to one or more of the activities during the hydrologic system's critical period. How this is done is detailed in chapter 8, where a fairly brief description of the model's development, its properties, and its capabilities is presented. More complete documentation, the data file, and related information are stored on tape for convenient use, perhaps for further work in an integrated approach to planning for the mix of rival uses for Yellowstone River Basin water.

Having described the approach to this problem and the way in which answers to many questions that are relevant to addressing the conflicting claims for water in the Yellowstone Basin can be obtained, we now ask, What are the results? In one sense we may claim that results of all of the work involved in refining the simulation model and developing the data file necessary for its use (chapter 8 and chapters 2 through 7, respectively) are presented in chapter 9. It would be unfortunate, however, to leave the impression that all of the utility that may be gained from this work has been extracted in the numerical analysis of chapter. 9. The numerical analysis has demonstrated the capability of the simulation model to carry out investigations of various sets of interdependent questions in a way that has not been done before. It is hoped that the federal and state agencies concerned with the allocation of water in its various uses in this study area will find the model useful to them. Even the Indian communities and the courts may find the simulator of interest in testing the quantitative implications of one or another modification of working assumptions used in analysis. In short, it is a mechanism of great utility as an aid in planning and policy analysis because it is capable of providing quantitative boundaries around tradeoff issues heretofore addressed largely only in qualitative terms.

Concluding Observations

Since the major federal- and state-owned coal deposits occur in the Tongue, Powder, and Mid-Yellowstone subbasins, it has been helpful to have a hydrologic simulator that can disaggregate sources of water for various uses by subbasin. Looking first to the Tongue subbasin, we learned that the minimally regulated flows of this stream are already overappropriated and that no supplies are available for expansion of either irrigation agriculture or energy unless more water-efficient methods are adopted by existing irrigators, or dry cooling is employed in the electrical generation or conversion processes. However, with the addition of proposed storage on the Tongue River of 450,000 acre-feet corresponding to the High Tongue stage II facility, there would be water available for meeting the most energy-intensive scenarios we have postulated,[2] provided the stored water were reserved for energy alone. Similarly, all of the irrigation subsumed under the irrigation reservations granted by the Montana Board of Natural Resources and Conservation (BNRC), existing irrigation water rights, and the assumed Indian reserved right claims applied to irrigation could be accommodated by use of such a storage facility, were it to be reserved exclusively for irrigation purposes. In this case, however, irrigation would be problematic because of the salinity that would attend such use without some instream flow reservations. Water used for irrigation will, because of the attendant soil leaching, cause water quality to deteriorate downstream in a manner that distinguishes it from its alternative uses either for energy or instream flows.

Better perspective can be obtained by viewing the various potential rival uses simultaneously within the context of the institutional and legal setting. Here we find that Indian reserved water rights loom as an important consideration. Without additional storage, there are insufficient dependable flows to meet existing irrigation rights during the irrigation season in many years quite apart from the reserved right claims of the Northern Cheyenne or any other uses. Given storage, however, and alternative criteria employed by the courts with respect to Indian reserved water rights (that is, following a restrictive *or* an expansive interpretation), the problem becomes very complicated. There are two proposed reservoir sizes, two criteria possible for estimating the range of Indian reserved right claims both of which depend on the amount of feasible irrigable land on the Northern Cheyenne Reservation (which itself is indeterminate at

[2] That is, conversion of 30 million tons per year through two 2,600-megawatt steam electric plants, and a 250-million-standard-cubic-foot-per-day (scf/day) coal gasification plant, with export of the remaining 70 million tons by either rail or slurry pipeline (RFF scenario IV); or, the conversion of 30 million tons per year with export of the remainder of the Department of Energy and Department of Interior 339 million tons per year (high projection for 1990 for Montana) by rail only. We hasten to add that this scenario may not be regarded as intensive against the backdrop of recent discussions of a massive synfuels program.

this time), and at least three major water uses—irrigation, energy, and instream flows. Accordingly, the amount of water allocable to the various uses represents a large number of plausible mixes. The interested reader is referred to tables 9-1 through 9-6 in chapter 9 for a view of a meaningful set of outcomes under a reasonable variation in assumptions regarding reservoir sizes and legal and administrative rulings. To summarize the results, the following may be said. Only with the larger storage facility (whatever its economic, including environmental, merits) can a significant part of all of the rival claims be met. In fact, it may be more accurate to say that only with the largest reservoir can anything but very sharply reduced claims all be met simultaneously. For example, were the Northern Cheyenne to be allocated reserved rights of 150,000 acre-feet per year to accommodate an ambitious irrigation level (50,000 acres), and were existing state irrigation rights and all of the state BNRC-granted reservations simultaneously implemented, then beginning with a full reservoir and reflecting Wyoming's share of water likely to be depleted, the rival uses excluding energy conversion could be satisfied for only about half the simulation period. If, on the other hand, it is assumed that the courts will grant the Northern Cheyenne reserved water rights consistent with our estimate under the restrictive criterion with water-efficient (3 acre-feet per acre) irrigation practices applied to a reduced irrigation level of 10,000 acres, and given the larger 450,000-acre-foot proposed storage reservoir, then the existing irrigation rights and all of the BNRC-granted reservations could also be met with sufficient water remaining in storage under the most adverse hydrologic conditions of record to support either the RFF 1985 or the U.S. Department of Energy/U.S. Department of the Interior (DOE/DOI) 1990 projected coal extraction for export by rail only. With the smaller 320,000-acre-foot storage facility, all of the activities listed immediately above could be accommodated for all years except one, with a single month reservoir shortfall for the scenario depicting 100 million tons per year for rail export only and a single seven-month period for the DOE/DOI scenario assuming 339 million tons per year mining activity for rail export from the region.

Suppose now that the water rights historically reserved for the Indian tribes were found by the courts to include water for purposes additional to irrigation agriculture. What might the effects of this be? This of course would depend on the interests and economic motivation of the Indian community. It *could* mean that the water necessary to meet any implied Indian industrial activity to the exclusion of state irrigation reservations or other junior claims would be reserved for the use of the Northern

Cheyenne. Given the apparent attitude of the Northern Cheyenne tribe as evidenced by its filing for a Class I air quality designation permit (prevention of significant deterioration), it would appear unlikely such water would be used for energy development on the Northern Cheyenne Reservation beyond the tribe's own needs. On the other hand, failure to use such water does not surrender the right, and the result would constitute simply instream flow. Since the Northern Cheyenne occupy the upstream position just below the reservoir site, it would mean downstream junior claims could be accommodated only at the sufferance of the Northern Cheyenne.

The situation in the Powder subbasin differs markedly from that in the Tongue in a number of important respects. There exist use (unrecorded) rights in the Powder subbasin for irrigation, much of it used for water spreading from spring freshets rather than full-service irrigation. Second, there are no Indian reserved right claims to the flow in the Powder subbasin. Third, the location of the subbasin with respect to Indian reservations is such that the issue of air quality deterioration associated with energy conversion is unlikely to arise. Just as with the minimally regulated flows in the Tongue, the unregulated flows in this subbasin are not sufficiently dependable to permit significant expansion of existing uses of the water. Thus the building of storage facilities, perhaps the Moorhead or Intake (on the Moorhead site) reservoirs, would be required for expansion of activities, such as energy conversion, that require more dependable stream flows.

While absence of some of the legal constraints suggests the possibility of water available for energy development, certain physical relationships may additionally reinforce this inference. The Powder River carries very heavy sediment and total dissolved solids (TDS) loads. The former means that a disproportionate amount of the storage capacity has to be dedicated to trapping the sediment flowing into the reservoir. However, if we consider the normal life cycle of energy conversion facilities and the "interim storage" set aside for sediment impoundment that would not be called upon before the end of the normal life of the former, a substantial amount of storage would still be available to meet the various demands that might be placed upon the Powder. Moreover, given the normally occurring TDS concentrations in the Powder River, it does not appear that the stored water releases would be conducive to the proper germination and growth of agricultural crops. Whether irrigation would be feasible or not, our simulation studies clearly indicate that with the larger Moorhead Reservoir, all of the BNRC-granted reservations could be accommodated along with any of the energy development scenarios postulated. With respect to salinity and the feasibility of irrigation, the problem does not relate only to the question of the leached salts in the return flow from irrigating crops. Once the reservoir is built, and assuming reasonably uniform mixing during the annual turnover, the TDS concentrations in the water that would have to be released from the reservoir itself during the irrigation season appear to be too high to avoid serious problems for the irrigation of crops.

The building of a reservoir may also affect the feasibility of water-spreading activities currently practiced during the higher runoff, more dilute TDS concentration months of the spring. Since the BNRC-granted irrigation water reservations are for water spreading rather than full-service irrigation, one cannot infer that the replacement of present water spreading by regulated flows too saline for irrigating crops would be to the advantage of those parties currently benefiting from the spreading activity. It is an issue, however, which would need to be resolved in the course of a decision to build the Moorhead Reservoir.

Considering the somewhat smaller Intake Reservoir at the Moorhead site, virtually all of the above conclusions would also apply. There would be increased occasions for dipping into the "interim storage" and one six-month period of reservoir shortfall for the most intensive development scenario under hydrologic conditions which would correspond to the most adverse of record. The larger reservoir, of course, would accommodate more intensive energy development than those we have postulated throughout. However, we have not investigated whether or not from an environmental point of view the Powder subbasin could even accommodate the concentration of energy development activities which we have postulated. It is clear, though, that insofar as water quality is concerned, the energy development scenarios indicate much less quality degradation than would attend the BNRC-granted irrigation reservations if actually implemented.

To summarize, since there is no issue of Indian reserved right claims in the Powder subbasin, nor substantial full-service irrigation, the Powder subbasin with the proposed storage appears to be the preferable subbasin in which to locate any energy conversion facilities, were any to be located in the Montana portion of the Fort Union Formation. This conclusion is reinforced by the probable occurrence of increasing salinity of water resulting from irrigation agriculture. These two potential uses, which may be competitive elsewhere, do not appear to compete in this case. Finally, the location of the Powder subbasin relative to the Indian reservations makes the problem of air quality deterioration less important than in the case of the Tongue subbasin. This does not suggest that all coal activities be restricted to the Powder, but only that because of the severe problems with conversion in the Tongue, some degree of specialization might be usefully accommodated considering the two.

Turning next to the Bighorn subbasin, what appears at first to be a simple, straightforward situation—an existing reservoir with a large volume of unallocated water—becomes one of the most complicated cases on closer examination. To begin with, the Yellowtail Reservoir is a federal facility with greater complications involved over the allocation of water than would be the case for state or privately built facilities on the Powder. Also, it is not known, pending a process of negotiation and the meeting of minds (or a process of litigation and their boggling), what if any influence the BNRC-granted water reservations ultimately will have on the operation of the Yellowtail Reservoir. But perhaps even more critical to the question of whether water will be available out of the Yellowtail Reservoir for energy conversion activities is the disposition of the Indian reserved water right claims. If both the Wind River Indian and the Crow Indian tribes are granted reserved rights equivalent to one Department of Interior-suggested "plausible" estimate under the expansive interpretation of the reserved rights doctrine, there would be little if any dependable flow remaining for the state of Montana to allocate. Now, it is conceivable that if Indian reserved rights are based on the expansive criterion, one or another of the Indian tribes may elect to enter into some contract with the non-Indian community (be they private parties or states) for the leasing of their reserved water for a specified time. But, whether or not that is a plausible option is arguable pending the resolution of the Indian reserved water rights litigation.

The availability of water from the Yellowtail Reservoir in Montana is also dependent on the intentions and ability of the state of Wyoming to claim effectively its share of the Bighorn under the Yellowstone Basin Compact. It is conceivable that in both cases, while there will be no surrender of rights to Bighorn River water, arrangements could be made for the upstream claimants to suffer the downstream state (Montana) to use flows without prejudice to their eventual "recapture" by upstream entities in Wyoming. Indeed, if we are thinking of a near term decision horizon (until 1985 or 1990, for example) and a guaranteed *status quo* with respect to upstream use of the Bighorn over, say, a thirty-year term in exchange for a consideration, then we can contemplate a number of additional options for the use of the Yellowtail Reservoir water in the Montana reach of the subbasin.

Let us assume for the moment that the federal government ultimately has jurisdiction over the disposition of the stored waters of the Yellowtail Reservoir and elects not to sell water to the state of Montana for instream purposes. Then it is conceivable that both the Crow and Wind River Indian tribes' reserved water rights under the restrictive interpretation of the reserved rights doctrine (with water-efficient irrigation practices) could be accommodated along with the BNRC-granted irrigation reservations and any one of the energy development options (including the most intensive) that *we* have postulated. Alternatively, granting that the previous assumption regarding the outcome of the Indian reserved rights litigation were to hold, but the less water-efficient practices were employed in Indian irrigation agriculture, it would still be possible to accommodate all of the energy development scenarios along with the Indian reserved rights and the BNRC-granted irrigation reservations.

Suppose, alternatively, that the federal authorities were to sell the state of Montana rights to stored water for instream purposes up to the amount granted by the BNRC whenever water were deemed surplus to other requirements, then this could be done if, and only if, we have previously postulated too high a sustainable claim for water by the Indians under the restrictive interpretation. Were our postulated results of the Indian reserved water rights litigation unrealistically high in terms of what the courts may eventually grant, then it is possible that the reduced allocation to the Indians, the BNRC-granted irrigation and instream flow reservations, and even the most intensive of the energy scenarios postulated could be accommodated by the release of stored water from the Yellowtail Reservoir. That is, if the close-to-900,000 acre-feet we postulated in the aggregate for the Indian tribes in the Wyoming and Montana portions of the subbasin were to be reduced to about 500,000 acre-feet per year, then such an amount, along with that granted by the BNRC and even the most intensive energy scenario postulated, could all be accommodated.

The compound probability of all of these positive "ifs" being simultaneously realized through negotiation and litigation before new storage capacity in the coal-bearing subbasins could be built is further reduced by the recent decision of the Ninth Circuit Court of Appeals in *Environmental Defense Fund (EDF) v. Andrus*. Here, while the court did not sustain the EDF position that the Bureau of Reclamation lacked authority to make sales under its enabling legislation except in support of irrigation agriculture, it did impose conditions which the sale of water for non-agricultural purposes must meet, conditions that constrain the latitude with which the Bureau of Reclamation may operate in its industrial sales program.

If our analyses have been correct, however, absence of the use of Bighorn water for energy development seems not to be a serious issue for energy development in the Fort Union Formation. While it is true that there is an existing reservoir with uncommitted dependable flows, it is somewhat physically removed from the coal-bearing Powder subbasin where non-Indian energy conversion activities are most likely to be feasible. Recall that with the Northern Cheyenne being granted their request for protection of their airshed against significant deterioration, the Tongue subbasin, bordering the Bighorn in part, is not likely to be a strong candidate for any conversion activities. In comparison with coal-fired steam electric generation or coal conversion, the water required in the Tongue to mine and export coal is minimal, *if* the coal is transported outside the region by rail. Indeed, it is not clear that any additional storage is required in the Tongue for mining for export only. What is required is necessitated by the BNRC reservations rather than coal extraction. If stored water from the Yellowtail facility is to be used for electrical generation or coal conversion, then it would need to be transported across the Tongue subbasin and into the Powder, to take advantage of the existing storage facility. Again we have the problem of resolving the outstanding issues regarding the sale of water from the Yellowtail Reservoir for nonagricultural purposes, and the process of purchase, condemnation suits, or both, to obtain the rights-of-way enabling construction of a conveyance system from the Bighorn into the Powder. Whether this prospect has a higher probability of early resolution than does the building of storage on the Moorhead site requires careful examination. Storage on the Powder, if otherwise justified, would provide sufficient dependable flows to meet even the most intensive energy development scenario we have postulated along with all of the BNRC-granted reservations. And it is not even clear that the irrigation reservations for the Powder can be implemented because of the salinity issues discussed previously.

Use of the mainstem flows on the Mid-Yellowstone poses a somewhat different set of considerations. There are no proposed storage reservoirs on this reach of the mainstem, and while the Bureau of Reclamation requested some offstream storage reservations, the BNRC assigned them the lowest priority. Moreover, in response to the considerable value of retaining the Mid-Yellowstone as a free flowing river, the BNRC provided for a sizable (5.6-million acre-feet per year) instream flow reservation, which, if honored, would effectively preclude flows available for other nonreservation purposes for as much as a third of the time, a condition not conducive to the conduct of industrial activities requiring an assured supply of process or cooling water. Accordingly, only the municipal water reservation of something under 3,000 acre-feet per year and water to irrigate 47,000 acres of land with a reservation of roughly 119,000 acre-feet per year could be accommodated in addition to the instream flows.

Although the above means that water would not be available for some levels and mixes of energy development in the Mid-Yellowstone, it does not imply a particular problem for extraction of the coal occurring in the Mid-Yellowstone reach. Indeed, recall that we have moved the demands of the *total* postulated levels and mixes of energy activities successively from one to another subbasin, including the Mid-Yellowstone, and failure of one subbasin or reach of the Yellowstone to have water sufficient for the total required does not imply failure for the Yellowstone Basin as a whole to do so. Indeed, the Powder subbasin, assuming the proposed Moorhead storage is in place, could accommodate the most intensive energy scenario we have postulated insofar as water supplies are concerned, while simultaneously meeting all of the BNRC-granted water reservations. Moreover, while the prospect of duplicating this feat in the Tongue with proposed storage and in the Mid-Yellowstone independently is not promising, the relatively limited water withdrawal requirements for extraction would permit the mining of a great volume of coal if destined for export by rail for conversion to other forms of energy *outside the region*. The Powder, particularly, affords opportunities for some energy conversion activities if proposed storage is in place. Whether environmental considerations, especially the issue of air quality deterioration over the Northern Cheyenne Reservation in the Tongue, would qualify these conclusions awaits a careful environmental assessment.

Index

DATE DUE

MAR 2 '87			
JAN 30 '93			

DEMCO 38-297